Language Diversity and Cognitive Representations

HUMAN COGNITIVE PROCESSING is a forum for interdisciplinary research on the nature and organization of the cognitive systems and processes involved in speaking and understanding natural language (including sign language), and their relationship to other domains of human cognition, including general conceptual or knowledge systems and processes (the language and thought issue), and other perceptual or behavioral systems such as vision and non-verbal behavior (e.g. gesture). 'Cognition' should be taken broadly, not only including the domain of rationality, but also dimensions such as emotion and the unconscious. The series is open to any type of approach to the above questions (methodologically and theoretically) and to research from any discipline, including (but not restricted to) different branches of psychology, artificial intelligence and computer science, cognitive anthropology, linguistics, philosophy and neuroscience. It takes a special interest in research crossing the boundaries of these disciplines.

EDITORS

Marcelo Dascal *(Tel Aviv University)*
Raymond Gibbs *(University of California at Santa Cruz)*
Jan Nuyts *(University of Antwerp)*

Editorial address: Jan Nuyts, University of Antwerp, Dept. of Linguistics (GER), Universiteitsplein 1, B 2610 Wilrijk, Belgium, e-mail: nuyts@uia.ua.ac.be

EDITORIAL ADVISORY BOARD

Melissa Bowerman *(Nijmegen)*; Wallace Chafe *(Santa Barbara, CA)*
Philip R. Cohen *(Portland, OR)*; Antonio Damasio *(Iowa City, IA)*
Morton Ann Gernsbacher *(Madison, WI)*; David McNeill *(Chicago, IL)*
Eric Pederson *(Eugene, OR)*; François Recanati *(Paris)*
Sally Rice *(Edmonton, Alberta)*; Benny Shanon *(Jerusalem)*
Lokendra Shastri *(Berkeley, CA)*; Dan Slobin *(Berkeley, CA)*
Paul Thagard *(Waterloo, Ontario)*

Volume 3

Catherine Fuchs and Stéphane Robert (eds)

Language Diversity and Cognitive Representations

Language Diversity and Cognitive Representations

Edited by

CATHERINE FUCHS

STÉPHANE ROBERT

JOHN BENJAMINS PUBLISHING COMPANY
AMSTERDAM/PHILADELPHIA

The paper used in this publication meets the minimum requirements of American National Standard for Information Sciences — Permanence of Paper for Printed Library Materials, ANSI Z39.48-1984.

Library of Congress Cataloging-in-Publication Data

Language diversity and cognitive representations / edited by Catherine Fuchs, Stéphane Robert.
    p.   cm. -- (Human cognitive processing, ISSN 1387-6724 ; v. 3)
Includes bibliographical references and index.
    1. Language and languages--Variation. 2. Cognition.
3. Psycholinguistics. I. Fuchs, Catherine. II. Robert, Stéphane. III. Series.
P120.V37L344   1999
401'.9--dc21   99-40994
ISBN 90 272 2355 6 (Eur.) / 1 55619 203 7 (US) (alk. paper)   CIP

© Copyright 1999 - John Benjamins B.V.
No part of this book may be reproduced in any form, by print, photoprint, microfilm, or any other means, without written permission from the publisher.

John Benjamins Publishing Co. • P.O.Box 75577 • 1070 AN Amsterdam • The Netherlands
John Benjamins North America • P.O.Box 27519 • Philadelphia PA 19118-0519 • USA

Table of Contents

Introduction   vii
   Catherine Fuchs and Stéphane Robert

I. SEMANTIC VARIATIONS AND INVARIANCE : COGNITIVE ISSUES   1

Diversity in linguistic representations
   A challenge for cognition   3
   Catherine Fuchs
Cognitive invariants and linguistic variability
   From units to utterance   21
   Stéphane Robert
Subjectivity, invariance, and the development of forms
   in the construction of linguistic representations   37
   Antoine Culioli
Language evolution and semantic representations
   A case study of the evolution from "subjectivity"
   to "objectivity" in French   53
   Christiane Marchello-Nizia

II. CONCEPTUALIZATION AND REPRESENTATIONS OF SPACE ACROSS LANGUAGES   71

Spatial orientation in some Austronesian languages   73
   Françoise Ozanne-Rivierre
Language space and sociolect
   Cognitive correlates of gendered speech in Mopan Maya   85
   Eve Danziger
Localization and predication
   Ancient Greek and various other languages   107
   Hansjakob Seiler

The expression of spatial relations and the spatialization of
    semantic relations in French Sign Language   123
  Christian Cuxac

III. LANGUAGE ACTIVITY :
    FROM LINGUISTIC TO COGNITIVE PROCESSES   143

From natural language to drum language
    An economical encoding procedure in Banda-Linda,
    Central African Republic   145
  France Cloarec-Heiss
Electrical signs of language in the brain   159
  Marta Kutas and Mireille Besson
Linguistic variations and cognitive constraints in the processing
    and the acquisition of language   179
  Michèle Kail
Universal vs. language-specific constraints in agrammatic
    aphasia. Is comparatism back ?   195
  Jean-Luc Nespoulous
Schizophasia and cognitive dysfunction   209
  Bernard Pachoud

INDEX   221

  Subject index   221
  Author index   225
  Language index   228

Introduction

Catherine Fuchs
and Stéphane Robert
CNRS-LTM and CNRS-LLACAN, Paris

It is hardly an exaggeration to say that language diversity is *the* primary theoretical issue for linguistics as the science which seeks to apprehend the human language faculty in and through the multiplicity of individual languages. It is no less important an issue for cognitive science insofar as language diversity also implies the construction and expression of different 'representations' of the world in each language, rather than a mirroring of some real or imaginary world by expressing a universal conceptual system in a particular form.

Linguists faced with interlinguistic (and intralinguistic) variation have traditionally approached the subject from an ethnolinguistic (and sociolinguistic) perspective. In the domain of *cognition*, however, the question has largely been obscured. It is true that D.I. Slobin introduced a cross-linguistic perspective on language acquisition some twenty-five years ago and that Bates and MacWhinney's model for psycholinguistics dates back ten years; in the field of aphasia study, Menn and Obler have also developed a cross-linguistic approach. Nevertheless, apart from these particular cases, most research in the domain of cognition largely overlooks the question of language diversity. In fact, it is ironic that the main disciplines dealing with language in the cognitive sciences (neuroscience, psychology, artificial intelligence, etc.) usually approach the language faculty through a single language (that of the researchers), or at best in the form of circumscribed crosslinguistic comparisons where the search for universals takes precedence over any consideration of variation. This is why it is not only essential but even urgent to open up the study of individual languages to the perspectives of cognitive science and conversely, to devote more attention, in cognitive studies, to the viewpoint and issues of linguistics.

Such is the motivation for the articles in this book, which bring together the contributions of individual language scholars, linguists, anthropologists, psychologists, and neurophysicians. These papers all focus on human cognitive processes involved in language activity and the impact of language diversity on them. The basic issue under consideration is how to correlate language diversity with the universality of the language faculty, i.e., where to situate the *invariant* factors which allow translation from one language to another and guarantee the unity of the language faculty with respect to the *variations* which give individual languages their specificity.

From a purely linguistic standpoint, this leads to the question of the metalinguistic representation of invariant and variant factors. From a cognitive viewpoint, it amounts to asking whether each language emprisons us in an irreducible 'world view' or whether the representations formed by different languages indeed have some common features — or at least provide crossover points. Can invariant semantic features be postulated to explain such interconnections, and if so, what are they like and how can they be defined? At the same time, how can we account for the observed variations among languages in both the way they conceptualize the world and the way they express notional content in utterance form (morphological, syntactic, semantic, and pragmatic constraints)? Finally, how are these representations and linguistic operations related to other cognitive processes, particularly perceptual processes? Can linguistic and cognitive representations be treated as identical without further ado, as 'cognitive grammars' seem to do? In such cases, what is the status of cross-linguistic variation? Does it involve variable neurophysiological or psychological mechanisms? More generally, what do we know of the neurophysiological processes involved?

'Language diversity', as the term is applied in this volume, concerns not only the formal diversity of morphology and syntax, but also, in a more critical way, the specific semantic content and pragmatic values of linguistic markers across languages. Both the semantics of units and their overall organization differ widely from one language to another. In fact, there is no pre-existent set of 'universal' concepts underlying various expressions across languages. The paradoxical nature of language lies in the fact that, on the one hand, individual languages yield specific meaningful constructs and organization, with lexical and grammatical units dividing up the world in different ways, so that no linguistic system is reducible to another; yet, on the other hand, it is always possible to build up equivalences between the specific meaningful constructs of each language (units, phrases or sentences), i.e., it is always possible to translate one language into another.

'Cognitive representations' precisely refer here to the meaningful constructs in languages and to the processes underlying their construction, functioning and usage. This includes a broad domain ranging from linguistic-specific processes to perceptual processes, including psycholinguistics and the pathology of

'Cognitive representations' precisely refer here to the meaningful constructs in languages and to the processes underlying their construction, functioning and usage. This includes a broad domain ranging from linguistic-specific processes to perceptual processes, including psycholinguistics and the pathology of language. When examining — in the light of language diversity — which cognitive representations are at work in language activity, one is then naturally lead to revisit the Sapir-Whorf hypothesis: apparently the specificity of individual language does not enclose the speaker in an irreducible system of thought, but rather provides him with tools for building up the expression of his thought content and induces privileged (and perhaps proto-typical) habits and paths in the activity of representing and conceptualizing. However, beyond the individual specificity of languages, a number of invariant processes obviously appear as well, particularly those proceeding from perception. The question remaining is how to define the nature and the extension of the invariant processes and their connections to the specific properties of individual languages.

Part I of this book includes a selection of papers dealing with the questions of *semantic variations and invariance* across languages, and the cognitive issues raised by these questions. C. Fuchs reviews the history and current import of the issue of language diversity for cognitive science. The next four papers examine data from various languages and attempt to analyze the dynamic processes underlying variations of representational constructs. Thus a number of quite general cognitive mechanisms can be defined on the linguistic level, over and above the diversity of the linguistic operations involved. S. Robert constrasts the variability of representations at the level of meaningful units and linguistic categories, with the common cognitive mechanisms involved in speech activity, where the construction of meaning is essentially characterized by non-linear semantic effects. A. Culioli accounts for the phenomenon of polysemy across languages due to the cognitive activity of the speaking subject involving abstraction, deformation and proliferation of forms (from a gestaltist viewpoint). The historical aspect of variation is also considered in a discussion of the causes of language change: C. Marchello-Nizia asks how some apparently stable systems can have been suddenly restructured, and what consequences the restructuring process has for the representations expressed by these systems.

Part II gathers a number of papers devoted to *representations of space* and how speakers use them. Illustrations come from languages as diverse as Maya (E. Danziger), Oceanic languages (F. Ozanne-Rivierre), Ancient Greek, Finno-

final paper, C. Cuxac presents the expression of spatial relations in French Sign Language and describes the use it makes of striking procedures of spatialization of linguistic representations.

Part III brings together papers which are more specifically devoted to *language activity* and connections between linguistic operations and cognitive processes. F. Cloarec-Heiss analyzes the structural and cognitive procedures at work in drum language involving a simplification which is nevertheless not a hindrance to understanding, despite the disymmetry between encoding and decoding. The following papers present the results of experimental studies in neurophysiology, psychology and psychiatry. Neuroscience reveals the first possibilities of correlating certain linguistic constraints or types of error with specific electrical waves in the brain, while showing marked differences in the cerebral activity involved in language and music (M. Besson and M. Kutas). Recent work in the field of language acquisition suggests connections between morphosyntactic variations and constraints on language development (M. Kail). Cross-linguistic studies in language pathology, still in progress, are attempting to distinguish 'cerebrally motivated' factors (i.e., those common to speakers of different languages), from 'linguistically motivated' ones, which vary from language to language, in the loss of grammatical markers observed in subjects suffering from de Broca's aphasia (agrammatism) (J-L. Nespoulous). Language disturbance in schizophrenics would seem, however, to vary little across languages and may be attributable to more general cognitive mechanisms associated with concomitant motor disturbances (B. Pachoud).

Acknowledgment: We would like to thank Raymond Boyd and Steven Schaeffer for helping with the translation of this book.

Part I

Semantic variations and invariance: Cognitive issues

Diversity in Linguistic Representations
A Challenge for Cognition

Catherine Fuchs
CNRS-LTM, Paris

1. Language and languages: Unity and diversity

Language diversity is a subject which has long been side-stepped in scholarly work on language, the verbal faculty. At best, any discussions have been purposely restricted to considerations of superficial syntactic variation. In recent years, however, cognitive science has shown renewed interest in this subject, in connection with the diversity of the signifying representations constructed in individual languages.

1.1 A subject mostly side-stepped...

As one of the characteristic properties of the human species, the language faculty is inevitably of central importance in cognitive science. Speech activity involves various mental processes which are of interest to the *psychologist*, as a student of individual linguistic behavior and of the ways in which children acquire language. The use of language relies on neural circuits within the brain, whose operation is described by the *neurophysiologist*, particularly through the observation of language pathology. Finally, speech output can be modelized, or even simulated, for the purposes of automatic processing, by the mathematician, the logician, or the computer scientist working on the formal aspects of *artificial intelligence*.

Language is thus central to all the primary disciplines involved in cognitive science. Now it so happens that all these disciplines, particularly when lumped together under somewhat equivocal compound appellations such as 'psycholinguistics', 'neurolinguistics', or 'linguistic information science' (see Fuchs 1993), claim to be dealing with *language in itself*, sometimes even using the term 'natural language' to refer to this faculty of the human species, rather than to any particular spoken language. Language as such can of course only be apprehended through some individual language, for which reason scholars in these disciplines always apply themselves to a given language, which is usually their mother tongue (thus mostly to English, but to French for work done in France). But for the exception of a few studies, most of them fairly recent, which are avowedly contrastive (concerning acquisition or pathology in different languages, or in some cases the observation of the performance of multilingual subjects), most work on language as a cognitive activity is based on a *single* language. Even more surprisingly, the language in question is not considered in terms of its own distinctive features with respect to other languages; rather, it is treated as some arbitrary representative of language in general. The ambiguity of the word *language* in English, which may stand either for the language faculty (cf. French word "langage") or for any individual language (cf. French word "langue"), has certainly helped to perpetuate this confusion.

The theoretical and methodological difficulties involved in contrastive work on more than one language are doubtless responsible for the fact that the study of speech activity is usually confined to a single language, a hard enough task in itself. All the same, it is easy to see how risky it might be to take any given language as representative of others, thus leading to unwarranted generalizations: first from that language to languages in general, then from all languages to the language faculty itself.

1.2 ...or with discussions purposely restricted

For the linguist, however, language diversity is an inescapable fact of everyday life. It is thus no surprise that one of best-known linguistic theories among cognitive scientists, Chomsky's generative grammar, comes directly to grips with this issue. What Chomsky and Lasnik (1993) call 'universal grammar' is a theory applying to syntax alone and postulating the existence of a set of universal innate *principles* (rules independent of any individual language) and a finite number of *parameters* which may vary within a limited range of values from one language to another. The purpose of the ongoing 'minimalist' program (Chomsky 1995) is to state the rules of universal grammar in an ever more unified and simplified way, justifying the description of this program by Epstein *et al.* (1996: 3) as "counter-intuitively postulating that there is, in effect, only one human language despite the appearance of unlimited diversity".

This strong hypothesis postulating a universal grammar thus allows the subject of language diversity to be circumscribed in two ways: first of all, only the field of syntax need be considered; and secondly, only a small range of formal variations need be mapped onto universal principles:

Thus cross-linguistic variation, as expressed by parameters, is assumed to be highly restricted. A recent even more circumscribed theory of the formal properties of parameters postulates that each parameter is expressible as an irreducible cross-linguistic difference in the value of (a circumscribed set of) morphological features associated with certain lexical categories – the so-called functional syntactic categories such as Inflection / Agreement, Complementizer, and Determiner (S. Epstein *et al.* 1996: 3).

The purpose of this theory is thus to show that, outside this extremely limited sort of parametric variation, actually involving only morphosyntactic features, individual languages would, as Chomsky himself says (1993: 3), use "a single computational (syntactic) system and a single lexicon".

This attempt to keep interlinguistic variation to a minimum stems from the fundamental postulates of Chomsky's theory, particularly the hypothesis of a central, autonomous *syntactic module* which, as terms such as 'generation' and 'free monoid' suggest, can be described in terms of operations with logical or algebraic symbols, without regard to meaning and use in context. This module is then assigned, as an adjunct, a semantic component of a purely interpretative kind associated with formal languages, and presumably a pragmatic component as well, to account for the relations between the linguistic system and its users.

The assumption of a homology between natural language and formal language, deriving historically from the development of mathematical language theory (see work by Schützenberger, as well as Gross and Lentin 1967) has led to the widespread use of formal approaches to syntax. It should however be remembered that most studies from this perspective, particularly for purposes of automatic processing, have involved only the most widely spoken languages; with the result that for many years, the issue of language diversity has been relegated to secondary importance.

The *modular approach*, which has been popularized in linguistics by generative grammar, has also been adapted to psychology (see for example Fodor 1983, who postulates the existence of a specific language module which is autonomous with respect to other cognitive activities) and to automatic language processing (particularly in systems with an architecture in the form of hierarchical layers, see Fuchs *et al.* 1993: 26). Clearly, the success of the modular approach is largely due to the operative nature of the calculations it allows. Linguistics can thereby be truely accounted a *calculus*.

1.3 A tradition long overlooked...

Outside generative grammar, of course, the subject of language diversity has often been a subject of concern and debate among linguists involved in language description, particularly those working with languages with structures and typological features quite unlike their own native tongues. Except for typological linguistics and studies specifically devoted to cross-linguistic grammaticalization (see below § 2.3.), one might say that within the field of structuralism, each linguistic system is treated in and of itself, and the postulation of universal categories and structures is carefully avoided, there being no reason *a priori* for restricting the range of possible interlinguistic variations. Martinet ([1960] 1964: 25) sums up this approach in the following terms:

> We may reserve the term 'language' for a doubly articulated, verbal instrument of communication...There is nothing outside this common denominator *which cannot vary from language to language.*[1]

In earlier times at least, descriptive studies were carried out within a structuralist framework. As opposed to generative grammar, they all have in common the tendency to stress the way languages differ. Each language is viewed as a unique system of contrasting signs, thus implying that the way the sound/meaning relationship is organized, and hence the way reality itself is categorized, may vary from language to language. Each language therefore dictates to its speakers what they can say, i.e., the set of meaningful linguistic patterns. As Hockett (1954: 116) puts it, interlinguistic difference consists less in "what it is possible to specify" than in "what it is relatively easy or hard to specify". From the ethnolinguistic standpoint, which often amounts to a prolongation of language description, language diversity parallels cultural diversity.

There are many reasons for cognitive science to have largely overlooked this descriptive tradition. Some are institutional and need not concern us here. Others, however, are theoretical in nature and so are of direct interest. Firstly, there are difficulties with descriptions which seem to be too locally targeted and exempt of wider perspectives, or too fine-grained, with data so complex as to discourage any attempt at formalization. In either case, they appear unwieldy. Another obstacle can be put down to the descriptivist rejection of universalism and exclusive attention to differences (and perhaps even a belief in the irreducible nature of these differences), which may suggest that descriptive linguistics is for collector types who are attracted more by curios than by generalization. This attitude also contradicts the intuitive impression that there must be a common underlying ground to account for phenomena of language transfer (going from one language to another, translation and multilingualism) and acquisition.

1.4 ...and now strangely back in fashion

Nevertheless, one of those swings of the pendulum so common in history now seems to be reawakening interest in language diversity within cognitive science after years of indifference. Symptomatic of this peculiar revival, which is doubtless attributable more to a realignment of certain theoretical issues in the field of cognition than to any specific concern for linguistic phenomena in themselves, is the rehabilitation over the past few years of B.L.Whorf (1897-1941), an ethnolinguist who specialized in Native American languages. His work is currently the object of a sympathetic reappraisal, after having been denounced for many years as 'psychologistic' and even racist, even though he explicitly distanced himself from notions such as Levy-Bruhl's 'primitive mentality'. Several 'neo-Whorfian' meetings have been held, where the relations between linguistics, culture, and thought have been reexamined in the light of Whorf's ideas. Likewise, a number of publications have recently been devoted to Whorf, including – in the current decade alone – Schultz (1990), Lucy (1992), Joseph (1996), Gumperz and Levinson (eds) (1996), and particularly Lee (1996), who draws on both published and unpublished sources to paint him as a pioneer whose daring views on the role of language in cognition are largely to blame for the misunderstanding and hostility directed at him by his contemporaries and by succeeding generations.

Despite Lee's evident bias in Whorf's favor, which at times leads her to find more in his thought than may be there, her work is relevant in two ways: first of all, she shows that the so-called 'Sapir-Whorf hypothesis' of linguistic relativism is not reducible to the caricatures that have often been made of it in the literature; secondly, she points out the profound theoretical affinities between Whorf's approach and a number of established positions in other disciplines.

A few words are now in order concerning 'linguistic relativism'. For Whorf, linguistic processes stem from cognitive operations located at the core of human conceptual activity. But these processes do not operate arbitrarily on undifferentiated experience data. They are rather secondary elaborations working up data which are already perceptually structured, and which provide a common basis for reference. There are thus universal configurations of experience, to which linguistic patterns of classification and categorization apply in varying ways. Whorf thus distinguishes 'isolates of experience' (abstracted from sense data already worked up on the interface between the organism and its environment on the basis of invariant biological processes) and 'isolates of meaning' (those features of experience which are involved in the construction of meaning and may be either socially and culturally acquired or purely personal). *The construction of meaning* thus amounts to a selective abstraction from the experience of certain salient or coherent patterns. In other words, the material for linguistic expression is already a structured reality, built up according to psychophysiological patterns which are identical for all mankind – though languages may *conceptualize* these data of experience differently in accordance with differences in culture. Ultimately then, a language can only build up its own particular 'world view' insofar as its community of speakers choose experiential isolates in a distinctive way, and invest them with a common meaning.

On this view, linguistic relativism is not a kind of philosophical skepticism which sees each language community as locked into its own irreducibly specific world view ("each language tells its own truth, i.e., has its own conception of the world"). It is rather more like the principle of relativity in physics, whereby the observer's position in space determines his view of a given object ("each language looks at reality from its own standpoint"). The following two passages from Whorf tend to support this understanding of him as holding that interlinguistic variations are like differences in the projection of a system of coordinates of observation on an invariant background of experience of the world:

> We are thus introduced to a new principle of relativity, which holds that all observers are not led by the same physical evidence to the same picture of the universe, unless their linguistic backgrounds are similar, or can in some way be calibrated ([1940a] 1956: 214).

> (...) users of markedly different grammars are pointed by their grammars toward different types of observations and different evaluations of externally similar acts of observation, and hence are not equivalent as observers but must arrive at somewhat different views of the world ([1940b] 1956: 221).

An explicit statement of the same idea can already be found in Sapir (1924: 153):

> The world of linguistic forms, held within the framework of a given language, is a complete system of reference, very much as a number system is a complete system of quantitative reference or as a set of geometrical axes of coordinates is a complete system of reference to all points of a given space. The mathematical analogy is by no means as fanciful as it appears to be. *To pass from one language to another is psychologically parallel to passing from one geometrical system to another.* The environing world which is referred to is the same for either language; the world of points is the same in either frame of reference. But the formal method of approach to the expressed item of experience, as to the given point of space, is so different that the resulting feeling of orientation can be the same neither in the two languages nor in the two frames of reference. Entirely distinct, or at least measurably distinct,

formal adjustments have to be made and these differences have their psychological correlates.

'Configurational linguistics', as Whorf himself called the theory that he set out to develop, seems to have been influenced by the methods of physics and chemistry. Linguistic units are not thought of as stable, pre-existing components which can be conjoined without effect in linear or sequential relationships, but rather as relatively indeterminate entities which can be structured according to the relational patterns in which they appear, a view reminiscent of the way in which modern physics rejects the mechanistic approach of classical physics. Likewise, linguistic structures are treated in terms of merger, fluidity, and dispersion, notions associated more with chemical processes than with logical calculus. Whorf himself explicitly invokes the parallel with the physical sciences:

> The mathematical sciences require exact measurement, but what linguistics require is, rather, exact 'patternment' – an exactness of relation irrespective of dimension (...) linguistics has developed techniques which, like compasses, enable it without any true measurement at all to specify exactly the patterns with which it is concerned. Or I might perhaps liken the case with the state of affairs within the atom, where also entities appear to alternate from configuration to configuration rather than to move in terms of measurable position. As alternants, quantum phenomena must be treated by a method of analysis that substitutes a point in a pattern under a set of conditions for a point in a pattern under another set of conditions – a method similar to that used in analysis of linguistic phenomena ([1940b]; 1956: 231).

As Lee consistently stresses, this holistic, dynamic, relational approach to the patterned construction of meaning has resonances in both Gestalt psychology and the connectionist theory of neural networks.

The renewed interest in Whorf's theory in the field of cognition is definitely no accident. Equally symptomatic is the fact that this well-organized reappraisal is associated with references to certain contemporary linguistic theories, in particular to the American school of cognitive grammar, whose links with Gestalt theory and connectionism have also been repeatedly pointed out (though to some minds, these grammars seem more concerned with relatively static mental structures than with truly dynamic processes, cf. Nuyts 1996: 154-5; for further considerations about dynamic approaches that take gradual change seriously, see below § 2.2.). Indeed, 'cognitive linguistics' shifts attention from pure syntax to the domain of *semantics and conceptualization*, whence the primacy assigned to metaphor as a linguistic phenomenon (represented by notions such as 'fictive motion', 'mental spaces', and so forth), and the attention devoted to describing the linguistic representation of conceptual fields such as time, space, deixis, etc., in terms of very general underlying cognitive structures of language (cf. work by Langacker, Lakoff, and Talmy). It may be noted in passing that cognitive grammars have numerous points in common with various less internationally renowned European linguistic theories, such as Culioli's (1990) 'utterance-based' (situational) approach or to some extent Guillaume's (1969) psychomechanical theory of language, both of which share some of the theoretical assumptions cited above.

2. Variation and invariance

The diversity of the ways in which languages represent reality is a core issue for linguistics, demanding a theoretical basis for linking variation and invariance. Analogous situations exist in other scientific disciplines, e.g., biology, where the phenotype/genotype articulation is crucial. This issue is equally important to cognitive science: the overall view of how language, thought, and cognition are related intimately depends on how variation and invariance are apprehended.

2.1 The range of variation

The way in which the linkage between language and thought is theoretically expressed is decisive for the view to be taken of the nature and importance of crosslinguistic variation in the construction of representations.

'*Computational*' approaches conceive of language and thought as two autonomous modules, each carrying on its own computational processes. In the words of Jackendoff (1996),

> Thought is a mental function completely separate from language and can go on in the absence of language (p. 2); Although language expresses thought, thought itself is a separate brain phenomenon (p. 8); Language is just a vehicle for externalizing thoughts, it isn't the thoughts themselves (p. 19).

Various scholars using this modular, computational approach (cf. for example, Pinker 1994) would say that understanding a linguistic message consists of transforming sequences of words – ordered differently in each language – into syntactic arborescences, then interpreting the resulting trees as language-independent formulae of logical semantics (Fodor's 1975 'universal language of thought'). The mind, as it were, goes through a zone of formal variation before reaching the *terra firma* of universal conceptual semantics. Interlinguistic differences thus have no bearing on thought itself:

> Thinking is largely independent of what language one happens to think in. A French speaker or a Turkish speaker can have *essentially* the same thoughts as

an English speaker can – they're just in French or Turkish (...). If different languages can express the same thought, then thoughts can be embalmed in the form of any single language: they must be neutral as to what language they are to be expressed in (Jackendoff 1996: 6).

In this passage, the word *essentially* is vital to the reasoning. Indeed, Jackendoff appends the following note (note 2, p. 31):

> I say *essentially* here in order to hedge on possible 'whorfian' effects. There are undoubtedly *expressive differences* among languages in vocabulary, as well as in grammatically necessary elements such as tense-aspect systems and markers of social status (...) such differences must not be blown out of proportion; they are decidedly second- or third-order effects (...). They may create difficulties for literary translation, where style and associative richness are at stake, but no one seriously questions the possibility of effectively translating newspapers and the like.

This reference to 'expressive differences' as 'second-order' means that interlinguistic variation can only affect a minor aspect of thought, i.e., stylistic connotation, while denotative or referential meaning remains invariant in order to assure the possibility of translating informational content. Other writers in the same volume reject this view, cf. Barden's (1996: 66-7) remark:

> If different languages can express the same thought, the thought cannot be embalmed in the form of any single language (...). As soon as you allow that the thoughts might not be exactly the same, you open the door to the possibility that each of the thoughts is indeed embalmed in the form of a particular language.

Barden's reaction is typical of what might be called *'representational'* (as opposed to computational) approaches to language, whereby language is primarily seen as a means of representation of reality and intersubjective communication. These approaches tend to link language to thought by postulating a kind of 'thought language' inherent in all individual languages, while not excluding the possibility of extralinguistic thought. All this is implicit in Benveniste's ([1958] 1966: 70) particularly Whorfian remark:

> The sayable defines and organizes the thinkable. The speaker's language provides him with the basic configuration of the properties his mind attributes to things.[2]

From the representational standpoint, understanding a linguistic message would rather be conceived as a dynamic process: it implies the construction of meaning by the participants, using the meaningful patterns peculiar to a given language, which therefore *vary* from one language to another.

Philosophically speaking, computational and representational approaches fit into different theoretical paradigms. The former belong to the current paradigm of reference in cognitive science, the so-called *'cognitivist'* paradigm which uses the computational model of mind (and the brain, conceived of as a mere processing device for symbols, see Jackendoff 1987, and more recently, Pinker 1994). This model has, of course, given rise to considerable controversy over the years, cf. Searle's (1992) criticisms on philosophical grounds and Edelman's (1992) objections from the standpoint of neurobiology.

As for representational approaches, it must be admitted that there is currently no real alternative paradigm under which they might be subsumed. There are nevertheless various signs that such a paradigm, which has been tentatively labeled *'constructivist'*, is in the making. It would involve rejecting the idea that language should be treated as one (or more) specific, autonomous module(s), thinking of it rather as a property which emerges from the general mechanisms of cognition and has numerous homologous relationships with other cognitive activities, including perception. The notion of computation is thus replaced by the idea of a process of *construction* from which emerge typical, stable and more or less salient meaningful forms. Likewise, a formal apparatus of modelization must be sought, not within algebraic logic, but in dynamic topology.

2.2 From universals to invariant features

However much language-specific representations may vary, they are never irreducibly specific, since language transfer is always a possibility. One could therefore reasonably expect to be able to define certain crosslinguistic *universals of representation*.

Translatability is often cited as proof of the existence of such universals. For those who hold a *computational* view of language, the language-extrinsic universality of thought accounts – as we have seen – for the possibility of translation:

> The point of translation between languages is to preserve the thought behind the expression (Jackendoff 1996: 6).

Thought universals thus provide the common semantic and conceptual foundation for certain secondary variations deriving from differing forms of expression. The process of translation must then consist in eliminating superficial differences in order to reach the hard core which provides the standard of reference. This comes down to establishing an relation of equivalence, while seeming to retain a common informational content *pace* minor variations.

From a *representational* viewpoint, however, the actual possibility of translation, i.e., of constructing equivalents by transposition from one language to another, does not in itself constitute an argument for the existence of transcendent thought universals ready-made for use by individual languages. Many authors make the point that languages are not nomenclatures or stocks of labels for designating *realia*, nor are the vocabularies of individual languages sets of terms for expressing a universal *a priori* system of concepts. What is true of words goes for sentences as well, i.e., syntactic structures cannot be univocally interpreted in terms of universal logical formulae. In other words, any comparison or transposition of these structures can function simply on the basis of a given number of analogical properties and in no way requires the assumption of a common extrinsic content.

Contrastive studies of utterance organization in different languages have shown how each one uses its own lexical and morphosyntactic resources to build specific patterns of meaning involving different pragmatic schemes of orientation, i.e., different layouts of reality. If changing languages is indeed like adopting a new layout (as the quotations from Sapir and Whorf above suggest), then the very conceptualization of the referents must itself change, and the postulated equivalence must be seen in a *dynamic* perspective, somewhat as the way geometry apprehends invariance in the course of *spatial* transformations of figures (by rotation, translation, or dilatation).

One might even venture an analogy with automatic translation by contrasting the so-called 'pivotal systems', which seek underlying language-independent semantic and conceptual representations, with 'transfer systems', which have the more modest and realistic aim of constructing crossover rules for the semantic representations associated with texts in each language (Fuchs *et al.* 1993: 206-9).

Obviously, the theoretical issues of language-to-language translation can be correlated, *mutatis mutandis*, with those of *paraphrase* within a single language. Forms of expression which differ across languages have their correlates in the variety of specific semantic representations constructed by a given language, representations which cannot be reduced to a single logical formula capturing precisely the intersection which provides a common core for measuring difference in terms of quantitative distance. Here again, dynamic equivalences and *qualitative* differences are involved (see Fuchs 1994a).

This outlook replaces the notion of statically conceived substantive universals with that of *operative* universals, or functional invariants, to be viewed in dynamic terms. This would mean that languages construct meaning by an interplay of markers (not just lexical items, but grammatical elements and syntactic structures as well) which are (linguistic) operators – themselves issuing instructions for the elaborating of configurations or patterns of meaning – rather than symbols with substantive content.

2.3 In search of invariants

The search for crosslinguistic invariance in representations has, for many years, been the objective of *typological* comparative studies. These include Greenberg's work in syntax (particularly his 1963 paper and his 1966 work on constituent order and feature hierarchy, where he sets forth the notion of 'implicational universals', for which Vennemann proposed a 1972 generalization in terms of correlations) and Comrie's (1976, 1985, see also 1981) work on tense and aspect systems. Mention should also be made of the work done by the UNITYP group at the University of Cologne under the direction of H. Seiler (Seiler and Brettschneider 1985, Seiler 1994), and by G. Lazard's group in Paris, whose results have appeared in the house journal *Actances*. This trend is currently very much in vogue at the international level, as is shown by the creation in 1994 of the Association for Linguistic Typology and the appearance in 1997 of the first issue of *Linguistic Typology* under the Association's auspices.

The typological approach contrasts with the hypothesis-and-deduction approach of generative grammar. It is *inductive* and tries to generalize from observation and comparison of the largest possible sampling of languages (Greenberg 1973, 1974). It also applies equally to lexical and to grammatical markers (Lazard 1981).

Typologists make no assumption as to the existence of universal grammatical *categories*, but rather start from the fact of variation and look for invariants at the most abstract level of the very processes of category *construction*, i.e., *grammaticalization* mechanisms. To quote Lazard (1992: 431-2):

> Rather than crosslinguistic 'categories', there would seem to be invariant notions around which the categories of individual languages *tend to take form* (...). This means that, if we conceive the set of possible notions as located in a *multidimensional space,* 1) some regions of this conceptual space are such that perhaps all, in any case most, languages construct grammatical tools there (...); 2) some parts of the regions which act as 'fields of grammaticalization' have preferential status, i.e., are *'focal zones'.* The notions found there are much more frequently grammaticalized than others in the same field. Many languages thus have forms whose range of meaning contains one or more of these focal zones; but the *extent and shape of this range will vary* with the language, i.e., will include a given number of neighboring notions in addition to the primary one (italics added).[3]

This implies the existence of *invariants* at the level of both the field of grammaticalization and the focal zone. Nevertheless, each language marks out its grammatical categories in each field. The outlines vary since they are peculiar to each individual language, but the categories frequently include one or more focal zones (*ibid.*).[4]

As this quotation shows, the search for invariants underlying grammatical markers has all the characteristic features of constructivist approaches to language: the rejection of substantive universals, a definition of dynamic invariant features, the representation of meaning in terms of multidimensional space, and the dynamic construction of salient patterns. The notions of 'taking form' and 'focal zone' are symptomatic in this sense, though Lazard wants to avoid defining them too strictly:

> Semantic substance is *continuous* and unstable. Differences within it are *gradual*. Focal zones probably exercise a *variable force of attraction*, i.e., the notions they contain have a varying propensity to grammaticalization (*ibid.*, italics added).[5]

The notions of 'gradualness' and 'continuity' are important here as being characteristic of much recent work in the constructivist tendency (Fuchs and Victorri eds. 1994). They are terms which capture an essential property of natural-language semantics, viz., the deformability of meaning patterns to allow the 'deployment' of meaning, particularly evident in *polysemy*, a phenomenon which is massively attested in every known language and best handled by a dynamic approach (Fuchs 1994b). This is what motivates research into the underlying operative invariants of polysemic markers whose meaning varies in context (Victorri and Fuchs 1996). Notions of gradualness are essential to semantics where absolute constraints of the all-or-nothing variety are rare, but many *relative constraints*, i.e., the results of the interaction of many differently-weighted parameters which bend the meaning in different directions, and shift it gradually or sometimes abruptly, must be accounted for. This is why topologically dynamic tools are needed, algebraic tools having showed themselves inadequate for modelizing such situations whenever there are intermediate cases in continua or regularities which cannot be stated as rules.

Conclusion

It should by now be clear that the search for interlinguistic invariance and the search for invariants underlying semantic variation within a single language (both synchronically and diachronically) are equally reliant on an understanding of *gradualness*. They therefore require identical treatment at the level of theory and modelization, particularly in the form of tools which can go beyond binary oppositions and all-or-nothing conceptualizations, whence the usefulness of topologically dynamic types of modelization.

Allowing for gradualness means recognizing that all languages are by nature such that the relationship between form and meaning is subject to constant readjustments and that there is no ultimate state of equilibrium. Some states are nevertheless more stable than others. These states can be modelized by approximation in a static, discrete way using classic algebraic tools. The stability of apparently fixed patterns can, however, only be explained on the basis of an underlying mobility.

Notes

1. " (...) nous réservons le terme de langue pour désigner un instrument de communication doublement articulé et de manifestation vocale (...) hors cette base commune, *rien n'est proprement linguistique qui ne puisse différer d'une langue à une autre*".
2. "C'est ce qu'on peut dire qui délimite et organise ce que l'on peut penser. La langue fournit la configuration fondamentale des propriétés reconnues par l'esprit aux choses".
3. "Il existerait non pas, à proprement parler, des "catégories" interlangagières, mais des notions invariantes autour desquelles les catégories des langues particulières, en quelque sorte, *se cristalliseraient préférentiellement* (...). (Cela) signifie, si nous nous représentons l'ensemble des notions possibles comme situées dans un *espace multidimensionnel:* 1°) que certaines portions de cet espace sémantique sont telles que toutes les langues peut-être, beaucoup de langues en tout cas, y construisent des instruments grammaticaux (...); 2°) que, dans ces portions d'espace que sont ces "domaines de grammaticalisation", certaines régions sont privilégiées: ce sont les *"zones focales".* Les notions qui y sont situées sont beaucoup plus fréquemment grammaticalisées que d'autres du même domaine. Beaucoup de langues ont donc des formes dont l'aire (ou mieux: le volume) de signification contient l'une ou l'autre de ces zones focales, mais cette aire (ou ce volume) a *une extension et une forme variables* selon les langues, c'est-à-dire comprend, outre la notion privilégiée, telles ou telles des notions voisines".
4. "chaque langue découpe dans chaque domaine ses catégories grammaticales; ce découpage est *variable,* car il est propre à chaque langue; mais il est fréquent que les catégories recouvrent ou englobent l'une ou l'autre des zones focales".
5. "La matière sémantique est *continue* et mouvante, et les différences y sont *graduelles.* Les "zones focales" ont probablement une *force d'attraction variable,* c'est-à-dire que les notions qui s'y trouvent ont plus ou moins de propension à être grammaticalisées".

References

Actances (revue du groupe RIVALC), Paris: CNRS.
Barnden, J. 1996. "Unconscious gaps in Jackendoff's *How language helps us think*". *Pragmatics and cognition*, 4: 1, Amsterdam: Benjamins, 65-80.

Benveniste, E. 1958. "Catégories de pensée et catégories de langue". *Les études philosophiques*. In E. Benveniste. 1966. *Problèmes de linguistique générale*, Paris: Gallimard, chapitre VI, 63-74.

Chomsky, N. 1993. "A minimalist program for linguistic theory". In K. Hale and S. Keyser (eds.), *The view from Building 20: essays in linguistics in honor of Sylvain Bromberger*, Cambridge Mass.: MIT Press, 1-52.

Chomsky, N. 1995. *The Minimalist Program*, Cambridge Mass.: MIT Press.

Chomsky, N. and H. Lasnik. 1993. "Principles and parameters theory". In J. Jacobs et al. (eds.), *Syntax: An International Handbook of Contemporary Research*, Berlin: de Gruyter, 506-569.

Comrie, B. 1976. *Aspect*, Cambridge: Cambridge University Press.

Comrie, B. 1981. *Language Universals and Linguistic Typology*, Oxford: Blackwell.

Comrie, B. 1985. *Tense*, Cambridge: Cambridge University Press.

Culioli, A. 1990. *Pour une linguistique de l'énonciation*, Paris: Ophrys.

Culioli, A. 1995. *Cognition and Representation in Linguistic Theory*. Texts selected, edited and introduced by M. Liddle, Current Issues in Linguistic Theory 112, Amsterdam / Philadelphia: Benjamins.

Edelman, G. 1992. *Bright Air, Brilliant Fire: On the Matter of Mind*, New-York: Basic Books.

Epstein, S. *et al.* 1996. Introduction. In W. Abraham *et al.* (eds.), *Minimal Ideas: Syntactic Studies in the Minimalist Framework*, Amsterdam / Philadelphia: Benjamins, 1-66.

Fodor, J. 1975. *The Language of Thought*, Cambridge Mass.: Harvard University Press.

Fodor, J. 1983. *Modularity of Mind*, Cambridge Mass.: MIT Press.

Fuchs, C. 1993. "Linguistique, sciences du langage et construction du sens en contexte: le traitement de l'ambiguïté". In F. Eustache and B. Lechevalier (eds.), *Langage et aphasie*, Bruxelles: De Boeck, 267-289.

Fuchs, C. 1994a. *Paraphrase et énonciation*, Paris / Gap: Ophrys.

Fuchs, C. 1994b. "The challenges of continuity for a linguistic approach to semantics". In C. Fuchs and B. Victorri (eds.), *Continuity in Linguistic Semantics*, Amsterdam / Philadelphia: Benjamins, 93-107.

Fuchs, C. *et al.* 1993. *Linguistique et traitements automatiques des langues*, Paris: Hachette.

Fuchs, C. and B. Victorri (eds.). 1994. *Continuity in Linguistic Semantics*, Amsterdam / Philadelphia: Benjamins.

Greenberg, J. 1963. "Some universals of grammar with particular reference to the order of meaningful elements". *Universals of Language*, Cambridge Mass.: MIT Press, 58-90.

Greenberg, J. 1966. *Language Universals. With special reference to feature hierarchies*, La Haye / Paris: Mouton.

Greenberg, J. 1973. "The typological method". In T. Sebeok (ed.), *Current Issues in Linguistics*, La Haye / Paris: Mouton, 149-194.

Greenberg, J. 1974. *Language Typology (a historical and analytic overview)*, La Haye / Paris: Mouton.
Gross, M. and A. Lentin. 1967. *Notions sur les grammaires formelles*, Paris: Gauthier-Villars.
Guillaume, G. 1969. *Langage et science du langage*, Paris: Nizet.
Gumperz, J. and S. Levinson (eds). 1996. *Rethinking linguistic relativity*, Cambridge: Cambridge University Press.
Hockett, Ch. 1954. "Chinese versus English: an exploration of the Whorfian thesis". In H. Hoijer (ed.), *Language in Culture*, Chicago: University of Chicago Press, 106-123.
Jackendoff, R. 1987. *Consciousness and the Computational Mind*, Cambridge Mass.: MIT Press.
Jackendoff, R. 1996. "How language helps us think". *Pragmatics and Cognition*, 4:1, Amsterdam: Benjamins, 1-34.
Joseph, J. 1996. "The immediate sources of the 'Sapir-Whorf hypothesis'". *Historiographia Linguistica*, 23: 3, Amsterdam: Benjamins.
Lakoff, G. 1987. *Women, Fire and Dangerous Things: What categories reveal about the mind*, Chicago: University of Chicago Press.
Langacker, R. 1987/1991. *Foundations of Cognitive Grammar*, Stanford: Stanford University Press; vol. I: "Theoretical prerequisites" vol. II: "Descriptive application".
Lazard, G. 1981. "La quête des universaux sémantiques en linguistique". *Bulletin du groupe de recherches sémiolinguistiques*, Paris: EHESS and INALF, IV: 19, 26-37.
Lazard, G. 1992. "Y a-t-il des catégories interlangagières?". In S. Anschütz (ed.), *Texte, Sätze, Wörter and Moneme*, Heidelberg: Heidelberger Orientverlag, 427-434.
Lee, P. 1996. *The Whorf Theory Complex: A critical reconstruction*, Amsterdam / Philadelphia: Benjamins.
Linguistic Typology, Berlin/New-York: Mouton - de Gruyter (vol. 1: 1997).
Lucy, J. 1992. *Language Diversity and Thought: A reformulation of the linguistic relativity hypothesis*, Cambridge: Cambridge University Press.
Martinet, A. 1960. *Eléments de linguistique générale*, Paris: Colin (4th publ.: 1964).
Nuyts, J. 1996. "Consciousness in language". *Pragmatics and Cognition*, 4: 1, Amsterdam: Benjamins, 153-180.
Pinker, S. 1994. *The Language Instinct*, New-York: Morrow.
Sapir, E. 1924. "The grammarian and his language", *American Mercury*, 1, 149-155. In E. Sapir. 1949. *Selected Writings of Edward Sapir in Language, Culture and Personality*, Berkeley: University of California Press, 150-159.
Schultz, E. 1990. *Dialogue at the Margins: Whorf, Bakhtin, and Linguistic Relativity*, Madison: University of Wisconsin Press.
Searle, J. 1992. *The Rediscovery of Mind*, Cambridge Mass.: MIT Press.

Seiler, H. 1994. "Continuum in cognition and continuum in language". In C. Fuchs and B. Victorri (eds.), *Continuity in Linguistic Semantics*, Amsterdam: Benjamins, 33-43.
Seiler, H. and Brettschneider (eds.) 1985. *Language Invariants and Mental Operations*, Tübingen: Narr.
Talmy, L. 1988. "Force dynamics in language and cognition". *Cognitive Science*, 9:1.
Vennemann, T. 1972. "Topics, subjects and word order: from SXV to SVX *via* TVX". In Anderson-Jones (ed.), *Historical Linguistics*, Amsterdam: North Holland, 339-377.
Victorri, B. and C. Fuchs. 1996: *La polysémie: construction dynamique du sens*, Paris: Hermès.
Whorf, B. 1940a. "Science and linguistics". *Technology Review*, 42, 229-231 et 247-248. In B. Whorf. 1956. *Language, Thought and Reality: Selected writings by Benjamin Lee Whorf*, Cambridge Mass.: MIT Press, 207-219.
Whorf, B. 1940b. "Linguistics as an exact science". *Technology Review*, 43, 61-63, 81-83. In B. Whorf. 1956. *Language, Thought and Reality: Selected writings by Benjamin Lee Whorf*, Cambridge Mass.: MIT Press, 220-232.

Cognitive Invariants and Linguistic Variability
From Units to Utterance

Stéphane Robert
CNRS-LLACAN, Paris

Introduction

The question of diversity in linguistic representations is generally dealt with in terms of the categorization of meaningful units in different languages.[1] The purpose of this paper is firstly to show that this question must be approached differently at the level of the isolated units (lexemes or grammatical morphemes) and at utterance level, and secondly to define some of the mechanisms which connect these two levels.

Languages show the greatest diversity in their meaningful units, not just because referential strategies (categorization and referential paths, see 1.1. below) are extremely variable, but also because there is a *'depth dimension'* (see 1.2.) to the meaning of individual terms which differs from one culture to another, and even from one speaker to another. In fact the mode of designation or the way in which access to reference is constructed by a linguistic unit ('referential path') varies notably from one language to another, even when categorization is identical, i.e. for the same referent. Moreover, the representation assigned to a word fits into a complex network of formal and semantic relationships with other terms and also into a web of associations with physico-cultural context ('word depth'). This network belongs to the semantics of the word. It is also very different across languages and even differs from one speaker to another.

In language activity, virtual units undergo certain operations whereby they are incorporated into utterances. The overall meaning of an utterance and the meaning of the units it contains are involved in an *ongoing process whereby meaning is constructed* throughout the duration of the speech act. This process works by the creation of relationships which enable different levels to interact. At the utterance level, the relationship between thought and language can be apprehended in terms of 'projection' and *'dimensional conversion'* (see 2.1. below). In speech activity, multidimensional thought has to undergo a linearization process by which it is projected onto the syntagmatic axis. This process can be described as a dimensional conversion (and reduction) from the multidimensional space of thought onto the linear space of speech. In any natural language, the reduction of the dimensions of thought to the linearity of the utterance is made possible by a complex of relationships, between the units of meaning and the meaning of the utterance, and again, between the depth dimension of the words and the linearity of the utterance (see 2.3.). While language production is formally a sequence of units, the effect which their concatenation in the utterance has on *meaning is,* however, *non-linear* (see 3.).

The ongoing construction of meaning within the utterance places linguistic categories in the role of *tools* available at the outset of a uniquely instantiated process, and therefore loosens their relationship to the categories of thought. Languages thus make use of different tools, but do so within the framework of a common process of meaning construction, much of which has yet to be elucidated.

1. Variability of representations at the level of the meaningful units

It has long been clear that languages divide up the world in different ways through their vocabularies and grammatical categories.[2] Thus the body, presumedly the most universal and immediate of realities, can for example be shown to be divided up into different referential units in different languages. Depending on the scale of reference,[3] French *jambe* designates either the entire member (below the hip) or only the part below the knee, while Wolof *tànk* in the wider sense means the part below the knee, and in the narrower sense, the foot. Likewise, French uses "fingers of the feet" for English *toes*, while German has "hand shoes" (*Handschuhe*) for gloves. But there is more to the matter than this; different languages can also construct different 'referential paths' to reach the same object.

1.1 Diversity of referential paths

The way of naming a given body part can vary, e.g., the terms for the fingers can take quite different referential paths: in French, the index finger is the "one that shows, points", while in ancient Greek, it is the "one that licks" (*likhanós*).

Each of these units thus refers to the same object, but gains access to reference in different ways. This distinction between 'meaning' and 'reference', which has been common since Frege,[4] has been reformulated by several linguists in terms of 'referential path' (Corbin and Temple 1994: 9, also Langacker 1991a: 275 and 1991b: 5, 45). The diversity of referential paths accounts for both interlinguistic variation and some differences between synonyms within a given language.[5]

There is an essential property of language involved here. Words are only the 'representatives' of representations (Culioli 1990: 22), and the way reference is accessed is always a construct. This construction takes place through a choice of certain properties of the object in order to designate it, hence the variability of referential path. Thus, in the case of names referring to fingers, Greek and French have chosen different functional properties of the index finger, and name it according to what the most salient property is perceived to be. Thus in one case, this is its use for pointing, and in the other, its use for scraping. These choices of referential path are both motivated (the finger is named according to one of its properties) and arbitrary (only one property is chosen from among many possible ones). Lexical categorization here provides an example of how variation among languages can be neither stochastic nor strictly deterministic.

While the meaning of a word must not be confused with its reference, neither can its semantic content be reduced to its referential path. The *index* finger is not simply the "one that points". The referential path is nothing more than the 'typical property'[6] around which the semantic content of the term is organized, i.e., the means of gaining access to the various representations assigned to the word. The various semantic values of a lexical item can thus be described as a network of specific values, organized in family-type relationships around a common schematic value (Lakoff 1987: 105, 460; Langacker 1991a: 279-87). This schematic relationship among the various assigned representations is what optimizes the referential power of language, and in particular, what enables a single word to refer to more than one object. To take an example in French, the expression *un bleu* can designate a beginner, a new recruit, a work suit, a cheese, or a bruise,[7] all of which have, in different ways, the common property of 'being blue'. Polyreference is a correlate of linguistic motivation. *Bleu*, in each of its meanings, is however associated with different semantic fields, each with varying connotations.

1.2 Language diversity and word depth

Words call up representations which fit into a complex network of relationships. While most of these phenomena are well known, they do not seem to have been sufficiently modelized. This has led the author to refer elsewhere (Robert 1996: 169-76) to this network as a third dimension of language, called the 'depth dimension of language' (*l'épaisseur du langage*), as an addition to the syntagmatic and paradigmatic dimensions.[8]

In the first instance, this dimension contains the referential value(s) of a term (e.g., the different meanings of French *bleu*), which are culturally coded and make up part of every speaker's common knowledge, or the 'hyperlanguage' in Auroux's (1995: 28) terms. But word depth cannot be reduced to a term's referential values. It includes the various associations linking words to their physico-cultural context, e.g., the referential universes of the various sorts of *bleus*, and also variable connotations (the diverse connotations separating the terms *bleu* and *néophyte*, or *white* as the color of mourning in Chinese and marriage in French, and so forth), background 'scenarios' (e.g., the various types of market relationships underlying terms referring to trade[9] or, in the case of a *bleu* as a new recruit, the military context and the hiearchy of army, etc.).

Language in this way sets up not just a network of relationships which are internal to the meaning content of any given term (such as metonymy, metaphor, schematicity, and extension[10]), but also relations among terms, which can be supported by either meaning (synonymy, antonymy, etc.) or form. Thus, French *pardon* contains *don* "gift" (with a set of Judeo-Christian religious associations), while the corresponding Greek verb suggests shared knowledge (*syg-gignôskein* "pardon", lit. "know with"). Such morphological relationships (whether or not they represent true etymological derivations) produce resonance-like phenomena among the terms in a language: formal resemblance leads to semantic relationships among the notions, connotations, and values associated with each one. Thus, *Côtes du Nord* et *Côtes d'Armor* are the (former and present) names of a single French province, which are quite different in their semantic depth: one is associated with the north (cold, gray) and the other with Armor or Armorica (incorporating both Celtic legend and a formal resemblance between *Armor* and *Amor*).

The network of formal and semantic relationships among terms is made all the more complex by the fact that form and meaning do not change at identical rates. Thus, a French *plombier* ("plumber") is no longer a tradesman who repairs pipes made of *plomb* ("lead"); the depth dimension of the word (hence part of its meaning) has changed through its linkage to the history of the society in which it is used. Some linguistic relationships may nevertheless survive demotivation: the metonymy involved in using the word *plume* ("feather") in the sense of "pen" in French to denote a politician's speech writer is still active, even though writers no longer use feathers to write with. This complex and changing relationship between words and their meanings, between the history of form and the history of content, means that caution is always required in trying to capture cognitive representations through linguistic representations.

Thus words exhibit resonance properties, i.e. have the ability to respond, as if by resonance, to the material and cultural context as well as to other words. These resonance phenomena, due to notional associations, vary widely from one language to another, according to the context and the overall lexicon of each one. The depth dimension provides meaning content to words and, to continue the acoustic metaphor, creates a wide variety of 'harmonics' to the fundamental furnished by the semantic structure of the individual term. The depth dimension is a complex region where linguistic facts are associated both with other linguistic facts and with extralinguistic factors.

This is why word depth is not just language-specific but in the last analysis specific to each individual speaker, since individual experience also plays a part in building specific relationships among words. Thus the word *grandmother*, for example, is caught up in a web of variegated relationships, some of which are intersubjective, while others are strictly personal.[11] For this writer, *grand-mère* in French naturally calls up the domain and structure of kinship relations, but also ideas of *Little Red Riding-Hood*, a brand of jams (*Grand-Maman*), her own grandmother's blue eyes, her grandmother's sister who had a home on the Côte d'Azur, hence the Mediterranean, and so forth.

Clearly, this depth dimension is a functional property of human language. It plays a part both in the representational power of language and in the construction of the meaning of a term in utterances and in discourse.

2. From units to utterance: The dynamics of meaning

We have been hitherto concerned with virtual units which can be stored in memory with their potential values. But units never appear alone in language activity; they are always part of an utterance, where meaning is constructed through a dynamic process. The units therefore undergo certain operations as they are incorporated into an utterance. The various kinds of relationships which are established in the course of the speech production create a contextual linkage which constrains how the meaning of the individual unit is to be interpreted and fits it into the overall design of the meaning of the utterance.

2.1 Language and thought: Sequentiation and dimensional conversion

The communication of a thought content in linguistic form, whether successful or not, requires the progressive dissipation of an initial indeterminacy of the discursive space between speaker and hearer. Before I start speaking, the addressee does not know what I want to say or even, most of the time, what I want to talk about: we have, as common reference ground, only the material situation we share. In order to be expressed linguistically, the thought content has to be progressively built up through the act of speech. Linguistic communication therefore proceeds from a kind of empty common referential space between interlocutors to an increasingly specified referential space. Language activity means eliminating indeterminacy[12] in order to build up a referential space common to the participants. I have argued elsewhere (1996: 186-191) that this dissipation of indeterminacy takes place through a complex process which can be understood in terms of projection and dimensional reduction. In the speech act, the speaker has to project a *multidimensional* thought onto a *linear* axis and break it up into a sequence of discrete units. The physical properties of language (as sound produced over time) are such that verbal expression implies running thought through a specific code, which acts as a bottleneck. This projection of a multidimensional space onto a linear one takes the form of a dimensional conversion or reduction which is often a painful experience for the speaker, involving obliteration or deformation of the speaker's viewpoint: his words say less than he would like them to.

The greatest difficulty for linguistic analysis surely lies in the structural feature of language, which requires that words with individual meaning be used sequentially to build up the overall meaning of an utterance, but without allowing the meaning of the whole to be reduced to the sum of the meaning of its parts. Formally speaking, morphemes are units which are ordered sequentially to make up an utterance; but semantically, words are not units of thought which can be added together to yield the meaning of the utterance. The complex interaction between two levels of meaning (the meaning of the units and the meaning of the utterance)[13] sets up a dynamic process which proceeds throughout the speech act. This non-additive manner of building up the meaning of the utterance is precisely what allows the dimensional reduction of thought to language (and the reverse operation of interpreting the speech of others). The reason why the construction of meaning is not additive is that firstly, words have their own meanings and their own representational depth (the third dimension of language); and secondly, the utterance has structural features which shape meaning in non-linear ways.

2.2 Contextual linkage: The ongoing construction of meaning within the utterance

Using words in an utterance sets up a contextual linkage, creating in turn a frame of reference within which the potential semantic overload of the units (owing to their depth) and the initial indeterminacy of the utterance can be dealt with. This linkage *activates* one or another of the latent values for the given term and reduces its initial polysemy. Thus, in French *terme* can denote a word (as in *terme technique* "technical term") or a conclusion (as in *mettre un terme à* "put an end to"). It can also mean a mere temporal limit (*au terme de sa vie* "at the end of his life") or an outcome or qualitative limit (*une grossesse arrivée à terme* "a pregnancy come to term").

All contextual factors, whether lexical, syntactic, or pragmatic, play a part in building the meaning of a unit in the utterance. In the expression, *terme juridique* "legal term", for example, the connection between the meaning of the adjective and the meaning of the noun is responsible for assuring that *terme* is taken in the sense 'word'. In the plural, *les termes*, a fragmentation[14] is implied which makes it a count noun. But since words denoting a quality cannot be fragmented (**les blancheurs* "whitenesses"), the use of the plural eliminates the qualitative interpretation of *terme*. Likewise, the verb *arriver* "arrive at, reach" in *arriver à son terme* "reach its end" is telic and implies a dynamic process heading towards an intended end, thereby immediately eliminating the sense 'word', even when the preceding semantic context has to do with speech (e.g., *son discours arrive à son terme* "his speech is coming to an end"). The prototypical value of any term is thus more likely to be found in context-free or utterance-initial position.[15] Linkage takes place continuously within the utterance, enabling a term to take two different values within a single sentence, as in the advertising slogan, *au lieu de prendre$_1$ votre voiture pour une remorque, prenez$_2$ une remorque pour votre voiture* "instead of taking your car for a trailer, take/get a trailer for/as a car". Word order and the objects assigned to the verb *prendre/prenez* "take" assure it will have the meaning "consider to be" in the first occurrence and "choose, buy" in the second.

This linkage with the context is what makes communication possible: the depth dimension of the words is not constantly present in full. But the context does more than just filter semantic values, it creates its own. In French, *gueule-de-loup fanée* "withered snapdragon", where the name of the flower is a compound literally meaning "wolf's mouth", the adjective retroactively converts the preceding expression from a genitive construction into a compound noun referring to a flower.

2.3 Ways of connecting depth and syntagmatic dimensions

As we have seen, concatenation draws a guiding thread through the depth dimension of language, creating a semantic 'isotopic'[16] which orientates the meaning of any term towards an interpretation congruent with the semantic field established by what precedes it. Syntactic and semantic possibilities are restricted as the utterance proceeds, and the referential space becomes increasingly specific. This is why we often find ourselves able to anticipate the end of the utterance or to finish other people's sentences for them. The depth dimension of language nevertheless makes it possible to 'verbally hijack' the linearity of the utterance: the speaker can play on the different values of a polysemic term by setting up a set of concomitant isotopics. The activation of different isotopics in this way is the mainspring of most plays on words, much of poetry, and even the kind of explosive rhetoric so dear to politicians. A French deputy named André Santini, commenting on the falling opinion ratings of the prime minister, Alain Juppé, who had previously announced an intention to form a *gouvernement ramassé*, i.e., a "compact government" (with a smaller number of ministers) was quoted as sarcastically saying, *il voulait un gouvernement ramassé, il l'a* "he wanted a *'gouvernement ramassé'* ("compact government " /"government that has fallen flat"), well now he's got one!".

In this context a second meaning of *ramassé* is activated, namely the sense "fail, fall flat" assigned to the verb *se ramasser* in familiar speech, and referring here to the unfavorable polls. Two layers of meaning are thus formed within the utterance. Such layering is made possible by the twofold network of relationships among words: syntagmatic relations and relations in the depth dimension.

The effects of this dual articulation of a single expression which brings the depth dimension into play are all the more powerful when they appear at the end of the utterance and 'retroact' on all that has come before. The activation of the second value then spreads its connotations over the entire utterance, i.e. along the web of relationships established in the depth dimension of the words. This can be seen in the remark made by an important figure in the French Socialist party, Laurent Fabius, concerning the reappearance of the defeated presidential candidate, Lionel Jospin, who had let it be understood that he would withdraw for a time from the political spotlight: *en fait de traversée du désert, la traversée de Lionel Jospin a été celle d'un bac à sable* "more than spending time in the wilderness (lit. crossing a desert), Lionel Jospin has been spending time in a theme park (lit. crossing a sandbox)", i.e., "he could not keep away very long".

A semantic isotopic is set up by associating "desert" and "sand", and the utterance ostensibly compares the time required to "cross" them. But "sandbox" brings in an entire universe referring to children, and its connotations in the depth dimension are diffused throughout the rest of the utterance and retroactively associated with the politician. Here we see words used as time bombs to set off sudden associations of ideas.

3. The utterance: Formal sequencing and non-linear semantic effects

The utterance, then, has specific properties deriving from the connections between the semantic depth of words and its own sequential form.

3.1 The role of depth in semantic time bombs

Contextual linkage makes the information yet to come in a speech act more and more predictable,[17] but never entirely so. The guiding thread can always be broken. Unexpected information introduced at the end of an utterance can in this way have a surprise effect: the informational impact is made all the stronger by its arrival at an unexpected place, given the accumulated specifications created by contextual linkage. The dual network joining words both syntagmatically and through the depth dimension means that an unexpected word can shape meaning in a non-linear way. We have thus seen how semantic time bombs at the end of an utterance can have a retroactive effect by diffusing their connotations throughout the whole utterance. But the use of an unexpected term can also set up a syntactic isotopic with non-linear effects.

This sort of reversal of the information curve is a mainspring of rhetoric, and also of advertising, as Grunig (1990: 115-45), from whom the following examples are taken, has shown. Many advertising slogans make their impact by allowing an unexpected term with a high informational value, owing to its improbability, to intrude into familiar expression. One example is the advertisement for "Dim" hosiery: *en avril ne te découvre pas d'un **Dim***, based on an alliterative French proverb warning against the sudden return of cold weather in springtime, *en avril ne te découvre pas d'un fil* "in April, don't remove a stitch (of clothing)". A similar case is the advertisement for a brand of mineral water, *aide-toi et **Contrex** t'aidera* "help yourself and Contrex water will help you", suggesting the proverb *aide-toi et **Dieu** t'aidera* (lit."help yourself and God will help you", the English equivalent being "God helps those who help themselves"), i.e., fortune smiles on the enterprising. The 'verbal hijacking' only works when the original proverb is there to back up the slogan. Language depth thus makes resonance effects possible, not just among words but among utterances as well. The insertion of a single term ("Dim" or "Contrex") in the utterance has non-linear effects insofar as it activates *two* utterances, the actual slogan and the backgrounded proverb, thereby creating layers of meaning with semantic interaction between the two utterances.

3.2 Intonation and other linguistic butterflies

Returning to the emblematic example of chaos theory, we may say that utterances are like the weather: the tiniest change can affect the balance of the whole system. Intonation is one of those linguistic butterflies which can change the semantic climate merely by a beat of their wings. Thus, depending on the intonation, a simple sentence like *he's coming* can be an assertion, an assurance, a question, or an exclamation of surprise. A change of intonation affects the meaning of the entire utterance.

In more general terms, any phenomenon of *scope* acting within the utterance can be responsible for non-linear shaping of meaning. Thus, the syntactic scope of the adjective in our previous example of *une gueule-de-loup fanée* "a withered snapdragon", brings about the syntactic reorganization of the phrase, whence comes a major semantic readjustment. The scope of focus within the utterance is another factor with non-linear effects. A change in intonation, for example, can bring about a change of focus which has a radical effect on the meaning of the utterance. Thus a French sentence like *ne l'achetez pas par pitié* can have two completely opposite values, according to the scope of the negation with respect to the focus. One meaning would be "have pity and don't buy it". Another, however, would have the scope of the negative *ne...pas* extend beyond the verb *achetez* which it directly modifies, in which case the sense becomes "do not buy it for reasons of pity (but buy it just the same)". There are many such elements in language whose semantic effects extend beyond the syntactic head of their immediate construction.

3.3 Utterance-modifying units

The sequential organization of the utterance is crossed by a variety of transverse structures which are flattened out in the syntactic structure (Robert 1993, 1996: 88-101). The informational structure and the organization of the utterance into topic and comment[18] are one of these. But the utterance has other modifiers on two different levels (Culioli 1978a, 1982) which account for as many types of structural organization within the utterance: the predicative level (where the predicative relationship is constructed) and the higher level of the speech act (where a predicative relationship is associated with a speaker and a set of time/place coordinates). The meaning of some morphemes is such that they bear on the whole predicative relationship in which they have a syntactic role. Thus, in French *Jean est admirable de travailler ainsi* "John is wonderful to work so (hard)", more idiomatically expressed as "it's wonderful of John to work so (hard)", the adjective *admirable* modifies the syntactic subject *Jean*, but it also expresses a judgment on the part of the agent of the speech act (i.e. the speaker or 'enunciator') concerning the predicative relationship <*Jean, travailler*> as a whole.

This category of 'enunciative' morphemes, whose meaning bears on the utterance as a whole so that they affect meaning in a non-linear way, includes both evaluative terms (Kerbrat-Orecchioni 1980) like the adjective *admirable* above and, more generally, the external modal markers which express the way in which the agent of the speech act (the 'enunciator') endorses the utterance, e.g., propositional modalities (affirmation, negation, question, command, wish, etc.), epistemic modalities, and evaluative modalities (Culioli 1978b).

The concomitant activation of more than one level of modifying relationships is made possible by the fact that the meaning of words can function on each level. The morpheme *I*, for example, is associated with both the level of the speech act (since it refers to the speaker) and to the syntactic level (since it designates the subject of the predicative relationship). Likewise, some members of any other morphosyntactic class may have both a syntactic function which connects them to another component of the predicative relationship and a role in expressing modifications which emanate from the agent of the speech act and bear on the utterance as a whole, e.g., verbs or adverbs expressing an epistemic modality: *it **seems** he's forgotten, he's **likely** to come tomorrow*; or evaluative adverbs such as: ***fortunately** he's gone*.

The fact that meaning can be shaped in a non-linear way thus depends firstly on the complex articulation between the utterance and the depth dimension of words, and secondly, on the incorporation of terms into different levels of modification. The latter phenomenon is a consequence of the dimensional reduction to a linear axis imposed by the nature of language, so that all terms are required to enter into a sequential syntactic relationship, whatever the level at which the modifying relationship is established. Thus, in the course of the construction of the utterance, the insertion of any given element creates both semantic resonances and a reorganization of utterance structure which have non-linear effects on the meaning of the utterance as a whole.

Conclusion

Languages vary widely in the way they assign representations to their units. The categorization set up by linguistic units undoubtedly plays an important part in memory storage and cognitive access to referents.

In speech activity however, units are always incorporated into, and at the same time acted upon by a process of linearization of thought in an utterance. If we accept that the specific meaning of the units is built up in the course of the speech act, the problem of the relationship between thought and language (particularly the question of whether or not languages lock us into a way of representing reality) moves elsewhere: linguistic categories are only the tools available for the construction of a uniquely signifying utterance.[19] Looked at from the utterance level, language diversity thus parallels language-internal variation (polysemy, synonymy, paraphrase[20]). The nature of the process whereby meaning is constructed within the utterance implies that linguistic categorization must not be thought of as establishing set mental categories, but only as playing a part *at a specific level* in the construction of linguistic representations. Between language and thought, as between the utterance and its units, a process of construction intervenes with its concomitant adjustments, approximations, and occasional misfires.

Furthermore, the ongoing construction of meaning within the utterance is characterized by the non-linear shaping of meaning. This is the result of the constant retroaction of the units upon one other, thus assuming the existence of 'reentry-type' cognitive mechanisms in language activity, which will require further study.

Notes

1. I would like to thank Raymond Boyd and Steven Schaeffer for help in translating this paper.
2. See for example Boas (1911) and Whorf (1940), who reach different conclusions.
3. On variation of scale, see Langacker (1991a: 283).
4. Frege ([1892] 1971: 103) discusses the fact that the two expressions "Morning Star" and "Evening Star", which both denote the planet Venus, have the same referent but different meaning.
5. Thus, as Corbin and Temple (1994: 10) have shown, French *électrophone* and *tourne-disque* have (or at least once had) the same referent, but differing referential paths. *Electrophone* describes how the sound is produced, whereas *tourne-disque* describes how the device works. Here, interlinguistic variation clearly parallels language-internal variation.
6. This is Culioli's (1990: 129) 'schematic form'.

7. For a detailed analysis of the differences between semantic and prereferential categories, see Corbin and Temple (1994), from whom this example is taken.
8. Word depth cannot be reduced to the paradigmatic dimension: a paradigm defines the classes of words which can be substituted for one another in a given syntactic function, but neither the representational depth of a term nor the semantic relationships between the members of the paradigm (synonymy, antonymy, metonymy, connotative variation, etc.).
9. See Fillmore (1982) on 'cognitive scenes' and 'semantic scenarios'; and Kerbrat-Orecchioni (1977) for a discussion of connotation.
10. See Lakoff (1987: 91-115) and Langacker (1991b: 2-5, 266-78) for discussions of the ways in which the values of a given term can be organized into networks.
11. For this reason, the word depth is a third dimension but not a space such that it is homogenously filled.
12. This concept of Culioli (1982) can be related to Shannon's information theory.
13. This particular relationship between the whole and its parts is what distinguishes language from music.
14. This is what Culioli and others following him have called the discrete nature of count words (Culioli 1978c: 191; Franckel *et al.* 1988).
15. Indeed, the depth dimension of words is criss-crossed by different poles of reference (or 'meaning attractors') which can attract interpretations. The prototype is only one of these. Individuals also have personal meaning attractors: a linguist will tend to interpret the word *instrumental* out of context as a case name, while a musician will think first of his cello. What makes communication possible is that contextual reference points working as meaning attractors take priority over all others, although there may be interference at any time from other sources of attraction.
16. The term is taken from Greimas (1966: 96), but has subsequently been redefined by various linguists. For a detailed analysis of the different kinds of isotopics, see Rastier (1987: 87-141).
17. In particular, see Givón's (1988) attempt at modelling connecting sentence structure and informational predictability of content.
18. The Prague school, in establishing a functional view of the sentence and its informational structure, foreshadowed the general theory of information (for a historical view, see Firbas 1974; also see Chafe 1994).
19. The various constraints imposed by individual languages at utterance level remain to be determined. Work undertaken by D. Slobin suggests there is an intermediate level of constraint between thought and utterance corresponding to what has been called 'dimensional conversion' above, and definable as 'thinking for speaking'. Distinctions involving aspect, voice, and noun modification, for example, constrain the speaker's linguistic representation of an event in different ways. But these distinctions "are not categories of thought in general but categories of thinking for speaking" (Slobin 1996: 91).
20. In particular, see Fuchs (1994).

References

Auroux, Sylvain. 1995. "L'hyperlangue et l'externalité de la référence". In S. Robert (éd.), *Langage et sciences humaines: propos croisés*. Bern: Peter Lang, 25-38.
Boas, F. 1911. *Handbook of American Indian Languages*. Reprint 1966. In P. Holder (ed.). Lincoln: University of Nebraska Press, 1-79.
Chafe, Wallace. 1994. *Discourse, Consciousness and Time: the Flow and Displacement of Conscious Experience in Speaking and Writing*. Chicago: University of Chicago Press.
Corbin, Danielle and Martine Temple. 1994. "Le monde des mots et des sens construits: catégories sémantiques, catégories référentielles". *Cahiers de lexicologie* 65 (2): 5-28.
Culioli, Antoine. 1978a. "Valeurs modales et opérations énonciatives". *Le Français Moderne* 46 (4): 300-317.
Culioli, Antoine. 1978b. "Valeurs aspectuelles et opérations énonciatives: l'aoristique". In J. David and R. Martin (éds), *La notion d'aspect*. Paris: Klincksieck, 191-193.
Culioli, Antoine. 1982. "Rôle des représentations métalinguistiques en syntaxe". *Collection ERA 642*. Paris: Université Paris 7.
Culioli, Antoine. 1983. "The Concept of notional domain". In H. Seiler and G. Brettschneider (eds.), *Language invariants and mental operations*. (Language Universals Series 5). Tübingen: Gunter Narr Verlag, 79-87.
Culioli, Antoine. 1990. *Pour une linguistique de l'énonciation. Opérations et représentations* (tome I). Paris / Gap: Ophrys.
Culioli, Antoine. 1995. *Cognition and Representation in Linguistic Theory*. Texts selected, edited and introduced by M. Liddle. (Current Issues in Linguistic Theory 112). Amsterdam / Philadelphia: Benjamins.
Fillmore, Charles. 1982. "Frame Semantics". In The Linguistic Society of Korea (ed.), *Linguistics in the Morning Calm*. Seoul: Hanshin Publishing Co.
Firbas, Jan. 1974. "Some aspects of the Czechoslovak approach to problems of functional sentence perspective". In F. Danes (ed.), *Papers on functional sentence perspective*. Prague: Academia, 11-37.
Franckel, J.-J. *et al.* 1988. "Extension de la distinction discret, dense, compact au domaine verbal". In J. David et G. Kleiber (eds), *Termes massifs et comptables*, Metz: Université de Metz, 239-247.
Frege, Gottlob. [1892] 1971. *Ecrits logiques et philosophiques*. Paris: Éditions du Seuil.
Fuchs, Catherine. 1994. *Paraphrase et énonciation*. Paris / Gap: Ophrys.
Givón, Talmy. 1988. "The pragmatics of word-order: predictability, importance and attention". *Studies in syntactic typology*. Amsterdam / Philadelphia: Benjamins, 243-284.
Greimas, A.-J. 1966. *Sémantique structurale*. Paris: Larousse.
Grunig, Blanche-Noëlle. 1990. *Les mots de la publicité*. Paris: Presses du CNRS.

Jackendoff, Ray. 1992. *Languages of the Mind: Essays on Mental Representation.* Cambridge Mass.: MIT Press.
Kerbrat-Orecchioni, Catherine. 1977. *La connotation.* Lyon: Presses Universitaires de Lyon.
Kerbrat-Orecchioni, Catherine. 1980. *L'énonciation. De la subjectivité dans le langage.* Paris: Colin.
Lakoff, Georges. 1987. *Women, Fire and Dangerous Things: What Categories Reveal About the Mind.* Chicago: University of Chicago Press.
Langacker, Ronald W. 1991a. "Cognitive Grammar". In F. G. Droste and J. E. Joseph (eds), *Linguistic theory and Grammatical Description.* (Current issues in linguistic theory 75). Amsterdam / Philadelphia: Benjamins, 275-306.
Langacker, Ronald W. 1991b. *Concept, Image, and Symbol. The Cognitive Basis of Grammar.* Berlin: Mouton - de Gruyter.
Rastier, François. 1987. *Sémantique interprétative.* Paris: Presses Universitaires de France.
Robert, Stéphane. 1991. *Approche énonciative du système verbal. Le cas du wolof.* Paris: Editions du CNRS.
Robert, Stéphane. 1993. "Structure et sémantique de la focalisation". *Bulletin de la Société de Linguistique de Paris LXXXVIII*: 25-47.
Robert, Stéphane. 1996. *Réflexions sur la dynamique du sens et la structuration des énoncés.* Mémoire pour l'habilitation à diriger des recherches. Université de Paris 7: U.F.R. de Linguistique.
Slobin, Dan I. 1996. "From 'thought and language' to 'thinking for speaking'". In J. J. Gumperz and S.C. Levinson (eds), *Rethinking linguistic relativity.* Cambridge: Cambridge University Press, 70-96.
Whorf, Benjamin L. [1940] 1956. "Science and linguistics". In J. B. Caroll (ed), *Language, thought and reality: Selected writings of Benjamin Lee Whorf.* Cambridge Mass: MIT Press, 207-219.

Subjectivity, Invariance, and the Development of Forms in the Construction of Linguistic Representations

Antoine Culioli
Ecole Normale Supérieure,
Université Paris VII

Introduction

This paper has two purposes: firstly, to show by way of a few examples that linguistic markers are the seat of various representational constructs which are dynamically "deployed" (in a technical sense) around an invariant meaning element (a schematic form with topological properties, see 3.2 below), through diverse processes of abstraction. This might illustrate one of the dynamic paths of language's unfolding and change. Secondly, I hope to show that this activity of constructing linguistic representations has as its source the cognitive activity of a thinking subject, who constructs both the invariance and the deformations which language develops, via polysemy, synonymy, and word history, as well as in translation from one language to another.

Moreover, I would like to stress the fact that cognitive research cannot exclude actual language from its domain, which means that it should avoid the reductionism based on logico-algebraic procedures which marks most work in Artificial Intelligence or the physicalist reductionism proffered by some biologists. Language is not apprehendable simply through linguistic artefacts and a handful of summary analyses, which miss the real complexity of the phenomena involved – whether they be the range of data from individual languages or the diversity apparent among different languages. Postulating complexity as a given and recognizing the universality of the language faculty as subsuming individual languages in their uniqueness must go beyond either mere declarations of principle, facile scepticism in the face of the intricacy of the data, or the use of a metalanguage which is basically concerned only with macrophenomena of a linear, classificatory nature.

Having said this, I shall now turn to the analysis of specific problems in order to illustrate my own approach and provide the interested reader with a reasoned discussion of a number of theoretical issues. Lack of space compels me to leave out technical definitions, and to restrict this paper to the bare essentials necessary for a good grasp of the theoretical framework. I refer the reader to other writings (Culioli 1990, 1994, 1995) for a more detailed development of the theoretical foundations of the following discussion.

1. Markers, invariant elements, and representations: The example of Vietnamese *phải*

I shall begin with a complex phenomenon which provides a good illustration of how empirical observations can be both language-specific and generalizable. Vietnamese has a marker, *phải*, which has five main types of use. These are as follows:

1.1 Spatial orientation

Phải designates "the right hand, the right side; the right side vs. the wrong side", i.e., one of the terms of an asymmetry based on the subject's representation of his own body, extended to the representation of space.

1.2 Value judgment

The spatial use leads to another order of representation: *phải* also designates "the state of being true, correct, proper, adequate". It is used to mean "be right" with *trái* "left, be wrong" as its opposite.

While such phenomena are commonplace, I must stress the fact that switching from representations of one order (the structuring of body and space, i.e., the contrasts involved in a construction taking the subject as the origin of the reference system) to those of another, involving assessment and evaluation, requires *abstraction*, i.e., "layering" (shifting from level to metalevel) and construction of a "form of forms" introducing an additional property. The process involved here is one of internal modelling which sets up and preserves an *invariant property* (the asymmetrical contrast), then *adds another property*, i.e., the shift from a form in space-time to a form which contrasts the stability of the true and proper with deviation from the 'good' value (through lack or excess), whence the need for the antonym *trái* ("that which is wrong"). Now the construction of this valuational representation ("be right"/"be wrong") involves a figure which is more complex than is at first apparent; for the representation of two possible orientations ("wrong" / "right") in a preference relationship (with "be right" as the positive term) assumes the existence of some external viewpoint from which the two orientations can be contemplated. *Phải* in the sense "be right" thus implies a complex figure with a) a neutral position from which the alternatives can be categorized and b) two alternative, diverging orientations, usually standing in an equiponderant relationship (a figure to be systematically designated hereafter as a *branching path*).

1.3 Negation

There is another use of *phải* which differs from the two preceding ones. Besides marking emphatic assertions and yes/no questions, *phải* can be used to negate a predicative relationship containing a nonverbal predicate (e.g., *của* "possession" or *là* "identification").

We thus find *là* in the affirmative utterance:

(1) Ông ấy là lính
 man / demonstrative / identifier / soldier
 that's a soldier

An utterance of this kind cannot, however, be directly negated since it contains a nonverbal identificational particle (which is unscaled and therefore unavailable for the construction of a contrast, Culioli 1990: 61). *Phải* is therefore used so that the contrast necessary for negation can be constructed (as with "left" / "right" and "wrong" / "right"), yielding a qualitative judgment of conformity between the "something" whose existence is asserted and the designation (attributive description) of that "something which is the case". The original utterance, with *phải* added, thereby becomes negatable as:

(2) Ông ấy không **phải** là lính

using the negative marker *không*.

Note that this operation results in a "layering" which paradoxically "disasserts" the predicative relationship and thereby allows *không* (etymologically "empty of") to apply, not to the positive value of the utterance ("that's a soldier"), but to its abstract representation ("it is not the case that that is indeed [= "right"] a soldier").[1]

We are thus able to follow the marker *phải* on its passage from a representation involving the body and space to its usage in the order of assertion, ultimately observable as a syntactic phenomenon, i.e., the provision of a negative form for propositions with nonverbal predicative markers.

1.4 Deontic modality

Phải also has a modal sense: "ought, should". The figure of the 'branching path' is thus retained, and a *goal-directed valuation* (teleonomy) added: the original "such is the case" / "such is not the case" is thus replaced by "path to a good state of affairs" / "path to a bad state of affairs". The branching path is again constructed with three possible positions for the experiencing subject:
- at the *starting point* or origin of the branching path (i.e., the neutral position corresponding to a state of affairs in which no commitment has been made to either of the paths);
- at the *outcome* of the action committing the subject to the *good* path (i.e., a state of affairs foreseen to be good and therefore sought after), an advantageous, beneficial *telos* is constructed to match whatever ethical, institutional, rational, or other stipulations exist;
- at the *outcome to be avoided*, i.e., the bad or harmful one.

There are thus three positions with respect to two differently valued paths.

The deontic value is obtained as follows: we assume a predicative relation <p> and a validity domain structured as Interior / Exterior. Let the path leading to Interior <p> be the 'good' one; it is thus positively valued and represents the beneficial *telos* (cf. "right hand", "be right"). Now let us block access to the 'bad' path. Only one path remains, whence its deontic value: it would be bad if <p> were not the case. Therefore, <p> *must be* the case and is the right outcome.[2]

Notice that the '*abstract form*' has been retained; only the valuational 'space' in which the form is immersed has changed, whence the additional values: anticipation and elimination of one path. In other words, the branching path is invariant; but either the starting point remains neutral and there is no dynamic in the system (1.1, 1.2, and 1.3 above), or the branches are constructed as paths with an outcome, in which case there is dynamic in the system, temporal distantiation, and agentivity (the fourth use). All this involves the 'superposition' (overlaying) of representations and the proliferation of semantic values; in judgment and negation (1.2 and 1.3), the "right side" represents, by deformation, that which is suitable and that which is the case. By another deformation, the fourth usage brings us to that which is good or upright, whence its deontic sense.

1.5 Marking diathesis

The final usage, attested in a regional form of Vietnamese, introduces a new order of categorization, diathesis (which corresponds here to passivization). In this case, *phải* can be translated as "undergo, suffer, contract (an illness)" or, as a main-verb modifier, "unfortunately for So-and-So" (with a detrimental value). We are thus no longer concerned with spatial positioning, assessment, or teleonomy (goal-directedness), but rather with an agentive relationship: the predicates involved are "transitory", "something happens to someone".

Let us again construct a branching path with its three positions. Let X_0 be the agent (in the broad sense of "the one who affects") and X_1 the "affected". By relating X_0 to X_1, we get the ordered semantic representation $<X_0 \ R \ X_1>$ which can be oriented through selection of the starting point (Culioli 1990: 138). Thus, either $<\mathbf{X_0} \ R \ X_1>$ (where the agent is the starting point), or $<X_0 \ R \ \mathbf{X_1}>$ (where the affected participant is the starting point). At the origin of the branching path, we thus have the representation of the unoriented relationship, with one of the oriented relationships on each branch.

How is it, for example, that in *nó phải bắt* (...) "he was caught up (and punished)" *phải* can be inserted between *nó* "he" and *bắt* "catch" (with no active/passive orientation in Vietnamese, or, to take another language, Chinese)? The answer can be obtained by comparing the two orientations, $<\mathbf{X_0} \ R \ X_1>$ and $<X_0 \ R \ \mathbf{X_1}>$.

$<\mathbf{X_0} \ R \ X_1>$ assumes an agent with a purpose, implying a conative space and possibly success. The purpose may or may not be clear; this is of little importance. The main thing is to reach a result while avoiding harm. The relationship of $\mathbf{X_0}$ to X_1 is thus *not deterministic*, since the path can branch at any time (that is what is meant by conation), leading to failure rather than success.

The process involved in $<X_0 \ R \ \mathbf{X_1}>$, on the other hand, is organized around the state of X_1 (the affected participant): X_0 no longer has the same role, since his action is effective. X_1 is thus affected by what is the case, i.e., the agent's (generally unspecified) action. Consequently, there cannot be two paths, as there is no alternative. The situation is *deterministic*: what is cannot be otherwise. For an agent, being unable to do anything else is being compelled to do what he does; while for the patient, it is being unable to react (which clearly shows how "re-act" marks action in return, impossible in the case of a detrimental value). The adverse value (*phải* as "undergo") derives from the (teleonomic) two-valued relationship between the ability to choose one's path and the inability to do anything else: "being unable to be an agent" is construed as undesirable, whence the detrimental value of what one would like to avoid but cannot prevent.

It should be pointed out that Vietnamese has markers other than *phải* for the relationship between passivization and goal-directed value assignment (teleonomy: "good", "bad", "indifferent"). For the beneficial, there is *được*, for which the convergence of two contextual usages is revealing: one meaning is "get (something good)", e.g., "get a good welcome"; or when asking a child his age. The other is "happen, turn out, be possible, be able". This marker can also mean "fortunately, happily", as in a sentence such as "he bought a big house". The relationship between teleonomy and agentivity on the one hand, and agentivity and modality on the other, is clear. We are thus led to a transcategorial relationship between teleonomy, agentivity, and modality when systems of different orders are superposed on a double-branching path –with one branch leading to the good, the real, what should be or is possible, and the other to the bad, the harmful, or what is undergone.

The marker *bị* "undergo, bear, be affected by something bad" is cognate with Chinese *bèi* "cover, be covered", whence "suffer, undergo". This phenomenon is familiar enough not to require a lengthy commentary. For the neutral value, there is a marker *do*, which can be translated as "be brought about by, result from", in short, as establishing a nonsubjective (hence nonvaluational) causal relationship.

At the conclusion of this first section, we should have a clear view of how cognition, subjectivity, and range of experience, working through epilinguistic (i.e. subjective unconscious metalinguistic) activity, directly shape (or perhaps provide structural models for) representations and markers.

2. Differentiation of meaning, or chance and necessity in the construction of representations: The example of *(ga-)mōtan*

Let us now consider a few more examples of similar "qualitative leaps" from one state, position, path, or facet to another.

2.1 From Greek to Gothic

Gothic *ga-mōtan* is the equivalent of one sense of Greek *khṓrein*, viz. "have, make room for, hold" (the noun *khṓra* means "place"). Nevertheless, an apparently simple case of New Testament translation from the Greek by Wulfila reveals, under careful analysis, an enlightening multiplicity of meanings.

The Greek verb clearly shows that the underlying representation associated with the notion of space ("place") is unoriented and indifferent to the category of agentivity. There are thus usages of two orders: the first involves movement in a given direction (agentivity), while the other involves room, i.e., position in or occupation of space, rather than movement between points. Thus,

1. Movement: *a.* "make way for (someone), withdraw (make room for)"
                b. "go forward", whence (with valuation) "get ahead, progress, be successful"
                c. "spread, get about (as a rumor)".
2. Capacity: "hold, have room for"; "be able to, capable of".

As we have already seen, our point of departure is a minimal representation: places located in a space within which movement occurs; space as a container, or a means of determining the position of any possible object. This minimal representation is the invariant meaning element. A range of usages connected with the experience of space, and particularly, of movement in space, are then established for any subject. The subject can thus move within the space, either in a linear fashion or by spreading, can assess the correspondence between a container and what it contains, or can distinguish between a foreseeable occurrence and its feasability, i.e., the likely path between an initial situation and a situation which can be imagined to exist at some later time. This proliferation of meaning values (which is relatively minor in this case) occurs by "deployment", starting from the minimal invariant element. The result is a *differentiation of meaning* regulated during the speech process by interaction with factors such as the discourse situation, the path opened by the utterance, and the textual context in general. This is what makes lexicography possible and gives the impression of having to deal with a classificatory system using a binary set of features (present / absent). At the same time, deployment, differentiation, and stabilization of usages are governed by no mechanism other than the *chance process* by which a given language community makes choices over time in changing circumstances. It is nevertheless *inevitable* that there should be some *regulation* and choice of *necessary* paths among the possible paths produced in the deployment of meaning.

2.2 Old English

If, within Germanic, we now look at the OE verb *mōtan* (which has the same origin as Gothic *ga-mōtan*), we find that the result is again what I call a deployment, i.e., a variety of usages associated in this case with the notion of "access" (establishment of relations among places through movement in space).

The entry for *mōtan* in the *Concise Anglo-Saxon Dictionary* gives the following translations: "to be allowed, to be able to, have opportunity to, be compelled to, must", with, in addition, "would that I might" for *mōste ic!*. Likewise, the French translations in Mossé's *Manuel de Vieil-Anglais* are "avoir la permission, l'occasion, la force de; pouvoir; devoir".

What is involved here is thus an (inter)subjective modal element such that:
- on the one hand, a subject as agent *anticipates* being able to perform an action to which there is no obstacle ("have the chance, power to, be able to");
- on the other hand, a subject is *submitted* to the agentive force of another subject, which may be simply fate itself ("be allowed, compelled to, have to").

"Be allowed to" links the first case to the second by its equivalence to "not be prevented from doing as one wishes": "X allows Y to" is formally equivalent to "X does not prevent Y from doing as Y wishes", "X does nothing to stop Y from acting as he will", etc.

"Be compelled", however, indicates access under pressure from another individual or from circumstances, yet access all the same. Only the volitive *mōste ic!* then remains to be explained. This expression marks the *fictive* construction of access to a favorable state of affairs (this indeed is what "wishing" is all about). *Mōste* is a past tense form with modal value, and the verb + person marker construction marks the optative hypothetical.

This analysis of *(ga-)mōtan* could be extended to the other Germanic languages. Here I need merely remark the presence in German of *müssen* "must, should" alongside *Musse* "leisure" and *müssig* "lazy, leisurely", which might seem unusual. If, however, we return to the notion of accessibility (and availability, i.e., "position in space-time with respect to"), we can see that:
- on the one hand, we have leisure, freedom from occupation, i.e., availability for access in the absence of commitment to any given path;
- and on the other, we have the commitment resulting from taking on any task or duty, so that "duty" constitutes the reverse side of the notional domain.

The same ambivalence of meaning associated with the notion of availability for access to an occupation can, of course, be found in Latin *ludus* ("game" / "school") or *vacare* ("be free to", whence "devote oneself to a task"), the latter prolonged in French *vacances* / *vaquer*; not to mention Greek *skholḗ* "leisure, nonchalance" / "school".

3. Aspects of the notion of 'representational construct': The example of French *tôt*

Let us now turn to another complex representation which associates:
- a subject's perception of the relative speed of two objects moving in the same direction, with one preceding or passing the other, so that one is ahead and the other behind;

- and a teleonomic (i.e., goal-directed) construct of the relative valuation of two eventualities, no matter whether their occurrence is to be desired and sought after, or feared and avoided.

There are many available examples, but we shall choose French *tôt*, which etymologically came to be associated with <quickness> through the connection between the notions (notional domains indicated by pointed brackets) of <heat> (latin *tostum* "roasted, grilled") and <speed>. To be brief, *tôt* gives rise to a differential representation of a point in time (instant, moment, etc.) on an oriented axis connecting it to some standard reference point (which varies from case to case). Thus, in the case of an interval of time, *tôt* refers to the beginning (that which is *early*); while in the case of an event, *tôt* signifies that that event significantly precedes the point serving as a standard of reference (the event thus comes *before* the reference point).

Both values are represented in:

(3) Je me suis levé tôt$_1$ parce qu'il fallait être tôt$_2$ à la gare
     I got up early because I had to be at the train station early

where *tôt$_1$* is "early in the day" and *tôt$_2$* is "early with respect to a temporal point of reference".

Consequently, *plus tôt* signifies what comes "earlier". If a choice is offered between P and Q, preferring P to Q means putting P before Q: *pre-* is, of course, etymologically "in front of, before". The alternatives are thus ordered, as if on an oriented axis, with P ahead of Q. Note, by the way, that this creates a valuational representation: the good, or the advantageous, is what is placed ahead of everything else. This provides the transition from *plus tôt* as "earlier, sooner" to *plutôt* "rather".

We could now continue our analysis in three different directions.

3.1 Comparison among languages

The first of these directions has us proceeding as we did with *mōtan* and looking for similar configurations in other languages. I need only make a remark here on English *rather*, which is etymologically the comparative of an obsolete adverb, *hrathe* "quickly" (note that use of *sooner* as equivalent to *rather* is now also antiquated).

3.2 Exploration of equivalences among markers

Another direction involves the analysis of the comparative implicit in *plutôt*. This is a topic which is worthy of consideration in its own right. I shall merely draw attention to a single point: saying that "P is more Z than Q" means saying

that no matter what degree of Z Q may possess, P is more Z than Q. Without going into all the detail of the relationship of comparison, we may clearly deduce from this way of putting the matter:
- first, that in the realm of Z-ness, P precedes Q (the analogy here between the comparative of degree and the temporal relationship is particularly enlightening);
- second, that with respect to the property Z, P's Z-ness is positively oriented towards the 'high-degree' (or extreme value), or more precisely, towards the 'attractor' (see below), while Q has no such degree.

This then brings us back to our '*branching path*':
- the neutral point here corresponds to the property Z insofar as there is no commitment to a specific attribution of it, the point of undifferentiation being that of two possible states of affairs: <Z oriented towards the attractor> (say, the lefthand path) / <Z oriented towards the Exterior> (say, the righthand path);
- the first (left-hand) path corresponds to the increasing scale ('more Z');
- the second (right-hand) path corresponds to 'less Z' or 'Z-less'.

The neutral point thus corresponds to $< \bar{Z}$ or $\vec{Z} >$, where the arrow marks orientation either toward the attractor or toward the Exterior, see below, 4.3). Now this configuration is empirically attested and has been brilliantly discussed by Benveniste ([1948] 1975) in his chapter on "The comparative", which deals with the ancient Greek marker ἤ "or". He assumes (1975: 137) a comparison between A and B involving a property

> which is not intrinsic to B, but rather conferred from without upon two objects which do not possess it naturally, one of which (A) has it to a degree which excludes the other (B) from having it. The proper domain for such comparison is that of a choice between two possible terms, whereby what is granted to one is refused to the other, i.e., exclusive disjunction. A and B thus no longer correspond, but are now disjoint, like the scales of a balance, so that even here, ἤ, which marks this disjunction, has its proper function of disjoining the terms of an alternative [...].

A look at the formal analysis conducted above will show that it accords perfectly with Benveniste's descriptive remarks. It is useful here once again to show how a given operation (comparison in this case) can lead to a multiplicity of equivalences among linguistic markers ("more...than", "be ahead of", "or"). These equivalences derive from a representation which constitutes their common invariant feature. This representation is a 'schematic form' (or 'schematic image' with topological and dynamic properties) which is topologically laid out in space with different positions and paths of access to the values associated with those positions.

3.3 The study of 'modulations'

Finally, there is a third avenue of study which involves (among other issues) showing how *plutôt* works in expressions such as *plutôt grand* "rather big", which can be interpreted as meaning either "pretty big" or "very big indeed". Once again, *stabilization* is not synonymous with *rigidity*.

4. Representations as complex constructs: On German *vielleicht* and diverse equivalents

Let us now turn to another representation, one which associates <lightness> and <ease>. It can be found, for example, in Germanic where the root **lenht-* has given *light* (in weight); also *lights* "lungs of a slaughtered animal", in English, and *leicht* "light (weight), easy" (also *gelingen* "succeed") in German. The crossover between lightness and speed is furthermore well attested, whence a notional complex associating <light, easy, fast>.

Now in German, *leicht* also appears in the adverb *vielleicht* "perhaps", in composition with *viel*, here, the intensive "very". How then can *vielleicht* have come to acquire this meaning?[3]

4.1 A complex operation

In order to analyse this phenomenon, let us construct a representation (a schematic form) of the notion involved. If we say, *Perhaps it will rain*, we set up a *fictive* construct for two foreseeable states of affairs: I) "at a given time in the future, <it is raining> will be the case" and II) "at a given time in the future, <it is raining> will not be the case" or "not <it is raining> will be the case". Now let us construct the point of *undifferentiation*, which is also the critical point in the system. It may correspond, for example, to the moment of speaking, a position which is neither I nor II, but from which both I and II are accessible. This means that, at a given time in the future, we will end up at either I or II. To sum up, then, the branching point provides us with a position from which we have access either to I or to II. *Perhaps* thus associates with three different relations:
- there must be a relation of 'otherness', i.e., process P must have more than one value; in fact, two values are sufficient, P (= I) and not-P (= II);
- there must be a ponderation ('weighing up') of the possibilities of I and II occurring; actually, this relationship is no more than equipossibility;

- there must be an equiponderant relation of accessibility, deriving from the preceding one: unobstructed access from the starting point to both states, I and II, must be available.

Fictive assertion of the existence of I or II actually comes down to canceling out the distance between the initial situation (the starting point) and the situation foreseen to be the case (I, II).

If we consider the various markers in this complex operation for <perhaps>, we will notice that any given language may distinguish any of the relations involved. A few examples are Spanish *tal vez*, lit. "such (and such a) time", *quizá*, etymologically "who knows" (placing us at the starting point); (classical and modern) Greek *ísōs* "equally", Dutch *misschien* (where *mis-* indicates diversity and *schien* "take place" marks the "times", the events, as with Spanish *vez* above), etc.

4.2 Accessibility

We may now return to German *vielleicht*, which marks accessibility to I and II: the absence of any obstacle (i.e. ease) places them within the scope of occurrence. Note that, conversely, the dative of classical Greek *skholḗ* "leisure, rest, laziness" (cf. supra) is used adverbially to mean "leisurely, taking one's time, slowly", whence its usage as a negation when preference is assigned to the path leading to not-P (cf. "at one's leisure, i.e. scarcely, hardly, not at all" in the Liddell-Scott dictionary, where "i.e." sums up all our remarks above regarding the relationship between <lightness-speed> and <success>, or the accessibility on which "success" depends, and obstructive <slowness>). The remarkable thing is that the notion of access, when applied to an alternative, brings us back to equiponderance. And once again, this (at first glance) trivial discovery clearly brings out the unceasing process of proliferation, differentiation, and stabilization involved in language activity.

4.3 The 'high-degree'

The matter does not, however, end there. *Vielleicht* is also found in emphatic exclamative constructions: *Du hast vielleicht starken Kaffee gemacht!* "you've really made strong coffee!".[4] Obviously, a translation with "perhaps" would be inappropriate here. Where does this usage come from?

It can be easily accounted for if we recall the structure of the notional domain (Culioli 1995: 45 sqq.) for <you have made coffee which has a given degree of strength>. All notional domains are assigned a center to organize the aggregate of occurrences; this center is either a 'type' or an 'attractor'. A type allows the extent of the match between an occurrence and a standard occurrence to be assessed. Representation as a type is what makes it possible to look at a woman/man and say, *That's a woman/man*. The attractor constructs the extreme value of an imaginary occurrence on a gradient, e.g., *a real woman/man* is a woman/man occurrence matching the type woman/man to the utmost degree ('attractor'), which cannot be verbally expressed in any other way than by reference to an absolute value: *what a woman/man she /he is! How womanly / manly she / he is!* In our "coffee" example, there is also a gradient involved, and the positioning is thus with reference to the *attractor*, which provides, not a definite value which can be situated in relation to a given object, but a representation constructed through a process of abstraction and converging towards an ideal limit. As such, it is inaccessible while still furnishing a stable value. Our example can thus be glossed as "the coffee is strong [stability of the central value] to an inexpressible degree [inaccessibility of the ideal limit]".

Returning to the branching path described in the analysis of *vielleicht*, we note that the only position providing an inaccessible value in the sense just described is the *starting point*. This point marks the construction of all the possible outcomes, which can only be differentiated, making a given value accessible, when a commitment is made to one of the branches. The position at the branching point only gives access to an unstabilized representation: a scan of the possible outcomes with no power/will to choose one of them.

Generally speaking, if an utterance indicates that the speaker is at this branching point, the utterance will have a value of instability, which may take the form of a question or a statement of possible values. Stabilization of the value designated by the utterance requires either that another subjectivity be called upon (as in a question) or that the possible outcomes be made explicit through fictive assertion or assignment of a stabilized value (in particular, by establishment of a relation to the attractor). In the latter case, there is an 'high-degree' construct, as in the example, *Du hast vielleicht starken Kaffee gemacht!*

Let us look at a few more elementary examples: first, <he, smoke>. Initially, we can produce one of the unstabilized utterances, then various values depending on how stabilization is carried out:

- question: *Is he smoking?* (yes or no?)
- possible outcomes: *Maybe he's smoking, maybe not*
- stabilized value: (a) path to the Exterior: *Him - smoke?!* (disbelief)
  (b) attractor (high-degree, the stable, inaccessible value):
  Does he (ever) smoke!!

Vielleicht thus marks the position at the branching point, whence the possibility of using it either to mark doubt ("perhaps") or intense degree in the exclamative construction. Other apparently unrelated phenomena can also be explained in the same way, e.g., the exclamative use of positive or negative questions, as in English *do I know him!! don't I know him!!* and French *suis-je bête!!*; or of indirect questions in French with the same high-degree value: *si je le connais!! si c'est pas malheureux!!* The equivalent in Dutch of English *whether* / French *si* (cf. supra) is *of* (German *ob*), which can also be found with a front vowel in other Germanic languages (in particular, in Icelandic, where *ef* is both equivalent to English *if* / French *si* and a noun meaning "doubt"). Note that Dutch *of* also means "or", taking us back to the same schematic representation according to which a marker for the critical branching point can be constructed to mark reinforcement, which accounts for German *Und ob!* (Dutch *En of!* French *Et comment!* English "And how!"). And the story could go on and on.

Conclusion

Throughout our discussion, we have been using metalinguistic concepts (admittedly without adducing precise definitions) which apply well to topological equivalences (homeomorphisms) constructed from a given invariant element, the result being a constant interplay of the continuous and the discontinuous, proliferation, differentiation, selection, and stabilization. We thereby obtain:
- a system which is both stable and flexible: closed to certain operations but at the same time open and adaptable;
- properties based on linearity and hierarchy, but without compositional features in utterance structure;
- a complex system avoiding all-or-nothing decisions and involving the interaction of heterogeneous subsystems (e.g., in the overlaying of different representations of a single marker), the manipulation of operations over domains, fields, and orientations, and the construction and transformation of representations.

It would be impossible, without subjectivity and intersubjectivity, to account for empirical observations reflecting our cognitive activity, particularly insofar as it expresses itself through language. A system of algebraic metalinguistic representations will invariably prove insufficient to explain the full range of observable data, rather than just a few subsets of quasi-observable facts, chosen for their unproblematic nature. Only an explanatory system which allows for formal layering, deformation, and proliferation, i.e., a dynamic topological system, in association with the notion of invariance, can open the way to a coherent understanding of the relationship between the uniqueness of individual languages and the universality of the language faculty.

In a word, there is a necessary relationship between the subject as cognitive agent and the diversity of linguistic phenomena (above all, the fact of interlinguistic variation itself), which is beyond the grasp of any computational theory whatsoever (so far) of mind and language activity.

Notes

1. On negation, see Culioli 1996.
2. A similar phenomenon exists in Japanese.
3. Provençal and Occitan *beléu* is composed in the same way: *ben* "(intensive) well" + *léu* < Latin *levis* "soon, fast". Space is not available here to deal with another term, *bessai* (*ben* + *sai* "I know").
4. This is a cursory exposition which leaves out prosody, positioning, as well as comparison with *aber* and *ja*.

References

Benveniste, E. [1948] 1975. *Noms d'agent et noms d'action en indo-européen.* Paris: Maisonneuve.
Clark Hall, J.R. and H.D. Meritt. 1962. *Concise Anglo-Saxon Dictionary.* Cambridge: Cambridge University Press.
Culioli, A. 1990. *Pour une linguistique de l'énonciation. Opérations et représentations.* vol. I, Paris/Gap: Ophrys.
Culioli, A. 1994. "Continuity and modality". In C. Fuchs and B. Victorri (eds.), *Continuity in linguistic semantics.* Amsterdam / Philadelphia: Benjamins, 21-32.
Culioli, A. 1995. *Cognition and Representation in Linguistic Theory.* Texts selected, edited and introduced by Michel Liddle. (Current Issues in Linguistic Theory 112), Amsterdam / Philadelphia: Benjamins.
Culioli, A. 1996, "Existe-t-il une unité de la négation?". *La Négation: une ou multiple?* Mémoires de la Société de Linguistique de Paris (Nouvelle série IV), Paris: Klincksieck, 33-44.
Mossé, F. 1950. *Manuel de l'Anglais du Moyen-Age, des origines au XIVème siècle.* (Vol. I: Vieil Anglais). Paris: Aubier.

Language Evolution and Semantic Representations
A Case Study of the Evolution from "Subjectivity" to "Objectivity" in French

Christiane Marchello-Nizia
ENS Fontenay/Saint-Cloud
Institut Universitaire de France

1. Historical linguistics: Questions about linguistic change

There exist three different modes of diversity in language. Firstly, we find diversity between languages. Secondly, there is the diversity functioning within each language. As sociolinguistics has revealed, each individual language is organized into a complex of sub-systems comprising a hierarchy of variables. Diversity organizes languages along social lines, unless it is the social structure which organizes the language's capacity for diversity, thus making a meaningful feature of it. Finally, diversity exists on the level of chronology: all natural languages change, without exception. It is now generally admitted that linguistic change, like geographical and social diversity, should be considered as a universal feature. And if this feature is common to all languages without exception, it may be considered as an inherent characteristic of language. The study of linguistic change is therefore the study of a *language universal*, and this study improves our knowledge of language as an aptitude.

Indeed, there is today no global theory of linguistic change. Some theories partly help to explain changes, such as the theory of parameters or a linguistic typology of syntax. Elsewhere one finds theories relative to just one type of change: such is the theory of "grammaticalization", developed mainly by E. Traugott, P. Hopper, C. Lehmann.

As a diachronic linguist, one is confronted with the appearance and disappearance of forms, paradigms, and even categories. In order to describe such changes, one cannot be satisfied with the notions which are used to describe either one of the synchronic states, that is, the source system and the current system. By definition, if there is change, there is a movement in the system, and there is in fact a change of system. It would therefore be inadequate to project the notional framework of one of the synchronic states onto the diachronic axis. If one contents oneself with notions which merely make it possible to describe one state or the other, one will miss something–precisely the "something new" which is the very object of diachronic studies.

Numerous examples could be given where a comparison between the source and the current systems proves clearly insufficient –where the common link between them was doubtlessly something quite different from what one imagines, since it belonged to a different grammar and a different system.

How should the notions and distinctions which are relevant be determined and presented? What is their nature? Once they are found, and one has abandoned the level of pure description, which is in any case biased by a teleological point of view, one reaches the level of explanation; change can then be described and explained. But there is also –and this is of capital importance– a cognitive interest in this reasoning; first, it casts new light on the faculty of language, as we have already said; and secondly, it reveals the nature of the notions which will prove relevant to the explanation we will now undertake to provide.

For example, in the cases we are going to discuss, we will need to resort to a notion which does not belong to either of these systems: the notion of "subjectivity", which is the representation or marking in morphology of the subject, both as enunciator and as utterer.[1] In most cases this is relative to semantic notions. We support the hypothesis that it is evolution, occurring on the level of just such notions, which governs certain changes within languages.

This is also the case for grammaticalization, which has already been alluded to in the preceding paragraphs: it often consists simply of encoding some subjective nuance in grammar which had been missing earlier, as has been shown in several studies by E.Traugott (1990, 1991, 1993). The changes which are studied here–which are not cases of grammaticalization and which do not in any way contradict those studies–reveal an altogether different, even diametrically opposed phenomenon. We see instead the disappearance of a grammatical or lexical encoding of subjectivity, and the appearance of "objective" semantic values.

We will deal here not with cases of terms or categories whose appearance always seems straightforward in retrospect, but with cases for which no reason nor necessity seems to justify the change that has actually taken place. We will deal with three phenomena: these are mainly the demonstratives and their evolution in French, and secondarily two other linguistic facts, both of a lexical nature.

2. A case of morphological reorganization: The evolution of demonstratives in French

We shall first take up one of the well-known questions in diachrony, broached many times. The changes which have occurred in the system of demonstratives in French have given rise to many studies in the past hundred years–the literature on this theme is not only rich, it is excessively abundant. It presents the advantage of now being well documented, thanks to the data bases of texts built up using computer techniques. Thus, we have had the opportunity of working on two different sets of data: the 12th and 13th century Old French data of about 700,000 words that our research group has collected, in which we have found more than 8,000 occurrences of demonstratives; and the data from the forthcoming "Dictionnaire du moyen français" (*Dictionary of Middle French, 14th-15th Centuries,* from now on, DMF), comprising 4 million words, among which more than 30,000 occurrences of demonstratives are to be found.

2.1 Deixis and anaphora

There is commonly assumed to be a link, whether from a diachronic or from a synchronic perspective, between deixis and anaphora, between deictics (which refer to the world) and anaphorics (which refer to the text). In our languages, deixis is mainly represented by demonstratives, anaphora by personal pronouns. But many languages have forms which may function as one or the other. Some demonstratives are, in a given synchronic system, both deictic (i.e. they refer to an object of the world, outside the text or the discourse) and anaphoric (they refer to the text: anaphora or cataphora); such is the case for *ille* or *iste* in Latin, of *cil* in Old French, *celui-ci* and *celui-là* in modern French. But apart from these forms, there are some which are only anaphoric, such as *is* in latin, *cil qui* in Old French, *celui qui/celui de* in modern French, and others which are only or mainly deictic, such as *-ci* in contemporary French.

This link can also be found in diachrony. It is well known that in various languages, personal pronouns and definite articles originate in demonstratives. Thus, the personal pronouns of Romance languages originate in a paradigm of demonstratives having a deictic value (*ille*); the definite determiners of the same languages have the same origin. This evolution characterizes the passage from Latin to Romance languages; it also characterizes the evolution of Germanic languages, and today even that of Finnish, which is developing a definite article taking the form of the demonstrative *se* (see Laury 1997). This link of semantic and formal proximity is often considered as a universal trait.

The problem we shall be dealing with here is not an additional illustration of this relation: the proximity shall be taken for granted, and it is with respect to this link that the changes we will look at now will acquire meaning.

The change in question here has in fact no meaning: it is a sort of mutation– not semantic but morphological– which takes place not between two different categories of morphemes, but within the system of demonstratives itself. There precisely lies the enigma which we will now consider.

2.2 The target system, the source system: Modern French, Old French

Let us first look at the target system; it is the system of demonstratives as it functions in contemporary French, without any change since the 17th century, at least, without any significant change as far as our topic is concerned.

Figure 1: The system of demonstratives in modern French

Pronouns

	Masculine		Feminine	
sg	**celui**	+ ci/là + de SN + qui/que	**celle**	+ ci/là + de SN + qui/que
pl	**ceux**	+ ci/là + de SN + qui/que	**celles**	+ ci/là + de SN + qui/que

Determiners

	Masculine		Feminine	
sg	**ce/cet N**	+ Ø + ci/là + qui/que	**cette N**	+ Ø + ci/là + qui/que
pl	**ces N**	+ Ø + ci/là + qui/que	**ces N**	+ Ø + ci/là + qui/que

In the 12th century, the system of demonstratives was completely different: it was based also on an opposition between two paradigms, but this opposition was not of a morpho-syntactic nature. In fact, both paradigms, CIL (originating in the latin *ecce + ille*) and CIST (originating in the latin *ecce + iste*), could function as pronouns and determiners, a trait which is no longer found in contemporary French.

Figure 2. Demonstrative pronouns and determiners in Old French (12th C.)

	Case	CIL	CIST
Masculine	Subject sg	(i)cil	(i)cist
	Object sg 1	(i)cel	(i)cest
	Object sg 2	(i)celui	(i)cestui
	Subject pl	(i)cil	(i)cist
	Object pl	(i)cels, (i)ceus	(i)cez
Feminine	Subject sg & Object sg 1	(i)cele	(i)ceste
	Object sg 2	(i)celi	(i)cesti
	Subj / Obj pl	(i)celes	(i)cestes,cez

In the 12th century, one could find just as frequently *Cil chevaliers vient* ("That knight is coming") and *Cil vient* ("He is coming"), *Cist chevaliers vient* ("This knight is coming") and *Cist vient* ("He whom we see is coming"). The same demonstrative forms were used as pronouns and determiners. The difference between the two paradigms lays in their semantics: the forms of the CIST paradigm were either deictic or anaphoric but referred only to the adjacent context. The CIL forms were anaphoric, but not necessarily in reference to a contiguous text, and were occasionally used as an unmarked form in place of CIST. Hence, one opposed *Cil vient* ("that one / he is coming") and *Cist vient* ("that one, whom we see, is coming").²

2.3 First steps of the change: **ces** then **ce** appear

At the end of the 12th century a new form appeared: *ces*. For a long time, this form was interpreted as a new graphic form for *cez* (see Figure 2 above), the masculine plural objective case form of the CIST paradigm. Indeed, at the end of the 12th century, the occlusive fricative [ts], written -z at the end of words had simplified into the fricative [s], and *cez* ([tsets]) had become [ses]. The written form *ces* had therefore been placed, in the grammars of Old French, next to *cez*. But there were a number of utterances in which clearly the form *ces* did not correspond at all to the meaning in the CIST paradigm. More recently, basing his work on a heavily documented phonological and dialectal analysis, A. Dees (1971)[3] showed that this written form *ces* also derived from the masculine plural objective case form *cels* (see Figure 2 above) in its unstressed uses; that is, when it is used essentially as a determiner. In the same way that *dels* (originating in the combination of preposition *de* + definite determiner *les*) resulted in *des* after the loss of [l] in front of [s] at the end of an unstressed syllable, and in the same way that *als* (from *a+les*) usually resulted in *as* (and sometimes remained *aus*, which has persisted in modern French), *cels* turned into *ces*. Thereafter, *ces* appears to have a double origin, and therefore as being the semantic equivalent both for the determiner *cez* and the determiner *cels*. This explanation, solidly confirmed by the data, makes it possible to account for some uses of *ces* which, as we have said, were difficult to explain if one only took into account its belonging to the CIST paradigm.

Having accepted this analysis, there are two ways of including the new form *ces* in the previously described system of demonstratives. One way is to include it with *cez* on the one hand, and with *cels* on the other hand, in the two primitive paradigms; but then, since the forms belonging to these two paradigms can be both determiners and pronouns, the fact that *ces* is only a determiner is glossed over. The other way is to put the emphasis on what is specific to this form compared to the other ones: its exclusive use as a determiner, its naturally unstressed character and the semantic neutralization implied by its double origin; thus, it creates a micro-paradigm of its own.

Two events immediately subsequent to the appearance of *ces* tend to prove that the second option should be retained. First, the extension of the use of *ces* to the feminine plural, in place of *cestes* or *celes*: *ces* feminine is found as early as the beginning of the 13th century. Secondly, and of even greater interest, is the appearance of the masculine singular objective demonstrative *ce*, in place of *cest* or *cel*, but not necessarily of *cestui*, *celui*, *icestui* or *icelui*. As it has been shown elsewhere, these "long" (*celui*) or "very long" (*icelui*) forms are used in some contexts where *ce* is not found, even though in some other uses, they seem to commute with *ce*[4]; in sequences where the demonstrative determiner has the same value, *ce* and *cest* alternate, as well as *ce* and *cel*.[5] Thus, with these forms – *ce* masculine singular and *ces* masculine and feminine plural – a real paradigm (even if it is a small one) is created, with demonstratives which are pure determiners, always unstressed and semantically neutralized; that is to say, which can be either deictic or anaphoric without any formal distinction, and which in the plural neutralize the gender distinction since *ces* can be used, as *cez* before it, for both the feminine and the masculine.

Several hypotheses have been formulated to account for the emergence of *ce*: is its origin *cel* or *cest*, whose final consonant(s) have disppeared in front of another consonant? If such is the case, *ce* should be found in all regions, since in this hypothesis, its origin is not linked to that of *ces*; but in fact, *ce* is found only in regions where *ces* also exists.[6] Is *ce* then a creation based on the analogy between the new demonstrative *ces* and the definite article *les*, modelled on the singular *le*? The new paradigm does present some of the morphological characteristics of the language spoken at the time: the paradigm of the definite determiners also had a masculine singular objective case form, *le*, a masculine plural objective case form *les*, and the same form *les* for the feminine plural. A. Dees, after H. Yvon, demonstrated that the only satisfactory answer is that of an "analogic" nature.

A further argument helps to confirm this explanation: some texts display the masculine subject case form *cis*; in those grammars in which it is included, it is interpreted as a derived or dialectal form of *cil(+s)* or *cist(+s)*; we think that it should be interpreted–at least in the texts and areas where *ces* is also found –as an attempt to complete the paradigm. In fact, *cis* is always a determiner, and appears mainly in 13th-century texts which also feature *ce* (*Le Roman de la Rose ou de Guillaume de Dole* by Jean Renart, *La Mort le roi Artu*, *les Récits d'un Menestrel de Reims*): *...ne ne cuide que cis grans doels soit pour ses freres* (Artu 100: "And he cannot imagine that this great misfortune is for his brothers").

2.4 The demonstratives in the 13th century: Three main paradigms and the appearance of an autonomous paradigm of determiners

One consequence of the appearance of *ces* as a determiner was the rapid disappearance in the early beginning of the 13th century of the *cez/ces* pronoun. Thus, a place in the paradigm was left free and the system of opposition between CIL and CIST became incomplete. A new form then appeared to maintain the opposition: *ceus-ci*, that is, the corresponding form of the CIL paradigm–but modified by the adjunction of the adverb *ci/la* as a deictic suffix– became the corresponding form of *cez* in the other paradigm. This is a very clear case of incorporation and grammaticalization[7] of an element which nevertheless remains an adverb. As A. Dees (1971) has shown, *ceus-ci/la* is the first composed demonstrative form to appear in French.

Later on, all other pronoun forms were likewise to accept the *ci* or *la* suffixes.

If one now reconsiders the system of demonstratives, one notes that a small independent group has been formed, comprising forms especially devoted to determiner uses. It is therefore adequate to give a different description of the system of the 13th century from the one given for the 12th century, as Figure 3 shows below.

Figure 3. Demonstrative pronouns and determiners in the 13th C

	Case	Pronouns and determiners		Determiners
		CIL	CIST	CES
Masculine	Subject sg	(i)cil	(i)cist	
	Object sg 1	(i)cel	(i)cest	ce
	Object sg 2	(i)celui	(i)cestui	
	Subject pl	(i)cil	(i)cist	
	Object pl	(i)cels,(i)ceus	((i)cez),(ceus-ci)	ces
Feminine	Subject sg & Object sg 1	(i)cele	(i)ceste	–
	Object sg 2	(i)celi	(i)cesti	
	Subj / Obj pl	(i)celes	(i)cestes,cez	ces

Here then we have new possibilities, such as:
- a substitution between the following: *Il voit cel chevalier* ("He sees that knight") / *Il voit cest chevalier* ("He sees this knight") / *Il voit ce chevalier* ("He sees that~this knight");
- the appearance of a gender-neutralized form: *Il voit ces chevaliers et ces dames* ("He sees these knights and these ladies");
- the creation of a new pronominal form with the suffix *ci* in the CIST paradigm: *Qui ceus ci porroit metre jus..?.* ("Who could smite these people?" – end 13th century)

2.5 Middle French: The forms which are specialized as pronouns

The first great change, which we have just examined, had to do with the constitution of a small autonomous series of purely determiner forms. The second –complementary– great change consists in the establishment, during the next period, of a paradigm of forms which functioned only as pronouns. We thus end up with the binary structure which prevails today for the demonstratives.

One can make out four steps in the establishment of this micro-paradigm of forms which became specialized in pronominal use. Those four steps are revealed by four strange phenomena which shall be now considered in detail.

The first step is the difference in treatment of the masculine singular or plural subject case *cist* on the one hand, and *cil* on the other. Until this point, their uses were parallel; after the third quarter of the 13th century, the situation was reversed: *cist* disappeared within less than half a century, whereas *cil* was still commonly used. The huge DMF data bank boasts about two thousand occurrences of *cil*, and not a single one of *cist* after 1320. Nothing is unusual about the fact that a subject-case form such as *cist* ceased being used at a time when bi-casual declension was disappearing in French. In fact, the form used as a subject was that of the corresponding objective case (*cest, cestui*). On the contrary, what is surprising is the fact that *cil* endured: why is it that, precisely at that time, the two forms diverged? There lies the enigma.

Cil was clearly less frequently used around 1400, and totally disappeared around 1430. Whereas *cist* disappeared completely between 1260 and 1320, *cil* endured one hundred and fifty years longer. But the time of its disappearance is not haphazard. *Cil* receded precisely at a time when the subject personal pronoun *il* was undergoing a thorough mutation; at that time *il*, which was, like *cil*, both singular and plural, both stressed and unstressed, was losing its autonomy. One ceased saying *Il qui vient...*("He who is coming") and in this disconnected use, the stressed form *lui* took its place: *Lui qui...*("Him-used-as-subject who is coming"). We therefore assume that *cil* thus followed the evolution of *il*. Just as the autonomous, stressed uses of the personal pronoun (which include the subject case) were henceforth to be assumed by *lui*, *celui* would later establish itself as the demonstrative pronoun.

2.6 15th and 16th centuries: Only some pronominal forms remain. Why those?

The remark we have just made is going to lead us toward a comprehensive explanation. Traditionally, the changes in the system of the French demonstratives were described as the specialization of the CIL paradigm in pronominal uses, and the complementary specialization of the CIST forms as determiners. But by the simple comparison of figures 2 and 3 with Figure 1, it can easily be inferred that this explanation is erroneous.

First, there were, in 12th-century Old French, seventeen forms of demonstratives (we do not take into account here the *i-* prefixed forms such as *icil*, etc.): eight in CIL, nine in CIST. But they were not all maintained: modern French has only eight forms, which correspond to four pronouns, coming from CIL, and four determiners, of which only two – *cet* and *cette* – come from CIST; the other two, *ce* and *ces*, are autonomous creations, as we have seen. Out of the seventeen forms of the original paradigm, only six have remained. Why is it these then, and none of the eleven others (among which figure some forms which were very seldom employed, but also others which maintained a high frequency of use until the 16th century, such as *cestui* as a pronoun, and *celle* as a determiner)?

If one observes those pronoun forms which remain nowadays, one notices a strange phenomenon: there is *celui*, which we have just dealt with, *ceux*, which was the only possible form after the disappearance of *cist, cil* and *cez*; there is also *celle*, in competition with *ceste* used as a pronoun and which, besides, was still used as a determiner, and finally, *celles*, a form which is also used as a determiner. Why have these forms remained, and only as pronouns, and none of the others?

Our assumption can be stated in a few words: the only pronominal forms which have remained are those which had a corresponding form in the set of stressed personal pronouns: *(ce)lui, (c)elle, (c)eux, (c)elles*. One can therefore analyze the demonstrative pronouns as resulting from the combination of the neutral *ce* with each of the personal stressed pronouns: *ce+lui, c(e)+elle, c(e)+eux, c(e)+elles*. And similarly, the only determiners which remain are those which formed, together with the other determiners, a paradigm: *ce (cet), cette, ces,* as *le, la, les,* as *mon, ma, mes,* as *un, une, des*.[8]

2.7 Assessment: The extension of a morphological pattern and the loss of a semantic contrast

What then has emerged from these upheavals?

Something which did not exist in the group of demonstratives has appeared: a morphological distinction now exists between one series of determiners and another series of pronouns. In fact, this distinctive feature extended to the demonstratives which in Old French concerned all the other representatives of determiners, excluding precisely the demonstratives. Thus one sees the gradual establishment, between the end of the 12th century and the middle of the 15th century, of a **meta-morphological pattern** in which pronouns and determiners are formally distinguished, a pattern in which the Romance languages, and more rigourously than all the others, the French language, is opposed to Latin.

What then has disappeared?

What has disappeared is an important semantic distinction, that which opposed a paradigm of plain demonstratives, CIL, to the CIST paradigm which explicitly referred to the situation of utterance or to the immediate context. This distinction is not maintained in modern French in the opposition between *celui-ci* and *celui-là*.

The evolution could be roughly summarized as follows: the passage to modern French accorded primacy to the current meta-morphological pattern and abandoned the semantic distinction specifying the reference situation of utterance. Morphological order prevailed over semantics, and especially over the explicit reference to the situation of utterance and to the utterer.

We shall now examine, more briefly, two other phenomena, different both in nature and as to the levels on which they take place. One concerns the verb *cuidier* ("to believe" or "to think"), the other, a pair of adjectives, *vrai* and *reel*. They will cast a new light onto what we have just presented (necessarily step-by-step and at great length), placing it in the context of a much larger semantic and cognitive evolution.

3. The extension to two other cases, and conclusion

3.1 The verb cuidier *and the utterer-enunciator*

In Old and partly in Middle French, there is a verb which has disappeared as such, but which has left two traces in modern French: the noun *outrecuidance* ("presumptuousness") and the adjective *outrecuidant*. This is the transitive verb *cuidier*, which could take as its complement either a noun, an infinitival group or a noun clause; it is this latter form which interests us mostly. The verb of the noun clause could be either in the indicative or subjunctive forms. It was in the indicative only if the three following conditions were fulfilled: the subject of *cuidier* had to be the first person singular pronoun *je*, that is to say, the only pronoun which refers specifically to the utterer; the verb had to be positive, and it had to be in the present tense: *Et je cuit qu'il le passera* (Chrétien de Troyes, *Yvain*, 2669: "And I believe he will go beyond the appointed date").

If only one of these conditions was not fulfilled, the complement noun clause was in the subjunctive, as in the following utterances, where *soit, seüsse, moreüst, truisse* are present or imperfect subjunctives (we have taken our examples from the same text, that is the novel by Chrétien de Troyes entitled *Perceval ou le Conte del graal*):
- If *cuidier* is in the first person, present but negative: *Mes je ne cuit que ce soit hui.* (id., ibid., 6592: " I fear it is not yet for today.")
- If *cuidier* is in the first person and positive, but the tense is not the present of the indicative: *Et je cuidai qu'il ne seüsse parler.* (id., ibid, 323: "And I thought, and I was wrong, he had not the power of speech")
- If *cuidier* is positive and present, but the subject is different from *I*: *Ele cuide que ele truisse ostel...* (id., ibid., 4865: "She believes she has finally found a dwelling")

This verb is usually translated in modern French as "croire" ("to believe") when it is in the first person, present tense, positive (the utterer as enunciator assumes and is convinced of the veracity of his words). It is translated in all other cases as "penser, s'imaginer que" ("to think, to suppose") where the words or thoughts of the (grammatical) subject are not "guaranteed" by the utterer-enunciator (see above: *je cuidai, je ne cuit*) or are reported by an enunciator who reckons that the grammatical subject is wrong or might be mistaken (*ele cuide*). In modern French, it is no longer possible to have a single verb in such a situation – apart perhaps from *prétendre*.

The verb *cuidier* disappeared between the 15th century and the 17th century –concurrent with the settling of the modern system of demonstratives–and with this verb, the possibility of seeing the speaker-utterer define the true or untrue character of the assertion given in the complement noun clause. *Cuidier* was succeeded by *penser* ("to think") or *croire* ("to believe"), where the subject-utterer ceases to be the possessor of the truth or error. With the disappearance of *cuidier*, as with that of the opposition between CIL and CIST, it is the primacy of the enunciation which disappears, or at least which becomes subordinate to an objectified notion of the opposition true/false or of the opposition internal/external to the situation.

3.2 The "Vrai" (true) and the "Réel" (real)

This third phenomenon is, superficially speaking, purely lexical: in Old French, there used to be one single word "vrai" (true) (or rather two synonyms, *verai* and *voir*), which refered both to a truth assumed as subjective (truth) as well as to a truth asserted as objective, exterior to any judgment (reality). We can therefore find utterances such as those shown below, for which the modern French translator must introduce the notion of realization precisely where Old French uses a word belonging to the same family as "vrai" (true): *Onques mes songes ne fu si averez.* (*Couronnement de Louis*, v. 299, 12th century: "Never dream came more true"); *Vray est que quand messire Looys d'Espaigne fut monté ou port de Garlande,...* (Jean Le Bel, *Chronique*, 14th century: "It so happened that when His Highness Louis of Spain reached the passage of Garlande, ...")

Here again, at the end of the Old French period and through the Middle French period, a change took place: a new word appeared – the word *real* – taken from the Late Latin *reale(m)*. This new word first appeared in a legal text which was very important in the history of French law, the *Coutumes de Beauvaisis* by Philippe de Beaumanoir (1283); its use then became common in wills and legal acts, before successfully expanding to philosophical studies.

Beaumanoir explains this word with great precision. He introduces the term to establish a distinction between *personnel* (personal), "which concerns persons", and *reel* (real),[9] "which concerns things"; the "inquiries in justice" (that is, the accusations, the complaints) should not be presented in front of the same courts if they concern persons on the one hand or things and material goods on the other:

> *Les demandes personeus sont qui touchent la persone, si come convenances, achas, ventes, vilenies fetes, obligations,... Les demandes reeles sont quant l'en demande eritages, si comme terres, bois, pres, vignes, eaues,... La resons pour quoi nous avons dite ceste division si est tel que, selonc nostre coustume, les demandes qui sont personeus tant seulement doivent estre demandees par devant les seigneurs dessous lesqueus li defendeur sont couchant et levant, et les demandes qui sont reeles et celes qui sont mellees doivent estre demandees par devant les seigneurs des queus li eritage sont tenu.* (édition Salmon, § 229-232)

> "'Personal' charges are those concerning people, such as contracts, purchases, sales, offences, bonds... The 'real' charges are those relative to inheritance such as lands, woods, prairies, vineyards, waterways (rivers, ponds)...The reason for which we introduce this distinction is that, in our customs, 'personal' charges must be brought to the landlord on whom the accused depends. The charges which are 'real' as well as those which are of mixed nature must be brought to the lord on whom the inheritance depends."

But quite soon, *reel* "real" was to be correlated with the notion of empirical, objective existence: Amyot would talk of *reale verité*, "real truth". Thereafter, *reel* ("real") was opposed to *virtuel* ("virtual"), *idéal* ("ideal"), *conceptuel* ("conceptual"), and to *vrai* ("true"), in a different manner – as what actually exists is opposed to what is envisaged in discourse. This conceptual step had been taken as early as the 13th century with the distinction made between "realism" and "nominalism", in the field of philosophy, and therefore in Latin. In French, the new term was first created in the legal field in order to express the distinction between what is connected to persons and what is connected to objects. But one can see what this distinction tends towards the disjunction between what is "truth" in the eyes of a speaker who stands as an enunciator possessor of the distinction, and what is "truth" empirically, because it is effectuated, actualized and existing in the world.

3.3 The loss of "subjectivity": Towards an "objectivation" of language?

With the terms *cuidier* and *vrai/réel*, we believe we have two converging phenomena.

When language has only *verai/voir*, it means that the enunciator[10] is the necessary mediator of the "real", first perceived then given as "true" by him.

With the introduction of *reel* as opposed to *vrai* in the 16th century, an opposition was institutionalized, "true" being kept for discourse, assertion, utterance and text, with possibly the world as a guarantee, whereas "real" was supposed to refer directly to the world "as it is", without the necessary intermediary – at least in language – of the enunciator.

The case of *cuidier* is in all respects identical. This verb implied obligatory reference to the enunciator (whether represented by the speaker or not), the necessary mark of the enunciator in language: "I am saying that I have reasons to believe..." / "I am saying that I wrongly believed / that he wrongly believes...". This verb was replaced by the verbs "to think" or "to believe", whose meaning in terms of truth (value) is ambiguous, and for which the truth must be measured in terms of reality or of an external truth; the vision of truth carried out by the enunciator represented here as a subject ("*je*") became secondary, and demanded precisions. In both cases, the evolution shows that the enunciator is less present, less clear; it shows, let us say, a tendency toward "objectification" in language.

Let us now return to the demonstratives. The distinction around which the system of opposition of the two paradigms CIL and CIST was organized was semantic; it relied on a form of deixis taken into account by morphology, since it enabled a contrast to exist between morphemes which necessarily implied reference to a contiguous element (for CIST), and those where it was not implied (for CIL). CIST was to be interpreted as: "I am saying that I am showing, and that what I am showing is close to me/us, in the immediate context of the text/world which surrounds me". We then had a system of opposition founded at the highest level on the situation of utterance, which then expressed, in morphology itself, the presence of the enunciator.

This is precisely what we noticed in the case of *cuidier*, construed according to the enunciator's vision of "truth" (whether or not he was represented), either with a noun clause in the indicative, which in Old French was the mode of the true-real, or with the subjunctive, mode of the virtual or the unreal-false. And in the same way, through the vision of an enunciator (not textually represented either), *verai/voir* organized the "real", i.e., the world.

The study – albeit brief – of these two phenomena, one lexical, the other syntactico-lexical, has enabled us to shed light on and interpret the first phenomenon of the demonstratives, which is now less enigmatic. The evolution of the demonstratives in French did have, in the beginning, a phonetic motivation – let us say that it was made possible by a phonetic phenomenon – that is, the simplification of the ending of two forms, *cez* and *cels* turning into *ces* ([tsets] and [tsels] becoming [ses]). But we also know that morphology always prevails over phonetics, and that this is the reason why the notion of "analogy" was invented in the 19th century. If a phonetic change takes place, when it endangers the equilibrium of a system (and it is the case here, as we have seen), it means that there was no obstacle to it. The evolution of the demonstratives, as it unfolded, follows the same pattern as what we have defined as two movements:

- the first, one which is meta-morphological: is the generalization to the whole of French morphology of a distinctive structure which was only primary in Old French (and which did not exist in Latin, as it is certainly a proto-Roman creation). The systematic distinction was made between the "pronoun" function and the "determiner" function, both functions being linked to syntax (whereas before that time, it was the semantic function of "representation", or of "anaphora" which concealed the morphological distinction);
- the second, which is semantic, and therefore cognitive is the disappearance in morphology and syntax, at least in the three cases we have examined (and the study should be pursued), of the marking of the subject-enunciator as the center and guarantor of what is "real". We have thus assumed that language underwent a process of "objectivation", an evolution which begins to be perceptible in French toward the end of the 13th century.

Notes

1. " Enunciator ": he/she who assumes or takes responsibility for his/her own utterance, *vs* " speaker " or " utterer ": who utters a clause regardless of whose opinion it is. See A.Culioli (1995).
2. About these distinctions, see G.Kleiber's articles.
3. See A.Dees (1971: 124)
4. See C. Marchello-Nizia (1995) *L'évolution du français, Ordre des mots, démonstratifs, accent tonique*, Paris, A.Colin, chap.4, p.139-144.
5. Thus: '*Ha ! Dieu, fet il, que pourrai faire De ce meschief, de cest afaire?*' (Anjou, v. 3553); and in *Le Chevalier a la charrette* by Chrétien de Troyes: *Et se reisons ne li tolsist Ce fol penser et cele rage,...* (And if reason had not taken away this mad idea and this rage,...). Examples quoted by Dees (1971: 65).
6. See also Dees (1971: 119-128).
7. The grammaticalization phenomenon we have here is comparable to the use that was made in Latin of the adverb *ecce* as a prefix to turn the demonstratives ISTE and ILLE back into deictics.
8. See C.Marchello-Nizia (1995: chapter 3).
9. The word *reelleté* was then created, following the same pattern.
10. See Note 1.

References

Texts in Medieval French

Bonnefois, Pascal (ed.). 1990. *Récits d'un ménestrel de Reims*. Thèse de Doctorat (Paris-7).
Frappier, Jean (ed.). 1963. *La Mort le roi Artu*. Genève: Droz.
Langlois, Ernest (ed.). 1966². *Le Couronnement de Louis*. Paris: Champion.
Lecoy, Félix (ed.). 1963. *Jean Renart, Le Roman de la Rose ou de Guillaume de Dole*. Paris: Champion.
Poirion, Daniel *et al*. (eds). 1994. *Chrétien de Troyes, Oeuvres complètes*. Paris: Gallimard (Collection La Pléiade).
Salmon, Amédée (ed.). 1970². *Philippe de Beaumanoir, Coutumes de Beauvaisis*. Paris: Picard.

Linguistic references

Culioli, Antoine. 1995. *Cognition and Representation in Linguistic Theory*, edited and introduced by Michel Liddell (Current Issues in Linguistic Theory Series 112). Amsterdam and Philadelphia: Benjamins.
Dees, Antonij. 1971. *Etude sur l'évolution des démonstratifs en ancien et en moyen français*. Groningen: Wolters-Noordhoff Publishing.
Dees, Antonij. 1980. *Atlas des formes et des constructions des chartes françaises du XIIIe siècle*. Tübingen: Max Niemeyer Verlag.
Kleiber, Georges. 1985. "Sur la spécialisation grammaticale des démonstratifs en français ancien". In *Mélanges H.Naïs, De la plume d'oie à l'ordinateur*, p.99-113.
Kleiber, Georges. 1987. "L'opposition *cist/cil* en ancien français ou comment analyser les démonstratifs?". In *Revue de Linguistique Romane*, 51, p.5-35.
Laury, Ritva. 1997. *Demonstratives in interaction*. Amsterdam and Philadelphia: Benjamins.
Marchello-Nizia, Christiane. 1995. *L'évolution du français. Ordre des mots, démonstratifs, accent tonique*. Paris: Armand Colin.
Marchello-Nizia, Christiane. 1989. "Le neutre et l'impersonnel". In *Linx 21, Genre et langage*. 173-180.
Marchello-Nizia, Christiane. 1992. "L'évolution du système des démonstratifs en français". *La Déixis*, PUF, 43-52.
Marchello-Nizia, Christiane. 1997. "Variation et changement, quelles corrélations?". *Langue française 115*, 111-124.
Traugott, Elizabeth C. 1989. "On the rise of epistemic meanings in English: An example of subjectification in semantic change". In S. Adamson, V. Law, N. Vincent and S. Wright (eds), *Papers from the Fifth International*

Conference on English Historical Linguistics. Amsterdam: Benjamins, 496-517.

Traugott, Elizabeth C. and König, Ekkehard. 1991. "The Semantics-Pragmatics of Grammaticalization Revisited". In E.C. Traugott and B. Heine (eds), *Approaches to Grammaticalization* (vol. I). Amsterdam: Benjamins, 189-218.

Traugott, Elizabeth C. and Heine, Bernd (eds). 1991. *Approaches to Grammaticalization,* Vol. I, Amsterdam-Philadelphia: Benjamins.

Traugott, Elizabeth C. and Hopper, Paul J. 1993. *Grammaticalization.* Cambridge University Press.

Part II

Conceptualization and representations of space across languages

Spatial Orientation
in some Austronesian Languages

Françoise Ozanne-Rivierre
CNRS-LACITO, Paris

Introduction

The conceptualization of space is an area which affords great scope for linguistic and cultural variation. It is also a field in which a great deal of research has been carried out in comparative and cognitive linguistics over the past few years: witness, for example, the substantial bibliography given in Svorou's work (1994) on "the Grammar of Space", or the work that has been carried out on the subject by researchers in cognitive anthropology from the Max Planck Institute (MPI of Nijmegen).

This variability is particularly manifest in the field of spatial orientation. The difficulties I encountered, while doing field work in New Caledonia as I tried to find my way following instructions given by local informants, cannot only be put down to my ignorance of local geography or to my lack of a "sense of direction". They are to be explained above all by the fact that the usual anthropocentric references familiar to a French speaker (in front of/behind, on the right/on the left) are practically never used by Kanak speakers to indicate direction or to say where something is located, even though the equivalent terms exist in all the local languages.

In these languages, as in most Austronesian languages, the main points of reference used for giving directions are not based on the visible axes of the human body, but are external to it and based on the surrounding natural environment.

Before I go on to present some of these Austronesian directional systems, how they are expressed in language and what sort of references they are founded on, I would like first of all to give some general indications which will help to understand not only how these systems compare with directional systems in general, but also how they compare with the system that can be reconstructed for Proto-Austronesian, and to try to assess to what extent and in what way the main features of this proto-system have been preserved in present-day languages.

1. Absolute and relative spatial orientation

Generally speaking, orientation in space can be either *absolute* or *relative*. Absolute orientation is based on fixed reference points such as the points of the compass or wind directions. Relative orientation depends on the circumstances, and relies either on external reference points found in the surrounding environment, such as the sea/land axis, upstream/downstream, or else on reference points based on oneself and on one's particular position in a given space at a given time (in front of/behind, on the left/on the right).

Languages usually alternate or combine these different types of reference points. In some languages, both systems may be used, but in different contexts. This is the case in English, where, in a small space, references are relative and anthropocentric ("look behind you", "turn left" and so on), whereas for larger geographical spaces the fixed system with cardinal points prevails ("north of Paris", "Eastern European countries", etc.).

In other languages, the same system is always used, whatever the scale. This is the case in Malagasy, an Austronesian language in which the same absolute system with four cardinal points is used both in macro- and in micro-orientation. Thus, instead of saying "the book which is on your right", they say "the book which is on the north (or the south) of the table".

However, the four points of the compass are not universal, and Brown (1983), in his study of the origins of cardinal systems in different linguistic groups, points out that in most languages, their lexical encoding appears to be a relatively recent development. The introduction of a technology such as the compass – and with the subsequent progress in navigation – undoubtedly contributed to the development of cardinal systems in Western languages. It is significant that the English terms *north, south, east* and *west* originally entered the Romance languages as nautical terms before replacing (at least in the standard variety of the language) local vernacular terms which corresponded (more or less) to them. Other factors, such as the development of a cosmology within an organized system of belief, may also have contributed to the appearance of a cardinal system in languages of other, very different families. Malagasy is an example of this, but other cardinal systems can be found in Australian Aborigine languages as well as in Maya languages. Finally, in some cases, the system may have been borrowed from another language.

In his dictionary of synonyms of Indo-European languages, Buck (1949: 870-73) shows that in these languages, the terms which correspond to the points of the compass have very diverse origins. In some languages these terms derive from words describing the daily movements of the sun ("dawn", "morning", "to rise" > east; "evening", "to set" > west; "midday" > south), whereas in others the original terms refer rather to the canonical position of a person looking towards the rising sun: "in front" > east, "behind" > west, "right" > south and "left" > north. Sometimes the north-south axis corresponds to the names of winds.

In any case, the widely different origins of these terms rule out the possibility of reconstructing a Proto-Indo-European cardinal system. Nevertheless, we can clearly see the crucial importance of the fixed axis of the rising/setting of the sun in the development of the different directional systems in this linguistic family.

2. Directional systems in Western Austronesian

In Proto-Austronesian we cannot reconstruct a cardinal system, but we can identify a directional system based not on the daily course of the sun, but rather on the opposition "inland"/"towards the sea", which clearly reflects the particular insular and maritime environment in which this proto-language was developed (Blust, 1984).

This basic axis for relative orientation has remained operational in most Austronesian languages, and there are two Proto-Austronesian terms, *Daya* "inland" and *laSud* "towards the sea", which are widely reflected with these meanings. In certain environments situated a long way from the sea, their meaning has been extended to "upstream"/"downstream". However, we shall see that in some languages these two etymons have lost their original topographical value and have become fixed points in a compass-like system.

This is what has happened in several western Austronesian languages, in which, as Adelaar (1997) has shown, to the sea/land axis has been added a further, fixed axis, one that is of essential importance to Austronesian navigators: that of the prevailing winds of their native region (the monsoon winds). These winds, which change direction from one season to another, can be reconstructed in Proto-Malayo-Polynesian as *timuR* "south-east monsoon" and *habaRat* "north-west monsoon".

2.1 The example of Malay

In Standard Malay (Adelaar, 1997: 59), there is nowadays a fixed east/west axis *(timur/barat)* which reflects the names of the monsoon winds, and which combines with a north-south axis *(utara/selatan)* to form the present-day cardinal system, used equally well to give directions in a large geographical space as to show the position of one object with regard to another. *Utara*, the term used for the north, turns out to have been borrowed quite recently from Sanskrit, whereas *selatan*, for the south, derives from *selat* meaning "strait".

As Adelaar explains, the original terms for the north-south axis in Old Malay continued the Proto-Austronesian divisions of **laSud* and **Daya*, "towards the sea" and "inland". The derived terms *laut* and *daya* are indeed still used in the compound directions *timur-laut* "north-east", *barat-laut* "north-west", and *barat-daya* "south-west". Their replacement is due purely and simply to a shift in cultural and political power which took place in the 14th century, away from the island of Sumatra and towards the Malaysian peninsula, which explains the loss of the old terms for "north" and "south", since they no longer fitted the new geographical environment. The term *selatan* for the south refers, of course, to the Malacca Strait which divides the Malaysian peninsula from Sumatra.

2.2 The example of Malagasy

Malagasy (Hébert, 1965), which we have already mentioned, provides another example of a fixed directional system. In this system, we no longer find the opposition "towards the sea"/"inland", but the monsoon winds (**habaRat* and **timuR*) are still featured as two fixed points (*a-varatra* "north" and *a-tsimo* "south") within a cardinal system, the importance of which has been underlined by all Malagasy specialists, both in everyday life and in symbolic uses. References on a four-directional basis (north-south-east-west) are used in Malagasy all the time and on all scales: in the country, in the village, in the house, in tombs, and for the location of people and of objects. Little use is made of notions such as "in front of"/"behind", "left"/"right". The cardinal points are even used to identify parts of the body, and to the customary greeting "Where do you come from?" the compulsory reply is "From the north" or "From the south", depending on the circumstances. However, it is clear that in all places and in all conditions, a Malagasy speaker sees himself and locates himself (and also locates all other objects and people) with regard to these four cardinal points.

2.3 The example of Balinese

We find a similar situation in Bali (Ramseyer 1977: 99), where the influence of Hindu culture is very strong. Here, we also have a cardinal system, which is not only used to describe everyday movements, but is also, as in Madagascar, the reflection of a very strict cosmic order. This compels all Balinese people to orient themselves all the time with regard to the four directions which structure their space, in order to avoid behaving wrongly.

However, unlike the Malay and Malagasy systems, the Balinese system is not a fixed one, and depends on one's geographical position. The basic axis of *ke-lod* "towards the sea" / *k-aja* "towards the mountain" is a reflex of the Proto-Austronesian **laSud /*Daya* axis, whose topographical value it has retained. So, when these relative directions are translated (as they often are) by "south" and "north", and when people say that in Bali the points of the compass are inverted according to which coast one is on, this is a Eurocentric view which is completely misleading.

To these directions – which revolve around Mount Agung, the central mountain (as well as the sacred mountain) of Bali, and which have nothing to do with the points of the compass – another, absolute axis must be added, which corresponds to the rising/setting of the sun: *k-angin* "east"/*k-auh* "west". The Balinese system of orientation is, therefore, a mixed system with two axes, only one of which is fixed.

Not all Western Austronesian languages have developed a cardinal system of this kind. In the Philippines, for example, N. Revel (1990: 85) has shown that the Palawan divide their space according to an "upstream"/"downstream" (*daja / napan*) axis, with a further, non-oriented, transversal axis (*dipag*).

As we shall see, this topographical axis, inherited from the Austronesian ancestor, has remained operational as a fundamental organizational principle in directional systems of Eastern Austronesian languages, that is, in the Oceanic area.

3. Directional systems in the Oceanic Area

The gradual move of Austronesian speakers eastward throughout the Pacific area brought most of them away from a monsoon-type climate. This kind of reference therefore ceased to be operational as a means of giving directions. However, as a number of Polynesian and Melanesian examples will show, the fixed axis of the prevailing winds (in this geographical area, the east winds) was nevertheless to remain the main indicator for orientation on a large scale.

Indeed, Oceanic languages generally have two directional systems: one is a relative system, based on topography, used in a small area, and the other is absolute, based on the direction of the prevailing winds, used over a large area.

We propose to illustrate these systems with examples from a Polynesian language, the language of the Marquesas Islands, and from a Melanesian language, Nemi, from New Caledonia.

3.1 A Polynesian example: Marquesan

In Marquesan, in the limited area of the valley, Lavondès (1983) describes a directional system with two axes, one of which (the one that concerns the valley) is vectorially oriented. We therefore have a tripartite division of space, to which correspond three verbs of motion:

oriented axis:	*hiti* "to go up"	*'i uta*	"inland, upstream"
	heke "to go down"	*'i tai*	"towards the sea, downstream"
non-oriented axis:	*taha* "to pass"	*'i ko*	"crossways"

In the larger context of the archipelago or for sea travel, only one axis is used, which is oriented "upwards/downwards" (*'i uka* / *'i a'o*), the orientation corresponding to the fixed points of east/west. On this scale, there is no transversal axis as such. If they want, for example, to indicate the position of a reef, they can use – besides the terms "upwards" (east) and "downwards" (west) – the terms of relative orientation already mentioned (*'i uta* "inland"/*'i tai* "towards the open sea"). In this context, as in Bali, we therefore have a mixed system.

In Lavondès' opinion, the assimilation of the east to the upward side and the west to the downward side is not related to the course of the sun, but rather to the way in which people used to sail. According to local informers from the islands, it is the axis of the prevailing winds (which blow from east to west throughout all the region) which is the main determining factor for orientation. This hypothesis has been largely substantiated by the correspondence of *east-upwards* and *west-downwards* in several languages of this Pacific area, where the prevailing winds are easterly. This is the case in Tahiti (Lemaître 1973), in Tonga (Churchward 1956) and in Fiji (Milner 1956: 107-8), where "upwards/downwards" indications corresponding to easterly/westerly directions are used most often in this way on the open sea, and are even glossed in Tahitian as "the side from which the wind blows"/"the side towards which the wind blows".

3.2 A Melanesian example: Nemi of New Caledonia

In New Caledonia (Ozanne-Rivierre 1997), as on the Marquesas Islands, the directional system varies according to the frame of reference. However, unlike Marquesan, which possesses various sets of particles to express relevant oppositions, the languages of mainland New Caledonia have only a single pair of terms, "up" and "down", which is used on all scales. As we will see, according to the scale they are used on, these terms can refer to quite different types of orientation.

3.2.1 On a small scale

In Nemi, the language spoken in the Hienghène area, in the limited context of the valley, of the village, and even of the house, orientation is relative and topocentric. Here we can see space divided up into three directions along two axes, only one of which is oriented: the up/down axis. The three directional suffixes, *-da* "up", *-dic* "down" and *-en* "across" are clearly derived from the corresponding verbs of motion, *ta* "to go up", *tic* "to go down" (for the oriented axis) and *hen* "to go" (for the non-oriented transversal axis).

In this three-directional system, the up/down oriented axis is used to express the following oppositions: inland/towards the sea, upstream/downstream, towards dry land/in the water (sea or river), inside the house/outside the house, and, when one is inside the house, towards the interior of the house/towards the door (Ozanne-Rivierre 1997: 86).

The directional suffixes *-da* "up", *-dic* "down" and *-en* "across" are also used to describe more isolated movements on a horizontal or a vertical level, e.g. *na-da* "to place something high up", *na-dic* "to place something low down", *na-en* "to place something horizontally". In all Nemi speech, these different types of movements are always strictly oriented, using the system we have just described. One does not go fishing, one "goes down", one does not go into a house, but one "goes up", etc.

We may note in passing that if one "goes up" when entering a house and "comes down" when leaving it, this is not only due to the way in which houses are generally oriented, but also because traditional Kanak dwellings used to be built on raised ground. Today, even with the multiplication of European-style houses in the towns and in the bush, the expressions still remain as a constant reminder of the old material culture, much in the same way that French people still cross the road "*dans les clous*",[1] even though pedestrian crossings are now signalled differently.

We can also note that this opposition between "up" and "down" does not only structure concrete space, but is also used to connotate social relations and the strictly codified systems of attitude in these Melanesian societies, which have highly-developed rules of etiquette. In the middle of the last century, the first missionaries noted that people always "went up" to visit someone of a higher social status. Even today, people will tend to say *na-di-me* "give me down here" instead of just *na-me* "give me", as a sign of respect.

3.2.2 *On a larger scale*

We come now to the wider context of movements throughout the country or over the sea: just as in the Marquise Islanders' language, there is no longer a crossways axis, but only one axis which has a name. This can be identified as an up/down *(-da/-dic)* axis, based this time on fixed points which more or less correspond to our points of the compass, with "up" referring both to the south of the country and the west coast, and "down" referring to the north and to the east coast.

If on this scale only "up" and "down" are available for giving directions, this is because, as I have previously shown (Ozanne-Rivierre 1997: 87-88), several different reference systems have in fact been superposed.

The axis which goes from the south ("up") to the north ("down") of the country is clearly based on the prevailing winds in the area. The trade winds (south-east winds) blow across New Caledonia all year round, and when you move along the coast (by land or by sea), towards the south-east, you are going into the wind and are therefore "going up", whereas if you go towards the north-west, you are going away from the wind, and are therefore "going down".

However, the other axis linking the west coast ("up") and the east coast ("down") has nothing to do with wind directions, nor has it to do with the geographical relief of the country. The significant direction here is "inland"/"towards the outside", the west coast being considered as the bottom of the country ("up"), and the east coast ("down") as opening out both onto the open sea and toward the other islands.

It should be noted that people do not only "go down" when they go towards the east coast, towards the Loyalty Islands and Vanuatu, but also when they go to Australia or France. So, when you leave the country you "go down", just as you do when you leave a house.

3.2.3 *Deictic Directional Markers*

These topocentric or geocentric directional markers can be combined, in a verb group, with deictic directional markers, either centripetal or centrifugal, indicating 'towards' (*-me*), or 'away from' (*-ec*), and which are centered either on the speaker in the context of an exchange, or on any other point that the speaker may have in mind in a narrative context. Thus, for the verb *fe* "to carry", we find the following combinations: *fe-da-me* "to bring up", *fe-di-me* "to bring down", *fe-da-ec* "to carry up and away", *fe-di-ec* "to carry down and away".

In fact, in any Nemi narrative (Ozanne-Rivierre 1979), most verbs of action ('to carry', 'to throw', 'to put', 'to arrive', 'to look', etc.) are almost automatically accompanied by suffixes indicating the direction of the movements carried out by the different protagonists. When we examine Nemi narrative structures, we can see that the frequency of these spatial markers (and their repetition in sequences that punctuate the narrative) is not gratuitous, and that their function is often to compensate either for the absence of an explicit subject, which is often omitted as the narrative develops, or else for the imprecision of a pronoun which could stand for the subject, but which is unmarked for gender. When, in a narrative, there are several protagonists intervening, the repetition of certain actions or sets of actions with these directional suffixes is a means of avoiding ambiguity, since they act as a constant reminder of the absent noun referent (Ozanne-Rivierre 1997: 89).

To these directional markers with multiple references we can add an incredibly rich and varied battery of toponyms, which are of capital importance for these small societies for whom space is paramount. In New Caledonia, the identity of an individual and his clan membership are defined by referring to particular points in space, and to routes which justify why such and such a group is located in such and such a place. It is customary to refer to a person by the name of the place he lives in, rather than by his own name. All Nemi narratives, from the most ordinary tale to the great historico-mythological narrations, abound in such toponymic references. It is clear that these oral traditions, firmly implanted as they are in local geography, are not only used to transmit values and to pass on stories, but are also a way to teach – in a very concrete way – the youngest members of the community about the socio-geographical space they occupy. For the older ones, it is a way of memorizing it. A Nemi storyteller who knows the main plot of a narrative by heart, but who has forgotten certain toponymic references, will prefer not to tell his story.

Conclusion

In conclusion, we can underline the permanence of the reference points used in linguistic directional systems in the languages of the Austronesian family. Even when the Austronesian etymons are no longer attested, we can see that indications of direction remain predominantly geocentric rather than anthropocentric, whether we are dealing with space on a large scale or on a small scale. We have even seen that in some languages a very strict system of points has developed, based on these indicators, used on all scales, and determining a system of absolute angles in spatial descriptions.

This goes against the prevalent belief among researchers in human spatial cognition that the system based on the human body with its dissymmetrical (in front/behind) and symmetrical (left/right) axes provides the most natural structure for conceptualising space, and that the egocentric and anthropocentric model which characterizes most Indo-European languages could be a valid universal model.

Austronesian languages are not the only ones that show that such a system is not necessarily the only natural linguistic system. We can find systems of spatial description which are almost completely independent of the human self in language families as diverse as those of the Australian aborigines, those of Papua-New Guinea and a large number of American Indian languages.

In Tzeltal, a Maya language spoken in the south-east of Mexico, Brown and Levinson (1993) have shown that the terms *ajk'ol* "uphill" and *alan* "downhill" are used in an absolute sense to localize things on an idealized slope going from south to north, which of course corresponds to the slope from the Highlands in the south to the Lowlands in the north. This slope has become so fundamental for the conceptualization of space among these mountain-dwelling people that it provides a means of absolute spatial description, allowing people to locate objects with regard to each other and with regard to the speaker, in micro- as well as macro-orientation. In the immediate field of vision, the coordinates of "uphill" (south)/ "downhill" (north) can also be used to refer to a vertical axis, "above" and "below" the speaker (or any other point of reference). These coordinates can even be used to express relative distances, to show a region situated further away from the speaker ("uphill") or closer to the speaker ("downhill").

In Andoque, an Amazonian language from Colombia, Landaburu (1985) has described a similar absolute directional system, determined this time by the hydrographic system, oriented from west to east and conceptualized by the coordinates of "upstream" (west)/"downstream" (east), around which a whole cosmology has been developed. The grammaticalization of these concepts in the verbal morphology of Andoque, together with two deictic directional markers showing movement towards or away from the subject, is strikingly parallel to the structure of the verb group described previously for Nemi in 3.2.

This cognitive ability to decentralize direction in space outside of oneself in everyday life, and to develop absolute systems of spatial description which can be used in all contexts, makes it obvious that natural languages do not necessarily all build their spatial descriptions around relative, anthropocentric notions, just because our own perceptual system happens to have been built in this way.

Human beings do not have, in their genetic make-up, the capacity that migrating animals have to perceive magnetic fields in order to direct themselves, and the conceptualization of space in human languages is therefore largely the product of culture acting on experience. The questions put to cognitive research by languages like Malagasy, Tzeltal or the Australian languages that use these systems of spatial description that are completely decentralized with regard to the human persona are the following:

How is such a system acquired? At what age is it mastered? How do people find their directions when they are far away from their familiar surroundings?

In any case, it is absolutely necessary to take into account the evidence provided by the languages, more numerous than is usually admitted, which have developed these kinds of spatial cognitive strategies, if we are to develop meaningful general theories about the conceptualization of space.

Notes

1. Literally, "inside the rivets". French pedestrian crossings used to be indicated by lines of large-headed rivets. Now they are indicated by painted lines, but the old expression has remained.

References

Adelaar, K. Alexander. 1997. "An exploration of directional systems in West Indonesia and Madagascar". In Gunther Senft (ed.), *Referring to Space. Studies in Austronesian and Papuan languages*. Oxford: Oxford University Press, 52-81.
Blust, Robert. 1984. "The Austronesian Homeland: A Linguistic Perspective". *Asian Perspectives* 26 (1): 45-67.
Brown, Cecil H. 1983. "Where do cardinal points come from?". *Anthropological Linguistics* 25: 121-161.
Brown, Penelope, and Levinson, Stephen. 1993. "*Uphill* and *downhill* in Tzeltal". *Journal of Linguistic Anthropology* 3 (1): 46-75.
Buck, Carl Darling. 1949. *A dictionary of selected synonyms in the principal Indo-European languages*. Chicago: The University of Chicago Press.
Churchward, C.M. 1953. *Tongan grammar*. London: Oxford University Press.

Hébert, Jean-Claude. 1965. "La cosmographie malgache", *suivie de:* L'énumération des points cardinaux et l'importance du nord-est". In *Taloha 1 Archéologie, Annales de l'Université de Madagascar*, 83-195.

Landaburu, Jon. 1985. "El tratamiento gramatical del espacio en la lengua andoque del Amazonas". *Revista de Antropologia* 1 (Universitad de Los Andes), 34-40.

Lavondès, Henri. 1983. "Le vocabulaire marquisien de l'orientation dans l'espace". *L'Ethnographie* 79(1): 35-42.

Lemaître, Yves. 1973. *Lexique du tahitien contemporain.* Paris: ORSTOM.

Milner, G.B. 1956. *Fijian grammar.* Fiji, Government Press.

Ozanne-Rivierre, Françoise, en collaboration avec Poindi Tein. 1979. *Textes nemi (Nouvelle-Calédonie).* 2 vol., Paris: SELAF.

Ozanne-Rivierre, Françoise. 1997. "Spatial references in New Caledonian Languages", in Gunther Senft (ed.), *Referring to Space. Studies in Austronesian and Papuan languages.* Oxford: Oxford University Press, 83-100.

Ramseyer, Urs. 1977. *L'art populaire à Bali.* Fribourg: Office du Livre.

Revel, Nicole. 1990. *Fleurs de paroles: histoire naturelle palawan.* Paris: Peteers.

Svorou, Soteria. 1993. *The grammar of space.* Amsterdam: Benjamins.

Language Space and Sociolect
Cognitive Correlates of Gendered Speech in Mopan Maya

Eve Danziger
Department of Anthropology
University of Virginia

Introduction

It is widely acknowledged that languages differ from one another in all sorts of ways. What is less clearly understood is the nature of the relationship between variation in language structure and non-linguistic cognition. If languages differ in their classification of phenomena, does this mean that the way that their speakers make decisions about nonlinguistic categorization also differs? Data collected from languages around the world, and in particular from Mopan Maya – an indigenous language of Central America – suggest that this question can be answered, at least sometimes, in the affirmative.[1]

1. Cross-linguistic variation in the encoding of spatial information

The members of the Cognitive Anthropology Research Group asked speakers of many different languages to describe the six pictures below to a partner (Pederson et al 1998).[2] Both partners see an identical set of pictures, but neither can see what the other is looking at (this is usually accomplished by placing a curtain or screen between the partners, who sit side by side). The game consists in having the listening partner pick out each photo in turn, on the basis of the verbal description alone. Partners are free to discuss their descriptions and choices fully, and this discussion is videotaped. After all of the pictures have been described, the partners check the matches that they have made with one another. Data from three pairs of speakers is collected for each language.[3]

Figure 1. Men and tree (Pictures for description)

Many different strategies are used across languages to describe the pictures under these conditions. These strategies can, however, be grouped together according to the kind of information that is used to construct the answer (Levelt 1984, 1996, Levinson 1996). For example, speakers of many languages – including European languages such as Dutch and English, but also including Japanese for example – make reference to *the left and right sides of their own bodies* when making statements about the differences among the photos. For example, English speakers might say that picture 7 differs from picture 8, because in picture 7, "The man is to the left of the tree". Such speakers make use of elements of their own physiology as the coordinate system with which they anchor the relationship of the Figure and Ground, while they themselves remain construed as third parties, outside the scene and playing the role neither of Figure nor of Ground. I use the terms 'Figure' and 'Ground' in Talmy's (1983) sense, so that 'Figure' refers to the Relator or element being located – in the English example above, the *man* – and 'Ground' refers to the Relatum, or element with respect to which the Figure is located – in the English example, the *tree*.

In certain languages, however, reference to the speaker's own physiology is a rare occurrence when making these descriptions. For example, speakers of Arrernte – an Aboriginal language of Central Australia – describe the six pictures in terms of the cardinal directions that actually obtain at the moment the description is made. That is, depending how the pictures have been laid out for the players, the man in picture 7 may be described as being to the north, south, east, or west of the tree (data from David Wilkins. See also Haviland 1979, 1993, 1998). In Tzeltal Maya meanwhile (Brown and Levinson 1993), speakers describe the pictures in terms of the 'uphill' and 'downhill' relations between man and tree – again based on the realities of the surrounding terrain. These descriptions make use of what has been called an 'Absolute' frame of reference, and rely for the anchoring of their coordinate system on features of surrounding geography rather than on those of participants' physiology. Speakers of many of the languages of Oceania would be expected to describe the six pictures using this type of information (see Ozanne-Riviere, this volume).

The work of the Cognitive Anthropology Research Group has also shown that speakers of different languages find different solutions to non-linguistic cognitive tasks involving rotation, in just the directions predicted by their linguistic preferences (Danziger in press (a), Levinson 1998, Pederson et al. 1998, Levinson and Nagy ms.). In one experiment, for example, participants are asked to reconstruct an array of toy animals after they themselves (the participants) have undergone a rotation of 180 degrees (they are now facing precisely opposite to the direction in which they had been facing when they saw the original array). Speakers of languages in which information about speaker's and hearer's right and left – rather than information about surrounding geography – is used in verbal descriptions, reconstruct the array of toy animals in such a way as to respect the original right/left relationship of the array to their own bodies – even though this means violating the relationships of the original array to surrounding geography. On the contrary, speakers of languages in which information about surrounding geography ('uphill', 'seaward', 'north') rather than information about speech participants' right and left is used in verbal descriptions, reconstruct the array of toy animals in such a way as to respect the original relationship of the array to the local landscape – even though this means violating the relationships of the original array to their own bodies. Even the non-linguistic conceptualization of spatial relationships therefore appears to be at least partly a matter of construal. And the kind of construal an individual is likely to make appears to a large extent to correlate with variable aspects of linguistic practice.

2. Universal strategies: Figure and Ground only

Although the use of information about speech participants' left and right, and the use of information about surrounding geography varies across the languages in our sample, certain of the informational strategies used to describe the six pictures appear to be *universal* across languages (based on data collected by members of the Cognitive Anthropology Research Group in ten languages of eight different families, see Pederson et al 1998).[4] First, almost all speakers in all of the languages surveyed chose at times to construe themselves and/or their partner, either explicitly or implicitly as the nonce *Ground* of the spatial relation to be described, describing the position of the toy man, for example, with respect not to the toy tree, but to the speaker and listener themselves (eg. For English, picture 6, "He's got his back to us"; picture 7, "He's facing us"). Let us call this the encoding strategy that takes 'Self-as-Ground'. Second, almost all speakers, in all of the languages, often gave information about the *scene-internal* relationship of the toy man with respect to the toy tree. That is, speakers made statements about the relationship of the different parts of the toy man to the tree (eg. English picture 4: "The man has his back to the tree"; Picture 7: "The tree is to the man's left"). We may call this a 'Scene-Internal' informational strategy. Notice that since one internal element of the scene (the toy man) represents a human body, a 'Scene-Internal' statement can sometimes be made which makes use of expressions for "left" and "right". Picture 7 is illuminating here, and can serve as a diagnostic tool. Under a 'Scene-Internal' description, the tree is at the man's *left* hand. Making use of information about the physiology of speech participants however, one would describe the tree as being to the *right* of the man. It is thus possible to discover referential situations in which the difference between reference to the speakers' right and left and reference to the right and left of a Ground object which is not the speaker, is quite clear.[5]

The two information strategies that appear to vary in their distribution across languages – those that make use of speech participant right/left, and those that make use of surrounding geography – share certain properties which are not shared by the 'Self-as-Ground' and the 'Scene-Internal' information strategies. Both of the optional information strategies make use of information from *outside* the Figure-Ground scene, and they use this information to project a vector between Figure and Ground that locates these with respect to one another – and within a matrix of space which is external to them both (see Danziger 1996b). The 'Scene-Internal' and the 'Self-as-Ground' information strategies meanwhile are to-date universally encountered across languages, and make use only of information about the Figure and the Ground themselves.

3. Mopan speakers and the picture description task

Three pairs of Mopan speakers were consulted in the picture description task. Like speakers of all the languages surveyed, these six Mopan speakers made use both of 'Scene-Internal' information, and of a nonce construal of the 'Self-as-Ground' in order to describe the location of the toy man with respect to the tree in the 6 pictures shown above.

(1) Mopan use of Self-as-Ground Strategy. Picture 6 is described.

Käx-t-e'   a   tz'ub'   a...
seek-TR-SUBJ DET child   DET
Find the child who...

chun-pach   a   tun-cha'an   waye'-ji.
only-3A-back DET DUR-3A-look   DX1-SCOPE
only his back is looking here.

(2) Mopan use of Scene-Internal Strategy. Picture 4 is described.

Ka'   a-käx-t-e'   a   nene' tz'ub'   ada',
CONJ 2A-seek-TR-SUBJ   DET little child   DX1
You should find this little child,

a   t-u-pach   ke'en-Ø   a   t'opo.
DET at-3A-back be-located-3B DET flower
who has the flower at his back.

What is striking about the Mopan data is that these are the *only* informational strategies used. These speakers never referred to surrounding geography to make their descriptions of these pictures, and their reference to speech participant's right and left was also nearly nonexistent. In the one instance that such a reference was made, it was rejected by the partner. It is clear from that exchange that the listening partner (M.) interprets all instances of the (borrowed) Mopan words *suldeero*, *lef* ('left') and *rait* ('right') as referring only to the elements internal to the scene.

(3) Mopan Use of Speaker's Right-Left Strategy. Picture 7 described.

D. Käx -t-e'   a   tz'ub'   a   w-a'an-Ø   yok'ol   tunich.
   seek-TR-SUBJ DET child   DET stand-STAT-3B on   stone
   Find the child who's standing on a stone.

   Toj-Ø   u-che'   ti   yan-Ø.
   straight-3B   3A-stick at   exist-3B.
   His stick is quite straight.

   I   suldeero   ke'en-Ø   u-che'.
   and   left   be-located-3B   3A-stick
   And his stick is on the left.

M. Puuro   ich   rait.   Ma'   suldeero
   only   in   right. NEG   left
   It's only on the right. It's not on the left.

D. U-che'   ab'e'?
   3A-stick DX3I
   You're talking about his stick?

M. Mmhm.   Puuro   ich   rait.   Ma'   yan-Ø   a—
   AFFIRM.   Only   in   right.NEG   exist-3B   DET
   Yes. It's only on the right. There aren't any —

D. Yan-Ø   u-che'   ke'en-Ø   suldeero.
   exist-3B 3A-stick   be-located-3B   left
   They exist with his stick on the left.

M. Ma'   yan-Ø   ich   lef-i!
   NEG   exist-3B   in   left-SCOPE.
   There aren't any on the left!

   Puuro   ich   rait   ke'en-Ø   u-k'ä'.
   only   in   right be-located-3B   3A-hand
   His hand is always on the right.

Figure 2 shows the distribution of the four kinds of information strategies (Speech Participant RL, Geographical, Self-as-Ground, and Scene-Internal) just outlined, as they appear in the distinguishing propositions used by three speakers of Dutch, three speakers of Arrernte, and three speakers of Mopan Maya to describe the six pictures in this interactive game.

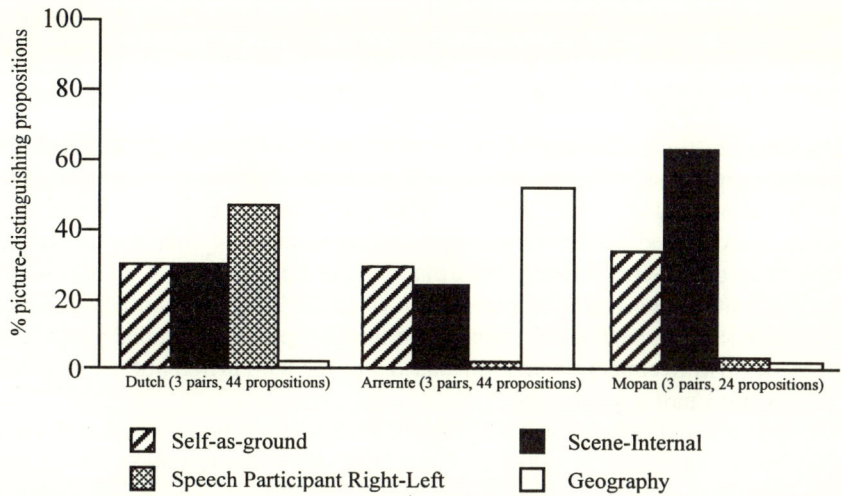

Figure 2. Distribution of Information Strategies in three languages: Man and Tree pictures - (Data: E. Danziger, D. Wilkins, FGKA)

The pattern of descriptions provided by Mopan speakers shows us that while use of 'Scene-Internal' and 'Self-as Ground' information strategies appear to be cross-linguistically universal in this context, the use of *any* kind of information external to the Figure-Ground scene – whether about 'speech participant right/left' or about 'geographical' information – is apparently dispensable. The distribution of information strategies across languages suggests that we should now see the encoding of spatial relationships in language in terms of two distinct components – one universal and obligatory in this kind of context, and one variable, contingent and optional in the same context. Where the optional slot for scene-external information is filled, the kinds of information resorted to are culturally variable, and they have different consequences for preferred solutions to non-linguistic tasks.

This cross-linguistic distribution should be of interest to psychologists, since we know from the work of previous scholars (Piaget 1928, Piaget and Inhelder 1963 [1948]) that use of scene-internal information to encode spatial relations is acquired very early, when compared to scene-external or 'Projective' kinds of information. This priority of scene-internal and self-as-ground information is also the general finding in language acquisition studies (Johnston and Slobin 1979, Tanz 1980). The information strategies based on information from outside the Figure-Ground scene (those based on speech-participant physiology and surrounding geography) meanwhile, are usually acquired late and must often be formally taught. As we have now seen, these are actually culturally contingent and quite optional habits of speech, for the kind of situation represented by the pictures in Figure 1 – and they are not in fact taught or acquired in all speech communities.

In another intriguing branch of the cognitive science literature, Jackendoff has explicitly proposed (1987) that the immediate product of visual processing has direct input privileges to language. According to Marr's theory of vision, this product is described as an 'object-centered 3D model' – that is to say it incorporates only Scene-Internal information (see Levinson 1994). This model may well provide the common ground for visual and linguistic encoding, upon which additional properties are erected: culturally optional, linguistic-cognitive edifices of spatial conceptualization based on speech-participant's right and left, or on surrounding geography.

The data presented here, and the place of Mopan in particular, makes it clear that as far as linguistic encoding is concerned, the representation of spatial relationships in terms of a dimensional matrix of absolute space is a cultural option, and one not taken up in all cases. Can the same be said of non-linguistic conceptualization in the realm of space? Could it be the case that Mopan individuals who speak this way actually also conceive of spatial relationships in a way analogous to their descriptions?

We can examine this question, making use of the fact that the Mopan speakers' characterization of pictures number 3 and number 5 (in Figure 1) has some interesting properties – pictures 3 and 5 are near reflections of one another. As we have seen, while using very different types of information, the speech-participant's right/left strategy and the surrounding-geography information strategy nevertheless readily characterize these two photos as quite different from one another. All of the six Dutch and the six Arrernte speakers whose utterances are summarized in Figure 2 made this distinction. However, not one of the six Mopan speakers represented in Figure 2 distinguished linguistically between these two pictures. This is of course directly related to the fact that the Mopan speakers made no use of information about speech participant's right and left or about the surrounding geography.

(4) Mopan description of picture 5

Ka'   a-käx-t-e'   a   nene'   tz'ub'
CONJ   2A-seek-TR-SUBJ   DET   little   child
You should find the little child,

a   t-u-ta'an   ke'en-Ø   t'opo.
DET   at-3A-chest   be-located-3B   flower
who has the flower at his chest.

Not surprisingly, when this type of description is given and is accepted as complete, picture 3 and picture 5 are frequently selected as matches for one another. It is of interest however to note that when the players check their matches at the end of the session, such matching of picture 3 with picture 5 *may be accepted as correct,* even by players who readily reject non-mirror-image mismatches (say, of picture 4 with picture 6) as obvious errors.

This is a startling observation. It suggests that the Mopan tendency to describe 2D left / right mirror image reflections in identical terms (using Scene-internal information only) goes hand in hand with an analogous psychological phenomenon. This phenomenon, also found elsewhere in the world (Verhaeghe ms., Levinson and Brown 1994, Verhaeghe and Kolinsky 1991) consists in treating the perceptual difference between mirror images as conceptually unimportant. The nature of an individual's judgements in this respect seem often to depend upon his or her previous exposure to cultural experiences in which this distinction has been made functionally salient. Verhaeghe and Kolinsky (1991) show for example that literacy is a major experiential variable affecting judgements about mirror-images. In their study, literate individuals strongly rejected mirror-images as not the same, while many non-literate subjects accepted them (see also Danziger and Pederson 1998).

In short, the convention of counting 2D left/right mirror images as different from one another is culturally learned and arbitrary, and has little importance in everyday life where particular cultural systems do not choose to emphasize it (Van Cleve and Frederick 1991). Various sorts of cultural experience can serve to teach it. What then of habitual language use? Levinson and Brown (1994) posit a link between the common intuition among Tzeltal Maya speakers that 2D mirror images should be considered as the same, and the very infrequent use of terms for 'right' and 'left' in the Tzeltal (Mayan) language.[6]

4. The Mirror Image task

Levinson and Brown's results were obtained in an experiment designed by Stephen Levinson and Bernadette Schmitt, and based on techniques pioneered by Stephen Palmer (1977). The implementation of techniques of this kind in the context of cross-linguistic research was inspired by the work of Arlette Verhaeghe and Régine Kolinsky.

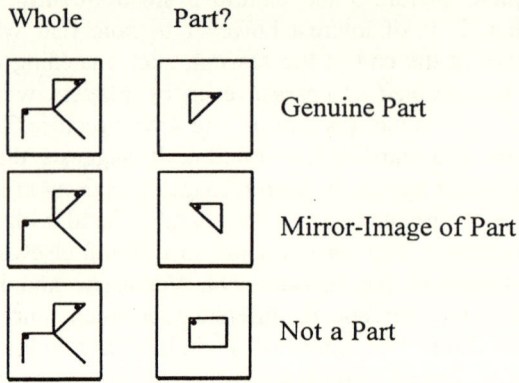

Figure 3. *Mirror-Image Part task design*

In the task, an individual is shown two different plastic cards with simple abstract line drawings printed on them. He or she is asked to judge whether or not the figure on one card can be found as part of ("inside") the figure drawn on the other. There are five full figure cards. Each is shown three different times, once in conjunction with a true part, once with a clear non-part, and once with a figure that is the left/right mirror image of the true part. Participants were presented with such Part/Whole pairs and asked to decide "if there isn't this one inside that one as well".

(5) Mopan Instructions, Mirror Image Task

```
Ka'     a-wil-a'              waj   ma'  yan-Ø    ada'
CONJ    2A-see-TR-SUBJ   Q     NEG  exist-3B     DX1
You should see if there isn't this one

ichil    ilik    akana'
inside   same    DX2
inside that one as well.
```

Using transparencies, participants were taught to accept the Genuine Part and to reject the clear Non-Part. Among those Mopan participants who completed the protocol, all were able to do this successfully on a subsequent practice trial. Participants were at the same time explicitly trained to *reject* the mirror image match.

Data was analyzed only for participants who accepted at least 4 Genuine Parts and who rejected at least 4 Non-Parts over 5 trials each. Over 5 trials involving Mirror-image Parts, the rejection rates of 34 Mopan subjects were very low indeed. On average, the Mopan participants accepted 2.7 mirror-image parts over the 5 trials. These Mopan results are significantly different from European results (Dutch), where virtually 100 % of the mirror image parts are rejected. This result systematizes what had been an anecdotal observation from Mopan. With the language transcripts, this result shows systematic and quantifiable parallel performance in linguistic and in non-linguistic Mopan treatment of spatial phenomena.

But the phenomenon of mirror-image part acceptance in Mopan is not sociologically undifferentiated. We know from previous studies that literacy has been a significant facilitating factor in the acquired intuition that mirror images can count as different from one another. And literacy is also a significant variable in the Mopan results. The tendency to accept mirror-image parts (average: 3.8 mirror-image-parts accepted over 5 trials) for Mopan speakers who told me that they could not read and write (n = 20) was significantly greater than chance. The tendency to accept these (average: 2.1 mirror image parts accepted over 5 trials) among Mopan speakers who reported that they were able to read and write (n = 14) was not significantly greater than chance, although the acceptance rate even among Mopan literates is still well above the rate in the Dutch sample.[7]

At the same time, Mopan men and women also show interesting differences on this task. The tendency for Mopan women (n = 21) to accept mirror image parts on this task (average: 3.3 mirror-image parts accepted over 5 trials) was significantly greater than chance. The tendency for Mopan men (n = 13) was not (average: 2.0 mirror-image parts accepted over 5 trials), although once again, even this latter group showed an acceptance rate well above that of the Dutch sample.

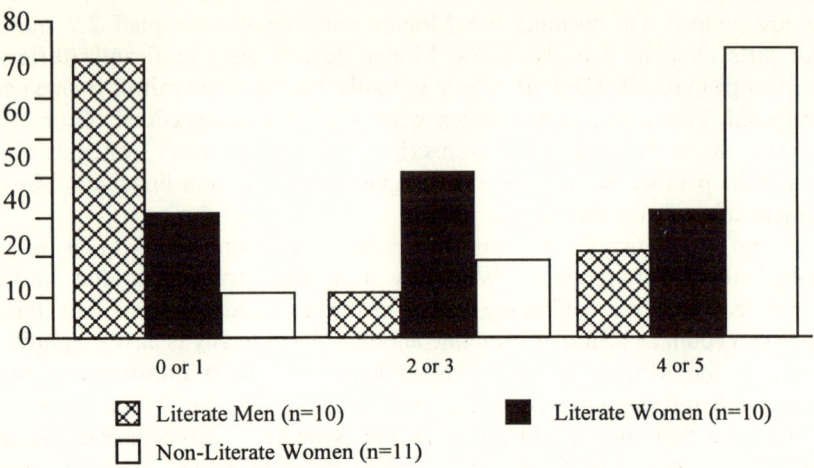

Figure 4. Gender and Literacy in Mopan: Mirror-Image Part Task (% participants, by number of acceptances over 5 trials).

The two sub-populations of Mopan speakers for whom mirror-image part acceptance is significantly high – non-literates and women – are confounded in the Mopan sample, since almost all non-literate Mopan speakers are women (11 of 14). The two appear to be independent factors however, as we can see if we examine separately on the one hand the contrast between men and women in the literate sub-population, and on the other the contrast between literates and non-literates in the female sub-population. The literate Mopan speakers in the sample are equally divided among men (n=10) and women (n=10). The rate for literate Mopan men who succeed at *rejecting* mirror-image parts is significantly greater than chance. The rate for literate Mopan women is not significantly greater than chance. Meanwhile the tendency for non-literate Mopan women to *accept* mirror-image parts in this task differs significantly from chance occurrence.

Figure 5. Distribution of Mopan Mirror-Image Parts Data across social groupings

	Mopan literates (n=20)	**Mopan non-literates** (n=14)
Mopan men (n=13)	Significant *rejection* of mirror-image parts (n=10) Average Accepted: 1.6	Insufficient sample size (n=3) Average Accepted: 3.3
Mopan women (n=21)	Acceptance/ rejection of mirror-image parts is like chance. (n=10) Average Accepted: 2.6	Significant *acceptance* of mirror-image parts. (n=11) Average Accepted: 3.7

As has been found in other studies, literacy is a significant factor here – one which apparently makes it easier for individuals to follow the instructions on this task. But the effect of literacy is much more pronounced in Mopan men than it is in Mopan women. Analogously, being female is also associated here with the acceptance of mirror-image parts – but much more so to the extent that one is not literate. It seems clear that not only literacy, but also gender are important variables in this sample. (Recall that the response pattern of literate Mopan women, characterized as 'near chance', still means that half of the individuals in this group are accepting a majority of mirror-image parts – such a pattern is very different for example from that of Dutch speakers).

5. Discussion of gender

The Mopan people (there are about 5000 today) are peasant farmers who make a living by working small plots of land for themselves in the Highlands of Central America. The society is extremely egalitarian, and every farmer has access to substantially the same subsistence resources. There is little social stratification and few if any occupational specialities. The main basis for economic division of labour is gender. Men work in the fields, and they also usually deal with the world outside the household and outside the village when that is necessary. Women work inside the house, and at domestic tasks inside the village. In particular, the grinding of maize into a form that can be processed for cooking is an extremely time-consuming task that is still often done by hand. Children acquire Mopan as a first language, and, in the community in which I have worked, both boys and girls today usually attend the (non-Mopan) village school sporadically for several years (Crooks 1997). But in this community it is still rare to encounter an individual who has actually completed a full course of primary education, and it is quite common to meet adults – especially women – who never went to school and who cannot read or write.

The differences observed here between Mopan men and Mopan women are without doubt the products of cultural socialization. In other investigations of spatial cognition cross-culturally, where gender differences have been found (Stewart van Leeuwen 1978, Segall et al 1990) such differences have been clearly related to generalized differences in socialization practices, such that a general emphasis on gender separation (usually associated with peasant agriculture and accompanied by an insistence on conformity and obedience in childhood, especially for girls) also correlates with gender differences on standardized cognitive tasks.

Considerable differences in life experience and in cultural style divide men and women in traditional Mopan society (Gregory 1984, Danziger in press (b)). Mopan boys and Mopan girls are socialized very differently, and adult Mopan men and Mopan women have access to very different types of cultural experience. Although the previous cross-cultural studies which have found differences in men's and women's performance on spatial tasks have not discussed language issues, the Mopan constitute a cultural case in which we are not unduly surprised to find socially correlated gender differences in responses to a spatial task.

6. Gender and spatial language in Mopan

We accept that the difference between Mopan men's and Mopan women's performance on the mirror-image part task is due to experiential variables. But could some of the relevant experience be linguistic? It so happens that the characterization of Mopan speech given in Figure 2 above was based on women speakers only (just as was the characterization of Dutch). In light of the analysis of the data from the non-linguistic task involving mirror-image parts, it seems reasonable to ask about Mopan men's linguistic descriptions of the pictures in Figure 1. Recall that our hypothesis links the emphasis on use of scene-internal information in speech (characteristic of Mopan female speakers as seen in Figure 2), to the possibility that non-linguistic tasks would be approached also on a scene-internal basis, resulting in the intuition that 2D left/right mirror image counterparts should be treated in the same way.

On my most recent field trip I collected linguistic data which strongly suggests that among the many experiential and cultural differences between Mopan men and Mopan women are certain habits of spatial language use. As we have seen, across three pairs of partners, Mopan women describing the 6 pictures in Figure 1 did not use terms for their own right and left. Instead, they referred to parts of the toy man's body (including at times, his own right and left) to locate him with respect to the tree. As we saw, this meant that across the three pairs of Mopan women partners represented in Figure 2, pictures 3 and 5 of Figure 1 were never linguistically distinguished from one another.[8]

Figure 6 repeats the data already shown in Figure 2 for Mopan women speakers. In figure 6, these data are compared to the data collected from three pairs of Mopan men. A heavy reliance on scene-internal information is apparent in the male as in the female data (one pair of male speakers used no speech participant right / left, or surrounding geographic information at all, and in this respect looks very similar to the female speakers' profile). However, of the three pairs of male Mopan speakers faced with this description task, two pairs also had recourse to linguistic informational strategies that would enable them reliably to describe the difference between 2D right/left mirror-images. One of these pairs made reference to surrounding geography in the form of local landmarks. The second pair made systematic use of reference to the speaker's right and left, as well as reference to surrounding geography. Of three pairs of female Mopan speakers, none had successful recourse to such an informational system.[9]

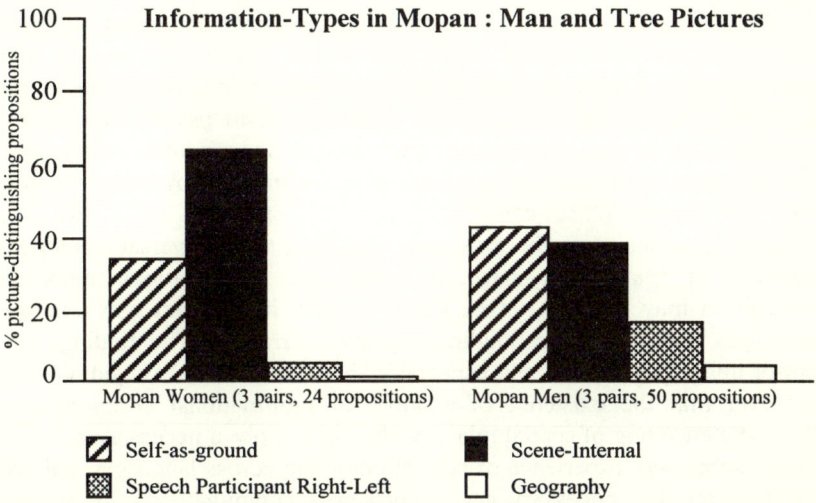

Figure 6. Compares propositional content of six male with six female Mopan speakers

I have been suggesting that the non-use of terms from speech participant's right/left strategies or from surrounding geography strategies in Mopan speech might be associated with the cognitive phenomenon of mirror image acceptance. The male Mopan speakers consulted in the picture description task show certain language choices which tend in the same direction as does the male data from the non-linguistic cognitive task. The additional speech data from male Mopan speakers supports the association between reliance on scene-internal information (characteristic of Mopan women's speech) and the intuition that 2D left/right mirror images ought to be treated alike (characteristic of Mopan women's reactions to the non-linguistic task).[10]

7. Discussion and conclusion

In comparing sub-populations with different sociolects from within a single speech community, we have surely reduced a large number of the unknowable additional cultural and linguistic factors that might play a role in comparisons across more widely divergent language varieties. I therefore would not hesitate to place this Mopan data alongside previous studies which compare spatial problem-solving strategies across languages. The Mopan case offers extremely suggestive data that indicates the existence of a relationship between habitual language use and conceptual construal in the domain of space.

The Mopan data is also interesting from a *typological* point of view. The fact that the use of information from speech participant right and left and from surrounding geography are both optional additions in describing the six pictures of Figure 1 is one that should be of some interest to psychologists, since the Scene-Internal Frame of Reference corresponds in many interesting respects, on the one hand to the kind of 'topological' space invoked by Piaget, and on the other to Marr's 'object-centered' perceptual encoding. This cross-linguistic evidence thus suggests the existence of a basic and universal object-centered encoding of relations in space. It seems that specifications about external orientation may or may not be added to this, in different ways in different languages, and with corresponding cognitive correlates. The findings from the mirror-image part task – and especially those from Mopan women – suggest however that the existence of a universal informational component to the linguistic encoding of spatial relations *does not* imply a necessary commonality of the subjective experience of spatial cognition across languages, cultures and sub-cultures, nor necessary agreement across communities as to what is the natural and basic way to look at spatial relationships. The cultural option to specify orientation *neither* in terms of speech participant's right/left *nor* in terms of surrounding geography brings with it its own conceptual correlates, in the form of intuitions about 2D left-right mirror-image reflections.

Finally, the Mopan case does more than bring another language and even another language type into the discussion of language and cognition in the area of spatial relationships. The fact that in Mopan we have dealt with *sociolinguistic* differences within a single speech community brings home to us the fact that we need to examine not only the relationship of language to thinking, but of both to 'culture' or 'subculture'. We will have to go beyond the referential (perhaps the most prototypically 'cognitive') function of language, and explore other, more social and communicative ones, in order to gain an understanding of why languages are the way they are, why they play the roles that they do – even in spatial reference– and why language varieties differ in the first place.

The gender data from Mopan make us particularly aware of this, since the differences between Mopan men's and women's speech are those of *sociolect*. They play the role of linguistic indices within the community, as well as that of linguistic symbols. It is not just for referential reasons, or for reasons of arbitrary language-historical convention, that individual speakers (thinkers?) choose and maintain a sociolect. The reasons also have to do with the individual's personal and often unconscious commitment to a particular social identity. Through this mechanism, sociolects also have to do with the symbolic maintenance of the very social order which gives rise to those identities in the first place. Mopan women's language use is part of a complex that *includes* the habits of spatial construal which we have tapped into in our experimental task, but which also clearly includes many other elements of 'language', of 'thought' and of 'culture'.

Appendix

Abbreviations used in Glossing

2A	2nd person Actor or Possessor	STAT	Stativizer
3A	3rd person Actor or Possessor	SUBJ	Subjunctive
3B	3rd person Undergoer	TR	Transitivizer
AFFIRM	Affirmative		
CONJ	Conjunction		
DET	Determiner		
DUR	Durative		
DX1	Speaker-proximal deixis		
DX2	Hearer-proximal Deixis		
DX3I	Textual Deixis		
NEG	Negation		
Q	Interrogative		
SCOPE	Scope		

Mirror-Image-Part Acceptance. Mopan Speakers

Participant	M/F	Lit/Non	# Mirror-Image-Part Accepted (/ 5)
1	F	N	5
2	F	N	5
3	F	N	5
4	F	N	5
5	F	N	5
6	F	N	4
7	F	N	4
8	F	N	4
9	F	N	3
10	F	N	2
11	F	N	1
12	F	Y	5
13	F	Y	5
14	F	Y	4
15	F	Y	3
16	F	Y	3
17	F	Y	3
18	F	Y	2
19	F	Y	1
20	F	Y	0
21	F	Y	0
22	M	N	5
23	M	N	3
24	M	N	2
25	M	Y	5
26	M	Y	4
27	M	Y	3
28	M	Y	1
29	M	Y	1
30	M	Y	1
31	M	Y	1
32	M	Y	0
33	M	Y	0
34	M	Y	0

Notes

1. This work was conducted with the support of the Cognitive Anthropology Research Group of the Max Planck Institute for Psycholinguistics. The ideas it contains are the product of intellectual exchange with many colleagues there, including in particular Stephen Levinson, Eric Pederson, and David Wilkins. Special thanks are due also to David Wilkins for permission to publish his data in Figure 2. Mopan examples are given in the orthography outlined in England and Elliott (1990). A key to the abbreviations used in morphological glosses is to be found in the Appendix. For more information on Mopan grammar, the reader is referred to Danziger (1996a).
2. This interactive elicitation technique draws on work by Clark and Wilkes-Gibbs (1986), and was adapted to the cross-linguistic elicitation of spatial language by Lourdes de León (1991). Figure 1 presents line-drawing renditions of photographs of toy objects. This series of photos was designed by Eve Danziger and Eric Pederson. A comparative semantic analysis based on the functional equivalence of distinguishing propositions used to describe these pictures across languages was developed by David Wilkins. Typological observations made here are based on that analysis.
3. Figures 1 and 3 are copyright of the Max Planck Institute for Psycholinguistics, and are published here with the Institute's permisssion.
4. Data was contributed by Balthasar Bickel (Belhare – Tibeto-Burman, Nepal), Penelope Brown and Stephen Levinson (Tzeltal – Mayan, Mexico), Eve Danziger (Mopan – Mayan, Belize), Kyoko Inoue and Sotaro Kita (Japanese), Sabine Neumann (Kgalagadi – Bantu, Botswana), Eric Pederson (Tamil – Dravidian, India), Gunter Senft (Kilivila – Austronesian, Trobriand Islands), Christel Stolz (Yucatec – Mayan, Mexico), Thomas Widlok (Hai//om – Khoisan, Namibia), and David Wilkins (Arandic – Pama-Nyungan, Australia). Dutch data was also collected and forms part of the sample.
5. This work owes much to Levelt (1984, 1996) and bears obvious similarities to the analysis proposed by Levinson (1996). Levinson correctly appreciates the importance of separating deictic Origo from spatial Ground, and therefore rightly distinguishes the kind of 'right-left' informational strategy discussed above, in which the point of reference for the calculation of spatial coordinates is the deictic Origo but *not* the spatial Ground (– in Levinson's terms, this is the 'Relative Frame of Reference') from other 'Deictic' Frames (Levelt 1984) in which the point of reference is an Origo that is *also* the spatial Ground. Levinson's proposal, however, classifies this latter kind of strategy, (here called 'Self-as-Ground') with all other cases in which the spatial Ground is the point of reference for calculation of spatial relations (here called 'Scene-Internal'). Levinson characterizes both of these as 'Intrinsic' (Levelt 1984), regardless of whether the Ground is or is not a speech participant. He thus restricts the number of informational strategies (Frames of Reference) to three. The four-way analysis proposed here was inspired by conversations with David Wilkins.
6. Tzeltal speakers make little use of speech participant's right and left to describe the pictures in Figure 1. They do however make exuberant use of information from surrounding geography (Brown and Levinson 1993). Literacy is also a significant factor in the Tzeltal mirror-image data (Danziger and Pederson 1998).
7. This statement and the succeeding ones involving probability are based on a simple Chi squared calculation in which the data are divided into two cells: The first cell contains the number of individuals accepting 0, 1, or 2 mirror-image parts over 5 trials. The second cell contains the number of individuals accepting 3, 4, or 5 mirror image parts over 5 trials. The raw data appear in the Appendix.

8. Scene-Internal reference to the left and right hands of the toy man will distinguish picture 7 from picture 8. But it will not distinguish picture 3 from picture 5. Nor will it distinguish between other mirror-image counterparts in which the elements are not considered animate (therefore having their own right and left sides).
9. Recall that it is possible to construct or discover situations in which reference to the speakers' right and left can readily be distinguished from reference to the right and left sides of non-speaker Ground (here, the toy man). It is not possible however, within the corpus of descriptions of these pictures, to discover situations which necessarily distinguish between uses of 'right' and 'left' that refer to the speaker's own parts, where the speaker is understood as a third point, outside the Figure-Ground scene (most explicitly stated, for example, of Picture 7 as "The man is to my right of the tree"), and those where the speaker is construed as also being the Ground of the spatial relation (most explicitly stated, for example, of Picture 7: "The man is to my right"). All too often, utterances take an ambiguous form – in Mopan as in English – such that they are best glossed simply 'Man on the right'. For the purposes of this paper then, which is primarily concerned with the issue of mirror-image description and distinction in the very specific contexts of the materials provided (for which both kinds of reference to speakers' right and left do equally well), all reference to speakers' right and left is classified together, and no such reference is considered an example of the Self-as-Ground, or of the Scene-Internal strategy. As a final characterization of the information strategies used in Mopan however, this will probably not be ultimately satisfactory. Elicitation and specific questioning, conducted with both Mopan men and Mopan women, indicates that Mopan understandings of the terms *seeb'* or *rait* 'right' and *suldeero* or *lef* 'left' are always two-placed rather than three-placed, even when they refer to parts of the speaker (Danziger 1996b). Mopan 'right' and 'left', for example, are not transitive, and the middle object of three placed across a consultant's line of vision cannot be understood to be in any kind of speakers' left/right relation to the two others.
10. It is worth noting here that of the original six Mopan women whose speech is represented in Figure 2, four are literate. The distribution is such that at least one member of each speaker-listener pair is literate. Thus, the data which showed Mopan speakers massively preferring scene-internal to speech participant right and left or to surrounding geographical information in describing the pictures of Figure 1, came from literate as well as non-literate Mopan speakers. There is an indication that literacy may also be a factor in speech patterns however. In the exchange in Example (3), it is a literate woman who initiates the use of speech participant 'left' which is rejected by her non-literate partner.

References

Brown, Penelope, and Levinson, Stephen. 1993. "*Uphill* and *downhill* in Tzeltal". *Journal of Linguistic Anthropology* 3(1): 46-75.

Clark, Herbert and Wilkes-Gibbs, Deanna. 1986. "Referring as a Collaborative Process". *Cognition* 21(1): 1-39.

Crooks, Deborah L. 1997. "Biocultural Factors in School Achievement for Mopan Children in Belize". *American Anthropologist* 99(3): 586-601.

Danziger, Eve. 1996a. "Split Intransitivity and Active-Inactive Patterning in Mopan Maya". *International Journal of American Linguistics.* 62(4): 379-414.

Danziger, Eve. 1996b. "Parts and their Counter-parts: Social and Spatial Relationships in Mopan Maya". *The Journal of the Royal Anthropological Institute N.S.* (incorporating *MAN*) 1:1-16.

Danziger, Eve. in press (a). "Cross-Cultural Studies in Language and Thought: Is there a Metalanguage?". In Carmella Moore and Holly Mathews (eds), *The Psychology of Cultural Experience.* Publications of the Society for Psychological Anthropology, Cambridge: U. Press.

Danziger, Eve. in press (b). *Relatively Speaking: Language, Thought and Kinship in Mopan Maya.* Oxford Studies in Anthropological Linguistics, New York: Oxford U. Press.

Danziger, Eve and Pederson, Eric. 1998. "Through the Looking-Glass: A Cross-Cultural Survey of Written Language and Mirror Image Discrimination". *Written Language and Literacy.* 1(2): 153-164.

England, Nora C., and S Elliott. 1990. *Lecturas Sobre la Linguistica Maya.* Guatemala: Centro de Investigaciones Regionales de Mesoamérica.

Gregory, James Robert. 1984. "The Myth of the Male Ethnographer and the Woman's World". *American Anthropologist* 86(2): 316-327.

Haviland, John. B. 1979. "Guugu Yimithirr". In R.M.W. Dixon and Barry Blake (eds), *Handbook of Australian Languages* (Vol 1). Canberra: Australian National University Press, 27-182.

Haviland, John. B. 1993. "Anchoring, Iconicity, and Orientation in Guugu Yimithirr Pointing Gestures". *Journal of Linguistic Anthropology* 3(1):3-45.

Haviland, John. B. 1998. "Guugu Yimithirr Cardinal Directions". *Ethos: Journal of the Society for Psychological Anthropology* 26(1): 25-47.

Jackendoff, Ray. 1987. "On beyond Zebra: The Relation of Linguistic and Visual Information". *Cognition* 26:89-114.

Johnston, Judith R. and Slobin, Dan. 1979. "The Development of Locative Expressions in English, Italian, Serbo-Croatian and Turkish". *Journal of Child Language* 6: 529-545.

de León, Lourdes 1991. "Space Games in Tzotzil: Creating a Context for Spatial Reference". *Working Paper* No. 4, Cognitive Anthropology Research Group, Max Planck Institute for Psycholinguistics. Nijmegen, The Netherlands.

Levelt, Willem J. M. 1984. "Some Perceptual Limitations on Talking About Space". In A. van Doorn, W. de Grind, and J. Koenderink (eds), *Limits in Perception.* Utrecht: VNU Science Press, 323-358.

Levelt, Willem J. M. 1996. "Perspective Taking and Ellipsis in Spatial Descriptions". In Paul Bloom, Mary A. Peterson, Lynn Nadel and Merrill F. Garrett (eds.), *Language and Space.* Cambridge: MIT Press, 77-107..

Levinson, Stephen C. 1994. "Vision, Shape and Linguistic Description: Tzeltal Body-Part Terminology and Object Description". *Linguistics: An Interdisciplinary Journal of the Language Sciences* 32 (4/5): 791-855.

Levinson, Stephen C. 1996. "Frames of Reference and Molyneaux's Question: Crosslinguistic Evidence". In Paul Bloom, Mary A. Peterson, Lynn Nadel and

Merrill F. Garrett (eds.), *Language and Space*. Cambridge: MIT Press, 109-169.

Levinson, Stephen C. 1998. "Studying Spatial Conceptualization Across Cultures: Anthropology and Cognitive Science". *Ethos: Journal of the Society for Psychological Anthropology* 26(1): 7-24.

Levinson, Stephen C. and Penelope Brown. 1994. "Immanuel Kant among the Tenejapans: Anthropology as Empirical Philosophy". *Ethos: Journal of the Society for Psychological Anthropology* 22(1):3-41.

Levinson, Stephen C. and Laszlo K. Nagy. ms. "Look at your Southern Leg: A Statistical Approach to Cross-Cultural Field Studies of Language and Spatial Orientation".

Ozanne-Rivierre, Françoise. this volume. "Spatial Orientation in some Austronesian Languages".

Palmer, Stephen E. 1977. "Hierarchical Structure in Perceptual Representation" *Cognitive Psychology* 9: 441-474.

Pederson, Eric; Danziger, Eve; Levinson, Stephen; Kita, Sotaro; Senft, Gunter and Wilkins, David. 1998. "Semantic Typology and Spatial Conceptualization". *Language* 74(3): 557-589.

Piaget, Jean. 1928. *Judgment and Reasoning in the Child*. M. Warden, trans. New York: Harcourt, Brace and Company.

Piaget, Jean, and Bärbel Inhelder. 1963 [1948] *The Child's Conception of Space*. F. Langdon and J. Lunzer, trans. London: Routledge and Kegan Paul.

Segall, Marshall H, Pierre R. Dasen, John W. Berry and Ype H. Poortinga. 1990. *Human Behaviour in Global Perspective* Pergamon Press NY.

Stewart van Leeuwen, Mary. 1978. "A Cross-cultural Examination of Psychological Differentiation in Males and Females". *International Journal of Psychology* 13 (2): 87-122.

Talmy, Len. 1983. "How Language Structures Space". In H. Pick and L. Acredolo (eds), *Spatial Orientation: Theory, Research, and Application*. New York: Plenum, 225-320.

Tanz, Christine. 1980. *Studies in the Acquisition of Deictic Terms*. Cambridge: Cambridge University Press.

Van Cleve, J., and Frederick, R. (eds) 1991. *The Philosophy of Left and Right*. Dordrecht, Boston, London: Kluwer Academic Publishers.

Verhaeghe, Arlette. ms. "L'influence de la Scolarisation et de l'Alphabétisation sur les Capacités de Traitement Visuel". PhD in progress, Department of Psychology, University of Lisbon.

Verhaeghe, Arlette and Kolinsky, Régine. 1991. "Discriminaçâo Entre Figuras Orientadas em Espelho em Funçâo do Modo de Apresentaçâo em Adultos Escolarizados e Adultos Iletrados" *Actas das I Jornadas de Estudio dos Processos Cognitivos*, Lisbon: Sociedade Portuguesa de Psicologia.

Localization and Predication
Ancient Greek and various other Languages

Hansjakob Seiler
University of Cologne

Introduction

The aim of this paper is to discuss the preliminaries to a specification of cognitive content on a conceptual level. The domains chosen are localization and predication. The paper starts from the assumption that such a conceptual level pertains to universality in language, and that there is no direct connection between universality and the facts of the individual languages. At least one intermediate level will have to be posited, which we might call the level of General Comparative Grammar. The approach will be presented in three stages plus an intermezzo. The three stages are: 1. The facts of an individual language (Ancient Greek); 2. Various other languages reflecting language diversity; 3. The more abstract level of General Comparative Grammar. The intermezzo will be on language acquisition in terms of non-linguistic maturation with reference to localization.

Localization must be understood in its close connection with predication. This may be illustrated with the following example: [1]

(1) (i) Carlo **va** in Germania
C. goes in Germany
LOCATUM LOCATOR LOCUS
Carlo goes **to** Germany
(ii) Carlo **vive** in Germania
C. lives in Germany
LOCATUM LOCATOR LOCUS
Carlo lives **in** Germany

The comparison between Italian and English shows a difference in signalling an allative *vs.* an inessive LOCATOR (= localizer). Whereas in Italian the difference resides primarily in the verbs (motion *vs.* position), in English the difference is represented by a combination of verb plus a different preposition. In both Italian and English the verb as the center of predication is an essential constituent in the representation of a localizer. What does this mean for cognitive content?

Cognitive representations are not given us for direct observation in a way that the utterances of an individual language are. However, cognitive representations may be intuitively perceived. We know what we want to say, *e.g.* express a locational relation. How can this knowledge be assessed in an intersubjective manner?

Our main research tool here is the continuum. For readers not yet familiar with my theoretical framework, I might provide a few explanations.[2] The continuum is first of all a metalinguistic ordering principle. An example is presented in section 1, figure 1, where the local preposition-adverbs of Ancient Greek are arranged in a continuous linear order that can be read from left to right or from right to left. The criteria for continuous ordering are presented in the form of several parameters, each with two opposite poles. They may be summarized by the following opposition: simple *vs* complex or, in functional terms: indicative *vs* predicative. 'Indicative' means that the common functional denominator of the continuum – in our case it is localization – is represented by way of pointing, or ostension, globally. This is certainly the case of the preposition *éni (en)* "in" marking inessivity in a nominal clause (*i.e.* without a verb), which holds true irrespective of one's point of view. 'Predicative' means that the common functional denominator is represented by "saying something about localization", *i.e.* by making it explicit and thus defining it. This is the case of such prepositions as *aná* "up hill", *katá* "downhill" (at the right end of the spectrum), forms always combining with a full verb (motion or other) and involving a supplementary deictic center (point of view of the speaker), and thus involving more expressive 'machinery' than the indicative *éni*. Between these extreme positions we find intermediate steps where the constructions with a nominal clause gradually give way to constructions with a verb of existence ("to be"), and further on with motion verbs and finally full verbs.

Now, such a continuum is not only a metalinguistic ordering principle. Its inherent dynamic actually reflects what speakers do. Evidence for this can be seen in diachronic developments, where the continuum is the *locus* of language change. This can go in either direction. From indicativity to predicativity: *éni* marking inessivity in Ancient Geek developed into the verb of existence *íne* "he/she/it is" in Modern Greek. From predicativity to indicativity: Ancient Greek *eis* "into", illative, replacing *éni* "in" which developed into an inessive *(ei)s* in Modern Greek:

(2) (i) Ancient: en têi Helládi
        in ART Greece

(ii) Modern: s tin Eláđa
     in ART Greece
     both: "in Greece"[3]

If we succeed in setting up comparable continua of localization in other languages, and if we can make similar observations about the order of acquisition of the relevant structures by children, this might enable us to uncover the principles according to which localization is being construed – on a general linguistic level and, eventually, on a cognitive-conceptual level.

1. The continuum of preposition-adverbs in Ancient Greek

The majority of Greek prepositions can also be used adverbially. They may then be separated from the verb (tmesis), come after their case (anastrophe), and shift their accent backwards (barytonesis). One peculiarity of some of these preposition-adverbs consists in their functioning as predicates, i.e. without a verb. Apart from this, we find their use as preverbs of the verb "to be": *estín* "he/she/it is". Here are two examples from Homer:

(3) (Il.14.216)

énth' **éni** mèn philótēs, **én** d' hímeros, **én** d' oaristús.
there in PT love   in PT desire   in PT lover's talk
[PT = Particle]
In there (i.e. in Aphrodite's mantle) (is) love, in there (is) desire, in there (is) lover's talk.

(4) (Od.10.45)

idṓmetha... hóssos tis khrūsós te kaì árguros askōi **énestin**.
see.1PL.SBJ.AOR how much IND gold and and silver bag.DAT in-be.3SG
[IND = Indefinite pronoun]
Let us see...how much gold and silver is in the bag

The first example, showing two variants of the preposition-adverb "in", is generally recognized as an instance of a nominal clause, i.e. a verb-less predication. It is not, as some handbooks still would have it, a matter of ellipsis of a verb "to be". As E. Benveniste (1950/1966: 151ff.) has convincingly shown, the nominal clause (as a predication of essence and permanence) contrasts with a clause showing the verb "to be" as a predication of circumstance and accidence. Applied to the situation of our preposition-adverbs, this means that in (3) *éni / én* with no verb present, signal a permanent and essential property of Aphrodite and her mantle, whereas in (4) with *én* plus the verb "to be", we have the very accidental situation of the companions of Ulysses, who want to know how much gold and silver is in the bag received from Aiolos.

Now, not all the preposition-adverbs of Ancient Greek exhibit this twofold use, viz. in nominal clauses – marking essence (E), and in clauses with the verb "to be" – marking circumstance (C). There are some that are limited to this latter use. A synoptic chart is given in the appendix. Here I will confine myself to going through it rapidly. Both essence (E) and circumstance (C) may be predicated with *én*, *ení* "in, inside", *epí* "on", *pará* "near, beside", *metá* "amidst", *perí* "around", *amphí* "on both sides", *apó* "from, since", *hupó* "beneath". Circumstance (C) alone is predicated by means of *estín* "is" with *hupér* "above", *pró* "ahead", *prós* "toward", *sún* "together with", and *eks* "out(side)". The remaining five occur neither in nominal clauses nor in bound form with *estin* "to be". If *aná* "upwards" occurs without a verb, it is in function of an imperative: *ána* "(get) up!" with a full verb of motion being tacitly understood. We have thus crossed the boundary between verb "to be" and full verb (of motion or of position).

The explanations offered for the asymmetries between nominal clause, clause showing verb "to be", and clause exhibiting full verb insufficiently account for the phenomenon. It has been suggested (Wackernagel 1906/1953: 178) that our use E is bound up with disyllabics. Yet *hupér*, *diá*, *aná*, *katá* and *antí* are disyllabic and are not used within E. Moreover, *én / éni* –as the oldest attested item and which is active up to this day – combines monosyllabicity and use within E. It has also been noted (Schwyzer 1939: 423) that use E is mostly limited to preposition-adverbs of position, not of motion. Yet, *pró* "ahead", *sun* "with", *antí* "facing" may be used positionally, depending on the case with which they are construed.

I think that the real distinction in question here is between a **topological** and a **dimensional** relation – the terms being borrowed from an article of W. Klein (1991: 77ff.). A dimensional relation encompasses not only the object to be localized ("figure"), a localizer (preposition-adverb or verb), a reference object ("ground"), but also a deictic center (CD), i.e. a reference point for evaluating the spatial relation. Thus, for *katá* "downwards, across", starting point and end point of the movement are determined with reference to a CD. In a topological relation, there is no room for a CD. Thus, the relation of inessivity *én*, *éni* (e.g.

"inside a box") holds, irrespective of one's point of view. It follows from this that dimensional relations – expression and content – are more complex than topological relations.

Yet the decisive aspect of our analysis is the observation of a **continuum** underlying the entire series of preposition-adverbs and their respective constructions. There is a gradual transition from nominal clause to clause with verb "to be" and clause with full verbs. The use and frequency of each preposition-adverb is documented in detail in Liddell-Scott-Jones' Greek-English Lexicon (1940). There one finds that the use within a nominal clause is most readily attested for *én / éni*, and from there on gradually decreases in frequency to constructions with *-estin* (see Appendix). As already mentioned, *éni* has proved to be active during the entire history of the Greek language: witness the Modern Greek *íne* "he/she/it is", "they are", which etymologically derives from *éni*.[4]

As for *hupó* "underneath" in a nominal clause, this dictionary exhibits only one example shown in an inscription. In fact, *hupó* marks a turning point in the continuum: it is from this point on that verbal constructions take over, to the exclusion of nominal ones. The emergence of a deictic center makes for increased complexity. Directional meanings of the preposition-adverbs contribute to further complexity. The preposition-adverbs preferably appear in pairs of opposites: *hupó/hupér*, *pró/epí*, *eks/eis*, *aná/katá*. There is also a steady increase in figurative-metaphorical uses, culminating in *éks-estin* "it is possible, permitted", restricted to impersonal use. The last four items to the right of the continuum permit neither a nominal clause nor compounding with verb "to be"; they only take full verbs. Each of them shows metaphorical use alongside non-metaphorical use.

A graphical representation of this continuum would be as follows (Figure 1) (the top line shows the adverbial forms; for the respective glosses see the Appendix; the triangle and the t.p. mark the turning point):

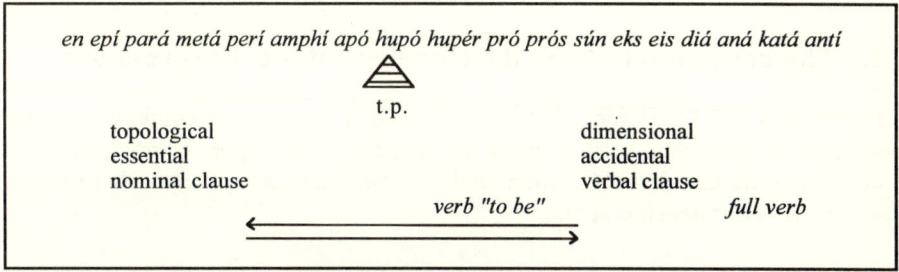

Figure 1: the continuum of prepositions-adverbs

The arrows pointing in opposite directions are meant to symbolize a dynamic that pervades the continuum: from left to right, they present a dynamic that takes us from lesser-marked nominal clause constructions (signalling a topological and permanent relation) by way of clauses with the verb "to be" toward clauses with a full verb (signalling more complex dimensional and accidental relations). In the opposite direction, the path takes us from the more complex and accidental to the less complex and permanent relation. By pointing out diachronic changes, we have seen (in the Introduction) that speakers do in fact proceed in either direction; this is, of course, one of the strongest arguments in favour of the linguistic reality of such a continuum.

To conclude this section, I should propose to correlate the preposition-adverbs of Ancient Greek with their respective localizing functions, arranged in continuous fashion (as in Figure 1). The schema is to be read from left to right for each line, and from top to bottom for each consecutive line. First line: topological relations; second line: turning point, area of inversion; third line: dimensional relations, preferably with motion verbs; and fourth line: dimensional relations with motion and other full verbs.

```
inessive - adessive - apudessive - mediessive - circumessive- abessive
  en         epí         pará          metá          amphí         apó
                        inferior / superior
                         hupó  /  hupér
         allative - comitative - separative - illative
          pró prós      sún          eks         eis
         translative - sursum   - deorsum   - adversum
             diá         aná        katá         antí
```

Figure 2: The continuum of localizing functions

2. The continuum of the development of local expressions

J. Johnston and D. Slobin (1979) investigated the ability of children between the ages of 2 yrs. and 4 yrs. 8 mths. to produce locative pre- or postpositions in English, Italian, Serbo-Croatian, and Turkish. Across languages, there was a general order of development:

IN / ON / UNDER < BESIDE < BACK$_f$ / FRONT$_f$ < BETWEEN < BACK / FRONT where BACK$_f$ / FRONT$_f$ refer to objects with inherent fronts and backs (e.g. people, cars, houses), whereas simple BACK/FRONT refer to objects without orientational features (e.g. trees, blocks, drinking glasses).

We recognize in this developmental series a progression from the topological toward the dimensional, comparable to our continuum of preposition-adverbs in Greek. This is an important parallelism, and all the more so as the authors investigated and discussed this development in terms of non-linguistic maturation, i.e. of universals of conceptual and communicative development. Naturally, they had to take into account the differences between those languages regarding their particular means of representing the semantics of local relations. Certain delays in the acquisition of a certain stage may occur, due to the structural make-up of the language under study. What is important, however, is not the particular stage *per se*, i.e. in isolation, but rather the dynamic between the stages. It is up to the linguist to try to better understand this dynamic. The procedure will follow two tracks:

- by further comparisons, and
- by reasoning on the basis of the data.

3. Continua of local relations across languages

W. Drossard (1993: 44f.) takes the Johnston-Slobin hierarchy as a starting point, as a *tertium comparationis*, which permits him to uncover suggestive parallelisms between languages of widely different structures. He examines, among others, languages showing different ways of representing case relations reflecting different degrees of complexity. The gist of it is that for representing inessivity, adessivity, and superiority, the noun for the reference object is followed first by case affixes that are mostly monomorphematic and originating from postpositions of nominal descent – whereas the more dimensional relations would be represented by the addition of more independant elements. Thus, among the Finno-Ugric languages, Finnish – with its distinction between "internal" and "external cases" – stops after stage two: that is, it represents inessivity and adessivity with postpositions ending up as affixes, whereas the remaining relations of the Johnston-Slobin hierarchy are represented by independent postpositions. Hungarian, on the other hand "advances by one further step" i.e. up to "superiority" in its stative function, whereas subsequent directional meanings would be represented by more independent means.

Drossard finds the most convincing examples among the Eastern Caucasian languages, where grammarians speak of series, i.e. increments that are differentiated according to the position of the particular local relation on the scale between the topological and the dimensional. For the languages of the Avaro-Andic group, he finds the following situation (op.cit.64; for brevity, only his translation equivalents in German are given here):

(5)   in - bei - auf - unter

realized as case affixes, whereas

(6)   hinter - zwischen - vor

would be realized as postpositions

By comparing the members of the Lesghian group, Drossard succeeds in setting up a perfect cross-linguistic "squish" ranging from Budux with seriation for two positions to Agul with seriation for all positions of the Johnston-Slobin hierarchy (op.cit.78) (Finno-Ugric is added for comparison). See table 1:

Table 1: A cross-linguistic squish

	in	bei	auf / über	unter	hinter	zwischen	vor
Finno/Ugrisch	LAP[5]	FINN[6]	UNGAR[7]				
Awaro-Andisch	+	+	+	+			
Cesisch	+	+	+	+			
Lakkisch	+	+	+	+	+		
Lesgisch							
• *Buduchisch*	+	+					
• *Udisch*	+	+	+				
• *Kryzisch*	+	+	+	+			
• *Lesgisch*	+	+	+	+	+		
• *Tabassaranisch*	+	+	+	+	+	+	
• *Aghulisch*	+	+	+	+	+	+	+

Our discussions from the preceding sections thus far show a striking convergence across languages: the linguistic representations of localizing relations can be ordered in the manner of continua which span from the less complex (both in form and in meaning), less informative (indicativity), less independent (affixes in section 3) to the more complex, more informative, more independent (postpositions in section 3). There is, in addition, an impressive parallel which comes from observations regarding the acquisition of locative expressions by children.

4. Localization and predication - *centralized* and *decentralized*

In this section, I want to show that the relation between localization and predication is one of solidarity, and that the two must be understood accordingly. Specifically, this would mean that the two behave in a solidary way with regard to the question of centrality to the utterance. When the predicate is low in agentivity, i.e., totally removed in a nominal clause, as in Greek, or a verb of existence, or a verb of position or motion, then location may potentially represent the center of the utterance. When the predicate is high in agentivity, as with a typical action verb, then location tends to be marginalized.[8] Consider the following examples (adapted from Premper 1993: 136).

(7) (i)   The doctor is in
    (ii) The doctor is in the office
    (iii) The doctor works in the office
    (iv) The doctor cured the patient in the office
    (v)   The doctor killed the patient in a fight

In (i) location is the center of the assertion. (i) is contained in / implied by (ii) and (iii). In (iv) the locative expression *in the office* shows adjunct status. Moreover, its syntactic relation is ambiguous: who is in the office – doctor or patient? (v) shows an action verb and a further marginalized locative expression characterized by metaphorization.

In order to fully understand the workings of this kind of solidarity, we need the more encompassing frame of reference, on a more abstract level, of General Comparative Grammar. It will permit us to bring to the fore the dynamic in the continua, as motivated by mental movements on a conceptual level. A closer look at the total structure of predication reveals that the interrelation between the predicate (prototypically the verb) and its arguments and adjuncts is characterized by bondedness in varying degrees. The variation may be captured by a hierarchy of the well-known sort where AGENT and / or PATIENT are highest, and LOCATION[9] is lowest in bondedness.

Now, it has been observed (Drossard 1992: 1 ff.) that the bond between LOCATION and the verb may be strengthened. We call this process centralization (Seiler 1994: 41), as the verb is considered to be the center of the respective constructions and is considered semantically to represent the center of the assertion. Centralization of LOCATION occurs when the verb is low in agentivity and instead carries or implies a locational meaning component. Consider the examples from Swahili (Drossard 1992: 17):

(8) (i) Juma a   - li   - weka   kitabu   meza- ni
    J.   he   - PAST   - put   book   table - LOC
    Juma put the book on the table

(ii) meza - ni   pa - li   -wek   - w - a   kitabu   na   Juma
     table - LOC 16- PAST -put   - PASS   book   by   Juma
     It was the table upon which the book was put by Juma

(ii) is an overtly passive construction; *pa* is the marker of local class 16 and conveys subject properties. Thus LOCATION, normally decentral, is moved to the center, *i.e.* to stronger bondedness; and the verb is a verb of movement.

Conversely, participants such as AGENT and/or PATIENT that are normally central to the assertion may become decentralized and assume LOCATION status when the verb does not carry or imply a locational meaning and is, instead, a verb of action. Consider the example of Awar (Drossard 1992: 24), where a LOCATIVE-ERGATIVE structure is preferred with appropriate verbs:

(9) Dica   l'abu - na   dos - da
    1SG/ERG   beat - PAST   3SG - SUP/LOC
    I beat him (lit. I beat on him)

Here, the PATIENT is encoded in the stative-positional case of the superessive series.

All the foregoing continua are the *loci* for corresponding mental movements, moving LOCATION to the center of the assertion in conjunction with verbs that are non-actional (and eventually totally removed as in the nominal clauses of Greek) and instead, carrying or implying a locational component (existence, position, or motion) - or marginalizing LOCATION as the status for decentralized AGENTS and/or PATIENTS. Localization and predication thus reveal themselves to be equipollent partners in a relation of solidarity.

Naturally, these statements are subject to further evaluation by means of the appropriate data – a task that is beyond the scope of this paper.

Conclusion

We promised to discuss the preliminaries to a specification of cognitive content on a conceptual level in the domains of localization and predication. The specification itself – being beyond the scope of this paper – would have to take into consideration the following results of the foregoing:
- The linguistic representations of localizing relations can be ordered in the form of continua which span from the less complex, less informative (indicativity), to the more complex and more informative (predicativity).

This can be observed within each of the individual languages which we have studied. Additional support comes "from outside", as it were, *i.e.* from observations regarding the acquisition of locative expressions by children.
- There obtains a dynamic in these continua which reflects what speakers actually do. This is corroborated both by the facts of language acquisition and by the facts of language change. The latter reveal mental movements that can run in two converse directions: either from lesser to more complex, or in the reverse.
- On the more abstract level of General Comparative Grammar, we found that the appropriate frame of reference would include both LOCATION and PREDICATION with its arguments and adjuncts. A relation of solidarity obtains between them all, which can be described in terms of centralizing *vs.* decentralizing movements.[10]
- This view on the solidarity relation between LOCATION and PREDICATION will have its consequences for the interpretation of the metaphor. The passage from so-called concrete local uses to so-called abstract non-local uses is in need of an explanation. It is made possible because both local and non-local relations share the same frame of reference. As Broschart (1993: 1 ff.) has convincingly shown, there is no need for postulating an *a priori* localism from which more "abstract" relations would be derived – and this in ways that are not altogether very clear.

If our view on the solidarity between LOCATION (represented by morpho-syntactic localization) and PREDICATION (represented by predication) is correct, this would mean that in each localizing expression there is a certain degree of predication, and in each predication there is also a certain degree of localization. And if this latter statement is correct, we would be in a postion to understand why verbs do not carry a special marker of *locus* whereas they do, obligatorily in principle, carry a *tempus* marker.

Epilog

The so-called cognitive representations – which, I repeat, are not given to us in a direct way – can be better approached now, through the debate on language diversity/unity. How should we go about stating this? There follow two remarks which derive from the preceding:
- We must distinguish between semantics (meaning) and sense - in keeping with the well-known precepts of E. Coseriu. Semantics (meaning) pertains to a particular concrete language, not to language in general. Sense pertains to

content, to the conceptual: this is the decisive level for all translation activity.
- Variation implies invariance, and vice-versa. Diversity implies unity, and vice-versa. Variation can only be thought of and described on the background of some idea of what is invariant. On the other hand, the invariant can only be arrived at by carefully studying the facts of variation.

The same holds for the relation between language diversity and unity. Are we thus moving in a circle? This is where the convergence with observations from adjacent fields comes in. It opens up new perspectives from "outside", thereby giving us the possibility of either leaving the circle or of entering it.

Appendix

Synopsis of the preposition-adverbs (-preverbs) of Ancient Greek

Adverbial form	being of essence (E) + being of circumstance (C)
en, ení "in(side)"	*éni* (E) "is in(side)", "is there" *énestin* (C) "is inside", "is present"
epí "there, near, above"	*épi* (E) "is there", "is at hand" *épestin* (C) "is on it", "is attached to it"
pará "by (the side)"	*pára* (E) "is near", "is copresent" *párestin* (C) "is there", "is near"
metá "amidst"	*méta* (E) "is among" *métestin* (C) "is among", "is one's share"
perí "around"	*péri* (E) "is around" *períestin* (C) "is superior"
amphí "on both sides"	*amphí* (E) "is at, by" * *amphíestin* (C)
apó "from, away from "	*ápo* (E) "is far (away)" *ápestin* (C) "is absent"
hupó "underneath"	*húpo* (E) "is underneath" *húpestin* (C) "is underneath", "is concealed"

	"being of circumstance" (C) without (E)
hupér "above"	*hupérestin* "is superior" (late)
pró "before, in front of"	*próestin* "is before" (temporal)
prós "towards", "hard by"	*prósestin* "is attached", "belongs"
sún "with"	*súnestin* "is with"
eks, ek "out of", "forth from"	*éksestin* "it is possible, permitted" (impersonal)
eis "toward inside"	* *eísestin*
diá "across"	* *díestin*
aná "upwards"	* *ánestin*
katá "downwards"	* *kátestin*
antí "opposite, over, against"	* *ántestin*

Notes

1. From Premper (1993: 122) after Stolz (1992: 17).
2. For detailed presentations see Seiler (1985: 14 ff.; 1986: 24 ff.).
3. More precisely we should say that Modern Greek *(ei)s* covers both inessivity and allativity with respective verbs of position *vs.* motion:
   (2) (iii) íne   s   tin   Eláða
            be.3sg   in   ART. Greece
            He is in Greece
       (iv) pái   s   tin   Eláða
            go.3sg   in   ART. Greece
            He goes to Greece
   Although the result of this development in Greek is the same as that in Italian as shown in (1), the paths of these developments are converse: from original inessivity to illativity in Italian, from illativity to inessivity in Greek. This shows that continua of the kind proposed in section 1 can be the *locus* of language change in converse directions. In either case, however, it is the verb, *i.e.* the predicate, that has a decisive role in the dynamic of such continua of localization.
4. This passage from inessivity ("inside") to a predicating element finds several synchronic parallels. Thus, in Welsh, *yn* "in" appears as a predicator (the examples are due to J. Broschart, 1993: 15f.):
   (a) concrete-local (with nasal mutation)
       (i) mae'r merched   yn   yr   ardd
           is-the girls   in   the   garden
           The girls are in the garden
   (b) predicative (with soft mutation)
       (ii) mae   Mair   yn   nyrs
            is   Mair   in   nurse

Mair is a nurse
(iii) mae'r merched   yn   ddel
      is-the girls   in   pretty
      The girls are pretty

Another parallel would be the use of French *en*:
(iv) en France
     in France
(v) Je vous dis cela en ami ~ étant ami
     I tell you this as one friend to another (lit. in friend~ as a friend)

5. = Lappic
6. = Finnish
7. = Hungarian
8. See also the work of W. Premper (1993: 136), who arrives at similar conclusions.
9. LOCATION (capitalized) refers to the more abstract, comparative level - as do AGENT and PATIENT. Localization refers to the level of linguistic, i.e. morphosyntactic representation.
10. In her article "Localization and predication in Yucatec Maya", C. Goldap (1993: 87s.) portrays the relevant scenario for that language as follows: "In Yucatec, almost all phenomena of localization are placed on a very high semantic and syntactic level; to speak syntactically: on the level of the clause or the verb phrase and not on the noun phrase level; to speak functionally: within the functional domain of predication and not so much in the functional domain of reference." - This might prompt one to outline a typology as follows. There are certain languages (English, German) that confer some of the local functions onto nominal, referential syntagms: e.g. the prepositional attribute. In other languages, like Yucatec, the functions of localization are almost entirely represented within the predicative-verbal domain. Perhaps it was an idea of that sort that led L. Talmy (1985: 57ff.) to positioning two types of lexicalization for the expressn of the PATH, which he calls respectively 'verb-framed' (e.g. French *entrer à quatre pattes* "crawl in/on all fours" lit. *enter* on four feet) vs. 'satellite-framed' (e.g. German **hinein**krabbeln.).

References

Benveniste, Emile. 1950 / 1966. "La phrase nominale". *Problèmes de Linguistique Générale* I, Paris: Gallimard, 151-167.

Broschart, Jürgen. 1993. "Raum und Grammatik oder: Wie berechenbar ist Sprache? (Mit Beispielen zu Kasusmarkierung, Aspekt, Tempus und Modus)". In Müller-Bardey and Drossard (eds.), 1-43.

Drossard, Werner. 1992. "Verbgebundene LOKALISATION *vs.* LOKALISATION von Propositionen". (Studien zur LOKALISATION II). *Arbeiten des Kölner Universalien-Projekts (AKUP)*, 87, 1-38.

Drossard, Werner. 1993. "Lokale Relationen: Vom Einfachen (Topologischen) zum Komplexeren (Dimensionalen) - Sprachliche Reflexe einer psycholinguistischen Erkenntnis". In Müller-Bardey and Drossard (eds.), 44-86.

Fuchs, Catherine and Victorri, Bernard (eds.). 1994. *Continuity in Linguistic Semantics* (Linguisticae Investigationes Supplementa: 19). Amsterdam / Philadelphia: Benjamins.
Goldap, Christel. 1993. "Localization and Predication in Modern Yucatec Maya". In Müller-Bardey and Drossard (eds.), 87-104.
Johnston, Judith R and Slobin, Dan J. 1979. "The development of locative expressions in English, Italian, Serbo-Croatian and Turkish". *Journal of Child Language*, 6:3, 529-545.
Klein, Wolfgang. 1991. "Raumausdrücke". *Linguistische Berichte*, 132, 77-114.
Liddell, Henry George et al. 1940. *A Greek-English Lexicon*. (2 vols), Oxford: The Clarendon Press.
Müller-Bardey, Thomas. and Drossard, Werner (eds.). 1993. *Aspekte der Lokalisation. Beiträge zur Arbeitsgruppe Lokalisation bei der Tagung der Deutschen Gesellschaft für Sprachwissenschaft in Bremen*, 1992, Bochum: Universitätsverlag Dr. W. Brockmeyer.
Premper, Waldfried. 1993. "Inhärente Lokalisation". In Müller-Bardey and Drossard (eds.), 120-138.
Schwyzer, Eduard. 1939. *Griechische Grammatik* I, München: C.H. Beck.
Seiler, Hansjakob. 1985. "Linguistic continua, their properties and their interpretation". In H. Seiler and G. Brettschneider (eds.), *Language Invariants and Mental Operations* (Language Universals Series 5), Tübingen: Gunter Narr, 14 ff.
Seiler, Hansjakob. 1986. *Apprehension. Language, Object and Order* (Language Universals Series 6), Tübingen: Gunter Narr.
Seiler, Hansjakob. 1994. "Continuum in cognition and continuum in language". In C. Fuchs and B. Victorri (eds.), 33-43.
Stolz, Thomas. 1992. *Lokalkasussysteme - Aspekte einer strukturellen Dynamik* (Pro lingua 13), Wilhelmsfeld: Gottfried Egert.
Talmy, Leonard. 1985. "Lexicalization patterns: semantic structure in lexical forms". In T. Shopen (ed.), *Language Typology and Syntatic Description*: vol. III, Cambridge: Cambridge University Press, 57-149.
Wackernagel, Jacob. 1906/1953. "Wortumfang und Wortform". *Kleine Schriften* vol. I, Göttingen: Vandenhoeck and Ruprecht, 148-185.

The Expression of Spatial Relations and the Spatialization of Semantic Relations in French Sign Language

Christian Cuxac
Département de Sciences du Langage
Université Paris VIII

Introduction

Sign languages, as well as congenital deafness, call into question many of the concepts which are considered as central to the social sciences, and indeed provide us with a starting point for their re-analysis.

With the present, I shall attempt to demonstrate that sign languages are linguistic objects which provide us with increasingly tangible means of accessing cognitive activity. This is possible by virtue of the existence in language of the visible, iconic manifestation of a dynamic process, which is set in motion by deaf signers to speak of experience outside of the situation of the utterance.

To begin with, I will limit my line of enquiry to so-called 'imagistic iconicity'; this seems to be the most basic and practical definition, that is, when there is a formal resemblance between the sign or signs and what is being referred to in the extra-linguistic world of experience.

1. The process of iconization for deaf individuals

Sign languages are equipped with a standard lexicon: this is a grouping of discrete items, which display referential iconicity to varying degrees (thus contained within an iconic continuum).

However, the great originality of sign language lies in the possibility of having recourse to other structures, endowed with great iconic value–but which function more or less independently of this standard lexicon. These structures are quite similar from one sign language to another, right down to the specific forms employed. They are what the deaf from different language communities use in order to communicate, both at programmed conferences and in chance meetings between individuals. The amazing thing about this is that the practice of any one particular sign language enables the signer to communicate efficiently with anyone practicing another sign language—thus transcending the specificity of any one particular sign language.

Even more fascinating is the fact that children born deaf (hearing-impaired) in an environment made up exclusively of hearing individuals constitute a unique group who yet manage to communicate: these individuals are placed in a situation where they derive no benefit from (verbal) solicitation by other members of the community, and where–given an average level of intelligence– they are unable to put into place the normal process of language acquisition, insofar as this concerns a first (spoken) language. Without being educated in specialized programs (for the learning of an oral language artificially), and without encountering other deaf persons already practicing a sign language (that is, the acquisition of sign language as a first language under the normal conditions of a linguistic environment), we might well wonder how they manage this communication with the surrounding population. And yet, few researchers have directed their efforts to studying this very basic problem. For it is only in the observation of such linguistic data that we can provide a solid foundation for theoretical developments.

This is precisely what one finds in Yau (1988), who collected a considerable body of data on the constitution of gestural languages (and particularly vocabularies) by isolated deaf adults. This research has shown firstly that the attested, ordered strata of signifying forms are indeed very similar, but are influenced at the same time by the cultural environment surrounding them– thereby indicating that, for any of the strata, such extreme hypotheses as "there are certain things which have yet to be named", and "only culturalized forms can be expressed" are in fact overly categorical responses which result from the problem being poorly stated. Secondly, it is clear from this research that as far as the closely related strata of signifying forms are concerned, the attested forms which support this finding are strongly resemblant from one individual signer to another.

The phenomena observed by Yau are corroborated by what we know about the creation of signs by deaf children growing up in a "hearing" environment. Before coming of school age, these children attempt to communicate with others by means of gestures of their own contrivance. If the family is indisposed towards these gestural creations and refuses to lend them any credence, the child will stop the creative process. If, on the contrary, the family adopts the child's signs, a familial gestural code will be set up. This code is formally similar to the vocabularies observed by Yau in isolated deaf adults.

These lexicalized gestural creations or signs, which provide proof of the human aptitude for categorizing, permit us to advance the hypothesis of stabilized pre-linguistic conceptual forms. The latter seem to be based essentially in visual perception or, to avoid over-simplification, in the perceptual-practical universe. The strong resemblance between the gestural forms which are retained for communication indicates that a process of (mental) iconization of experience has been set up, and furthermore that this process itself is based on the repetition and recognition of salient shapes, the description of the outlines of these shapes and/or the iconic gestural re-introduction of the salient shapes of categorized referents.

This hypothesis merits several remarks. First, the fact that these stabilized conceptual forms take on linguistic meaning by functioning as signs certainly reinforces their stability. Second, these categorizations seem to derive from a semiotic intent involving referential iconization processes of extra-linguistic reality expressed by means of gestural sequences; the latter have functions which are just as much categorizing as they are specifying. The difference between a sign representing a type and a sign representing a specified individual seems to reside in its being marked by the environment in which it occurs—whether in mime, in the gaze or in the context—which accompanies these gestural ensembles. Third, if there seems to be no gestural difference between the type and the manifestation of an individual example extracted from the type, the form of the signs thus created nevertheless exhibits a cognitive differentiation, separating referentially stabilized entities, and the events related to them. We find here a difference similar to that established by Langacker (1987) between "things" and "processes". Indeed, the former are rendered by signs which specify a shape or the outline of a shape, or by gestural complexes which associate a description of the outline of a shape and an action frequently associated with this shape; whereas the latter never have recourse to specifications of shape and are rendered exclusively either by personal transfers (cf. below), or by signs in which movements, representing actions, iconically play a major role. This all goes to show that the iconic differentiation between "things" and "processes" argues strongly in favour of the noun/verb opposition as a cognitive, pre-linguistic given.

This in turn leads us to formulate the hypothesis concerning the iconicity of lexical creations, that is, as a process of iconization conceived not merely as an aid to conceptualization, but rather as a construction (utilizing whatever means the gestural mode of signifying can provide) which simultaneously facilitates the co-construction of meaning by the addressee (for example, children seem to have a knowledge of other people's capacities for understanding very early on).

Along similar lines, but transposed into the framework of communication between adults, we might mention the utilization of the iconic process in international conferences, where an accumulation of strongly iconic characteristics produces generic forms (Cuxac, in press). Equally well known is the inverse process, whereby the iconicity of standard generic items is remotivated and is transformed into the specific ("that tree over there, that I'm pointing out"; "this house over here"; "like that", etc.) because the sign is placed in front of the gaze of the person creating it.

Taken together with the quite general value of this process of iconization representing the perceptual world, the strong iconic resemblance of the forms which are retained for use bear witness to the fact that deaf individuals in isolation repeat the first phases in the constitution of sign language in their familial microcosm.

We must never lose sight of the fact that–and this is the reason why congenital deafness is such a formidable analytic tool–firstly, all of the sign languages utilized in the world at present take analogous situations of communication as their starting point, although on the somewhat larger scale of the population in question (it is the univocity of the starting point, together with its dating, which constitute fictions); and secondly, the genesis of signs has always taken place more or less according to the same scenario. The serendipitous creation of small communities of deaf people in large cities (which one finds as early as the works of Plato), and later the institutionalized gatherings of deaf children in educational systems from the mid-eighteenth century onwards, did nothing more than extend–all the while accelerating–the process of semiogenesis brought into play by isolated deaf persons growing up in the midst of the hearing family.

As my point of departure, I will take a primary semiotic intentionality having recourse to a process of iconization which expresses both the generic and the specific, but which does not differentiate gesturally between the two. I will then try to account for the distinction between "great" iconic structures and the standard signs which today characterize the sign languages both utilized by large populations, and having a long history of institutionalized use.

With this aim in mind, I will advance the hypothesis that this primary iconization split into two sub-branches, according to whether or not the process of iconization serves the express aim of representing experience iconically: I shall term this "iconic intent".

2. Iconic intent and great iconicity

In the first case, iconicity is produced in a process of iconization, evolves over time and is perfected, whether one chooses to consider the ontogenetic development of the deaf child living with his peers, or the historical development of the deaf community. For example, this evolution has resulted in increasingly sophisticated specifications and transfers of forms (cf. below) made possible by paradigms of hand configurations, as well as increasingly complex types of movement which enable one to reshape sense experience in the signing space with extreme precision. If we take the most fundamental example–that of a past lived experience–the iconizing ambition corresponds to *"so, it happened like this"*, and one shows the experience while recounting it; *or "it was in a room like this"*, and one shows the room while describing it; or *"where a character like this one"*, and one shows the person while imitating them, and so on. This procedure is a bit like what is termed in criminology as the reconstitution of a crime.

All languages enable the speaker to construct such reconstitutions of experience, but spoken languages limit one to saying it without actually showing it (except for instances of gestural adjuncts: a fish *"this big"*, or the postural imitation of characters or voice imitation in reported speech).

Not so for sign languages, where the monstrative dimension *"like this"* can be activated at any moment through showing and imitating (as if I were the person of whom I speak, whatever his actions might be).

2.1 The structural characteristics of great iconicity

Great iconicity is the term I use to refer to the structural traces–in the realm of discourse – of a process of iconization which subserves the iconic intent; that is, when the monstrative dimension *"like this"* is conserved.

After considerable reflection, I have chosen to subsume the entirety of these structures under the heading of "transfers". This term seems appropriate in the sense that it is a matter here–beforehand–of transferring real or imaginary experience and slightly reshaping it, projecting it into a tridimensional discursive space we will call the "signing space", which is the space in which messages are made manifest.

As these structures, which are common to different sign languages have been catalogued elsewhere (Cuxac, in press), the rapid review which follows should suffice.

2.1.1 Transfers of size and/or form

Specification is an operation which is used to designate a transfer of a size and/or a transfer of a form. The corresponding hand configurations are discrete and limited in number. The movement involved refers to the use of the form in space and is part of a continuum. At the start of a signed narrative, specification refers to the places or characters in the story. It marks out the individual from the typical (specific from the general) and corresponds to what is indicated by *It's a...* in English, or *C'est un(e)...* in French.

2.1.2 Situational transfer

The most general example of situational transfer is as follows. Within a paradigm of a limited number of hand configurations, the subservient and immobile hand indicates a stable place ("locative") and in relation to which the dominant hand represents a mobile agent, particularized by its special configuration. The form of the immobile locative represents a trans-categorical referential shape (flat and vertical shapes, laterally projecting shapes, round shapes, etc.). The movement effected by the dominant hand is contained within a continuum. This structure corresponds to operations which are indicated by *There is a...which...* in English, or *Il y a un(e)...qui...* in French.

2.1.3 Personal transfer

In personal transfer, the signer disappears and 'becomes' a protagonist in the narrative; his gestures correspond to the gestures effected by the character he refers to, and whose place he has taken. Here, the hand configurations (limited in number) represent types of action, such as walking, seizing, and so on. Personal transfers usually correspond to those operations which are indicated by *and there s/he is, (do)-ing (something)...* in English, and by *et le/la voilà qui...* in French.

These extremely iconic structures do not have temporal-aspectual markers, their use being exactly like that of the English present progressive forms. They can be combined in double transfers, thus linguistically dividing the speaker's body – effecting situational transfers (with the signer's arm and subservient hand) and personal transfers (with the speaker's dominant hand, the whole of his/her body, and face, mimicry included, and the gaze).

All of these structures, insofar as movement is concerned, are a relevant part of a dynamic continuum. They are not discrete in the stucturalist sense, and their signifying form(s) cannot be transcribed into a written protocol (otherwise, the analogy loses its relevance). Their function is rather to represent the (monstrative) mode of *'like this'*, showing everything while telling

(specification and situational transfers) and the *'like this'* combined with *'as if'*, showing and acting out while telling (personal transfers and double transfers).

The inclusion of these structures in French Sign Language is necessary if there is to be mutual translation among the various languages. In fact, using only standard signs without any personal transfers, it is impossible to translate into FSL (i.e., French Sign Language, in French: Langue des Signes Française) such absurd statements as *'the chocolate eats the boy'*. Statements such as these require a personal transfer; the speaker must 'become' the chocolate.

Each of these iconic structures, which slightly reshapes real or imaginary experience through the iconicity of the image, can be classed with the reference types categorized by Desclés (1991) and is entirely compatible with the hypothesis of a perceptual (essentially visual) basis for language.

I would like to make one final comment as far as structuralist postulates are concerned. If the medium corresponds indeed to a phenomenon of substance, then the possibilities of iconicity, four-dimensionality, and analogic representations which the visual-gestural medium offers calls into question the (so-called) independence of form and substance.

2.2 The functional characteristics of great iconicity

The structures of great iconicity are present in all sign languages, and are used by the deaf in different cultural and linguistic communities when they feel the need to communicate among themselves.

These structures are most often attested in rather well-defined language activity, such as
1) in the construction of specific reference for actants;
2) in the construction of spatialized semantic relations (the localization and movement of actants in relation to a fixed reference point, relationship between the whole and its parts, etc.);
3) in the construction of temporal reference independently of the zero temporal reference point of the utterance act.

Here we are clearly dealing with a quite limited language, involving the specification of persons and objects (but not types), individual actions in the course of accomplishment, or specific references that reduplicate an experience. However, we are also concerned with considerations of a statistical nature, in the sense that (as we shall see later) great iconicity provides access to generic reference as well. It is interesting to note that when made dependent on an iconic intent and expressed as language, the cognitive apprehension of the real/imaginiary world enters into a very strict and closed economic structural framework. Thanks to its universality and extreme plasticity, a close examination of this great iconicity enables us to answer questions (limited, it is true, to an iconic intent) concerning basic cognitive filtering functions particular to the human mind. When this line of questioning is extended not only to the level of the central core of structures, but also to their linking in discourse (in a narrative, for example), it is possible to find, in the same way, interesting answers to questions concerning opposing relationships of form / ground, container / contained, localizer / localized, fixed / mobile, existing / new, as well as the aspectuality of a process, relationships of cause and effect, relations of simultaneousness in actions / processes, actant schemata and so on.

3. The construction of reference exclusive of iconic intent

The second sub-branch of iconicity mentioned earlier (cf.§ 2), exclusive of iconic intent, has contributed to a considerable increase in the standard lexicon. Here I am putting forward the hypothesis that this increase in the standard lexicon must have been concomitant with an evolution toward a formal resolution of signifying forms which was increasingly economical and systematic. However, this systematization of the lexicon was dependent on a logic of economical conservation with regard to iconicity, which accompanied both the constraints of an optimal adaptation to the reception of messages by the visual system, as well as constraints concerning ease of articulation. Here we find a classic pattern of the economical evolution of language (as advanced by both Frei and Martinet) which is structured around a logic of iconic conservation– which in a sense sets the possible limits for this evolution. This double structure of economy and iconicity is best illustrated at present by the creation of neologisms in the sign languages which pass through similar stages, only much more quickly than those we have seen up to this point. These begin with primary iconization, branching off towards generic reference with an economical resolution in the limited framework of maintained iconicity.

The development afforded by an economical evolution, coupled with the conservation of iconicity, has given rise to major structural characteristics; these have been analyzed in detail elsewhere (Cuxac 1996). If we leave aside the iconic intent for the moment, these characteristics (or structural parameters) can be listed under three headings for French Sign Language. First, there is the semantically molecular character of the standard signs, which can be broken down into configuration, orientaion and movement; second, there is the simultaneity of the gaze, mimicry and signs, as well as other facial and bodily movements; we find also a simultaneity within signs which, above and beyond the overall iconicity of the lexicon, iconically specializes each one of these three parameters at the syntactic level; the semantic relations between standard items utilizes space in an economical and relevant fashion to mark the whole range of locative relationships, including the greater part of relations between actants; the latter are represented as spatialized and animated "mini-scenarios".

As a conclusion to this paragraph, I should add that the major structural characteristics having to do with the relationships between signs are to be found in nearly the same form in the various sign languages which have been studied to date.

3.1 The molecular character of the standard signs

The simultaneity within signs allows one to see them as items having molecular structural characteristics, where each parameter in their constitution (such as configuration, orientation, positioning or movement) can in some sense become semantically specialized, and in this way make a specific contribution to the meaning constructed by the whole.

Moreover, we might wonder if a great many verbal items are not in fact simply miniature metaphors, whose meaning results from the accumulation of their constituent parameters. On this view, [TO REFLECT] is represented by a stirring motion of the hand (movement) and "question/scratch at" (configuration), signed at head level (positioning), an image equivalent to the expression "to rack one's brains". Similarly, [TO EXPERIENCE] includes contact at head level (positioning) and a configuration identical to [TO TOUCH]; the same holds true for [UPSET], which is represented by contact at heart level (positioning), using the "a relation of contact (same configuration as for [TO TOUCH]), and "a drilling motion, plus a negative, painful facial expression".

Without necessarily having a metaphorical function, actant relationships expressed by the standard signs are often represented as "mini-scenarios" which slightly reshape the real or imaginary experience to be transmitted. For example, [TO MEET] consists in fact of representing two participants (configuration) facing each other (orientation) and moving towards one another until they are directly opposite (positioning-movement-orientation).

In addition, the molecular character of the standard signs corresponds to the most exploited source of "word play" using (and on) signs, by means of a modification of one of their formative parameters. In this way (to mention only one example of metaphorical creation), the sign [TO OPEN A WINDOW] can be signed at head level, and will signify "open (the window of) one's mind"; or moved to heart level, "open (the window of) one's heart".

3.2 The simultaneity of information and the semantic specialization of signing parameters

When a message is transmitted by a sign language, several parameters combine simultaneously to construct its meaning: posture, body and facial movements, but especially the signer's gaze and its direction, facial mimicry, and hand gestures. Each of these last three parameters is essential to the elaboration of the meaning that is conveyed by the messsage. Irrespective of the particular sign language, each parameter appears to have a specialized and very specific semantic function.

3.2.1 The gaze

The signer's gaze governs the interaction and signals changes of discourse genre. In highly expressive iconic structures such as personal transfers or double transfers, the gaze of the signer is that of the character transferred. The end of a personal transfer is signalled by the signer's gaze meeting that of the addressee.

Apart from structures of personal transfer, the signer's gaze, directed at the signs he makes, indicates the referential value of these signs, drawing them into the realm of *'like that'*. Directed towards a point in space, however, the gaze not only signals that the construction of a reference is imminent; it also, (like the mouse attached to a PC), activates this portion of the signing space, creating a sort of secondary deixis belonging to the signed utterance.

3.2.2 Facial mimicry

Facial mimicry has considerable semantic importance, its values differing according to the context in which it is used. In standard utterances, it indicates the signer's state of mind, and possesses a modal value ('doubtful', 'interrogatory', 'detrimental', etc.). When mimicry accompanies nouns, its value is qualifying (*small, beautiful, spongy,* etc.) or quantifying (*a bit, a lot,* etc.). In personal transfers, it indicates the state of mind of the protagonist in the transferred phrase, or his manner of accomplishing the action.

I should like to add one parenthetical remark concerning facial mimicry. Due to the nature of the medium employed, one might say that sign languages lead us naturally to question the relevance of the generally allowed distinction between the verbal and the non-verbal. All else being equal, according to this distinction, the facial expressions and postures of the signing subject would be classed as non-verbal. The problem is that in personal transfer structures, when the signing subject embodies the character he is telling about, his mimicry, which could be assimilated to adverbs of manner, is attributed to the protagonist of the narrative action. This mimicry, however, is the same as that which characterizes the signer, outside of personal transfer, as the signing subject who participates interactively. It would be absurd to consider it as non-verbal in the latter instance and verbal in the former. Thus the distinction between the verbal and non-verbal blurs, thereby pushing back the frontiers of what is normally considered as 'language'.

3.2.3 Signs

Standard signs have an iconicity that is often metonymic when referring to a class of established referents. As discrete items, easily transcribed with *ad hoc* notational systems, they have four simultaneous parameters: positioning, hand configurations, hand orientation, and actual movement. Each parametric element entering into their composition can be exploited at a semantic-syntactic level (in contrast to their inherent 'atomic' value, which we have examined above (§ 3.1.).

Let us summarize with respect to standard verbal items. The modal value of facial expression (or mimicry), the interactive and referential value of the gaze, and the phatic value of head movements (small nods on the signer's part) all are superimposed on the verbal-gestural unit which, depending on its meaning, might include in addition:
- via hand configuration: the agent (verbs of motion), the instrument (e.g., [TO DRINK]), the patient (e.g. [TO EAT]);
- via hand positioning: the corporal locative (e.g., [TO OPERATE], [TO BLEED]) etc.;
- via hand movement: aspects of the action (such as 'repeatedly', 'inaccomplished', 'rapidly') etc.;
- via the orientation-positioning-movement complex: the semantic relationship governing the actants participating in the discourse process ('agent', 'patient', 'beneficiary').

3.3 The spatialization of semantic relations

Since by definition not everything can be said at the same time, the relationships between items are indicated essentially by spatializing these items in a relevant manner. We shall consider the case of non-specific references which involve spatial and temporal relationships, as well as actant relationships.

3.3.1 Spatial reference

Whatever the discourse genre to be represented, the general tendency is to use first-order iconic structures to express spatial relationships between (signed) items. Thus, even a sentence communicated by standard signs, such as *'each evening after eating, he watches television'* is usually ended by the repetition of [TELEVISION] as a great iconic configuration of the hand 'flat-surfaced rectangular object ', then by the standard sign [TO SEE] in semi-personal transfer posture with the associated mimicry of the transferred character directed (with passage toward a double transfer) toward the configuration (rectangular object...); both signs are effected by the dominant hand. In fact, this sentence in standard signs is followed by *'and it happened like this... '*.

For non-specific spatial relationships, standard signs are (wherever possible) spatialized directly, without recourse to first-order iconic structures. Let us take as an example [*coming home from work*]. [HOME /'house'] is first signed to the signer's right, and [TO WORK] to his left. [COMING HOME] is then signed by using the place where [TO WORK] was signed as a starting point, and that of [HOME /'house'] as the end point of the movement.

When standard signs cannot be moved (e.g. where there is contact with the body) the gaze-pointing combination comes into play. Thus, in order to speak of a person who has left for the United States to go on a training course, the sign [UNITED STATES] is made; at the same time the signer's gaze is directed up and to his left, activating that portion of space. The anaphoric use of pointing then relates [UNITED STATES] to the space activated by the signer's gaze. After this, the signs [TO WORK], [TO TRAVEL AROUND], [TO INVESTIGATE], [FOR A YEAR], are effected in the relevant portion of space.

As far as spatial relationships between nouns are concerned, the unmarked order localizer/localized, fixed/mobile, container/contained, ground/figure is compulsory; no recourse to isolated linguistic elements with the relational function of prepositions is necessary. Whenever possible (for example, with the standard signs [HOUSE] and [WINDOW]), signs which are the focus of the signer's gaze are placed in the signing space according to the spatial relationships each entertains with the other. Should this not be an option (when, for example, standard signs necessitate contact with the body), signs are re-introduced by a classifying hand configuration ('flat form', 'round form', 'form with lateral projections', etc.). The relationship is achieved via the hand configuration of the localizer (subservient hand) and another transfer of form representing the most movable object (dominant hand). A case in point is the part/whole relationship. The semantic specification of interrelated elements is effected via standard signs, then the relationship between them is conveyed via great iconic structures (specifying hand configurations which re-introduce standard signs and place them in relevant positions).

3.3.2 *Temporal reference*

Temporal relationships between items are also spatialized. The moment of the interaction and tense within the utterance are signaled in relation to the body of the locutor: forwards for future and backwards for past, with the distance from the body graduated accordingly.

When temporal relationships are independent of the moment of the interaction, a horizontal time-line is used whose direction (right-to-left or left-to-right) is not pertinent in an absolute sense, but becomes relevant depending on the circumstances. This time-line is always perpendicular to the movements marking tense within the utterance.

Thus, to take an example from data I myself have collected, a referential mark is constructed. First the standard sign is given [1978], followed by the signer's gaze activating a portion of space. Then there is the anaphoric re-introduction by the specific hand configuration, that is to say, a vertical referential marker (index finger of the subservient hand raised) effected at this same point in the signing space, a nod of the head to indicate co-reference, and pointing of the dominant hand toward the configuration of the subservient hand. Then the time-line is constructed. (In this example, 'before' is to the left of the mark, with 'after' and up until [NOW] being to the right).

Afterwards, a second referential mark [1970] will be established to the left in the same manner. These spatializations, imbued with temporal value, will be exploited continually thereafter. Thus the standard sign [THE DEAF] (dominant hand) simultaneously taken up anaphorically by the subservient hand to relate [THE DEAF] to the indicated space [1970], means *'the deaf of/at that time'*. Then [GOING AROUND TOGETHER] in the same position of space completes the utterance.

3.3.3 *Reference to actants*

In referential constructions, the gaze-pointing combination distributes the standard signs spatially, functioning in the same way as for spatial or temporal relationships.

The signer's gaze and pointing interact in the overall signing space, combining the enunciative space (i.e., the gaze) and the space of the utterance itself (i.e., pointing).

The gaze is employed before pointing. As the spatial dimension of FSL makes it possible to construct a three-dimensional situation which more or less reshapes reality, one could say that the use of the gaze constitutes a kind of paradoxical deictic process, to the extent that the situation or the reference always remains to be constructed.

Even where there is no express intention to reproduce experience spatially, there still can be a series of mini-scenarios in which actants and verbal notions are put into play together. The actants are signed into spatial relationships either directly or by pointing (in this case they are re-introduced anaphorically and assigned to a portion of space); the verbal items on the other hand distribute semantic roles, by virtue of their orientation and movement. One might therefore be justified in speaking of schematic iconictiy (I prefer this term to that of diagrammatic iconicity, which is commonly used), which is not subject to an iconic intent, and which is constructed in the signing space according to circumstance.

3.3.4 A review of referential pointing to selected portions of space

First of all, I should like to make an additional remark concerning pointing gestures, which are very frequently utilized. In a one-hour corpus of data I assembled, I was able to recense more than 1200 occurrences (excluding self-reference), of which approximately 950 were instances of referential pointing, and which we shall discuss here.

I will recall the fact that pointing is not an element which directly activates the pertinent portions of the signing space. It re-introduces or "re-activates" elements which have been previously assigned a spatial dimension and which are activated by the simple fact of the signer's gaze towards the place where pointing will occur; it is this last factor which plays an essential role in signing.

Since pointing does not actually create meaning, its true worth is dependent on its relation to the gaze (however, this is not the case with the simple re-introduction of actants by pointing at them). Its main function is rather to ensure discursive cohesiveness and coherence in a dialogic, referential space which is constructed through the focusing of the signer's gaze.

Then again, there can be instances of complex pointing, linking the actant to a temporal or locative referent. If such a temporal or locative construction has not yet been put into place, it would seem that a double pointing gesture (evidently preceded by the gaze) should be the usual way to go about it. If in fact a temporal or locative construction has already been put into place, a pointing gesture with one hand suffices (i.e., the re-introduction of the actant by pointing, assuring the temporal or locative link to a portion of space previously activated). The signer's gaze can be directed at these pointing gestures, although this does not seem strictly necessary.

There can also be instances of simple pointing at actants, that is, configurations corresponding to pronominal forms (*him/her*, *he/she* and so on). The gaze is not normally directed at these pointing gestures. However, the gaze must necessarily be directed at these gestures if the anticipated reference is of a spatial order (for example, if the actant is to participate in an action involving movement); and the gaze can, to a lesser extent, be directed at these pointing gestures if the relation to the actant to be constructed ("agent, patient, action") necessitates a relevant spatial orientation for the verb in the signing space.

Generally speaking, simple pointing is a form of anaphor, since the semantic specification contained in standard signs has previously been made manifest; nevertheless, examples of cataphoric forms do exist. At times, when this specification has already been made, it is possible for a pointing gesture to intervene before the standard sign is re-introduced a second time. In such instances, semantic specification can be compared to a form of insistence.

The complex functioning of pointing underscores our line of reasoning; pointing can extend from the simple re-introduction of a sign to a function linking two elements in the same portion of signing space, combining them semantically.

3.3.5 The creation of standard signs having a nominal function

I maintain, following Langacker (1991), that signs having a nominal function are part of an operation of instantiation. To put it another way, they are part of referential anchoring constructions, which make it possible to differentiate between the specific, instantiated individual and the type. There are concurrently two ways of instantiating in FSL, each competing with the other. The first is always subservient to an iconic intent, the second is not. In the latter case, we have pointing gestures with the various related functions mentioned above (pointing preceded by the gaze, underlined by the gaze, unaccompanied by the gaze; simple, double or repeated pointing; cataphoric, simultaneous or anaphoric pointing in relation to the standard item). In the former case, the utterance shifts into the monstrative mode "like this" through the reintroduction of the standard sign, which moreover always has an anaphoric value: this is accomplished by means of a hand configuration of great iconicity.

In general, these two means of instantiating standard signs, determined by an express intention, are compatible with the following relations of equivalence: whatever is not dependent on an express intention to represent experience iconically, or iconic intent, and therefore not a case of great iconicity tends toward generic referential value (genericity); on the other hand, whatever is dependent on an express intention to represent experience iconically, and which includes structures of great iconicity tends toward specific referential value. This equivalence is statistical, but by no means systematic in overtly generic utterances. For example, an utterance such as: "Cats are animals that love to sleep in armchairs", can shift effortlessly (at the termination of signing) into the "like this" mode of the iconic intent.

4. Iconicity and language as systems of differentiation

The inclusion of sign languages among the world's languages affects not only linguistic epistemology: there is also an impact on commonly accepted notions concerning language acquisition, such as the concept of a critical age. I personally know several congenitally deaf people who, educated among the hearing and for whom oral French could not be a first language, acquired FSL late (after ten years of age). Nevertheless, their practice of this language is completely similar to that of native signers. On the other hand, even if those deaf children to whom signing is forbidden suffer cruelly from a lack of linguistic communication (I speak of those, and they are numerous, who never really master an oral language), their behavior–although disturbed–cannot be considered outrageous. Despite their lack of a first language, they nonetheless manifest coherent and adequate behavioral patterns in their relationships to the world and to others.

Along the same lines, isolated deaf people spontaneously create signs (specification of size and form, personal transfers, standard signs) in order to communicate with the hearing population around them (Yau, 1988). I was present, and became extremely moved, when a deaf French adult was introduced to a young deaf Moroccan man who, for the first time in his life, was able to communicate with another deaf person. The dialogue took place via signs which the young man used with his hearing family, and which he had been inventing himself since his childhood.

All these observations lead one to consider that proto-linguistic conceptual stabilizations do in fact exist; they are categorizations of a perceptual-practical origin which are forerunners of linguistic grounding (Desclés, 1991, Petitot, 1991).

My observation of the creation of signs by isolated deaf people leads me to postulate the existence of a fundamental type of cognitive differentiation from which both nouns (referentially stable, and distinguished by their perceptual shapes) and verbs (recurrent, meaningful, discontinuous processes of daily experience) might originate. Some of these became central in man's specific development as man. I refer the reader to R. Thom (1972, 1980) and to that set of what he calls 'elementary morphologies'. (Whilst on this topic, it is impossible not to mention the marked similarity which exists between the graphs of these elementary morphologies on the one hand, and on the other, the movement of those signs in FSL which correspond to them semantically.)

One might be critical about limiting the object 'language' to the referential function. Where then would one fit in pragmatics or, more especially, the concept of language as a system of signs, the identity of each being that which the others are not? In short, is not iconicity, because it is associated with reference, a problem for the essential Saussurian concept of arbitrariness?

I believe that this criticism stems from a fundamental misreading of structural linguistics. In fact, two distinct meanings of the word 'arbitrary' are confused, based on this mistaken premise: the functioning of oral language units as parts of a system based on differences has been deduced from their non-iconicity.

I think that what is so characteristic of language, and differentiates it so specifically from other systems, derives from a capacity much more fundamental to human nature. This capacity simply adapts itself to language, as it does to non-linguistic behavior. It is the very same capacity which causes a child to replace the lid on a pot of jam from which he has eaten, despite having been told not to; the same capacity causes a human to remove all trace of his footprints; the same which leads humans to creates false tracks; the same which affirms the truth of what is known to be false, etc. This capacity consists in the application of two concomitant processes to a particular element in a behavioral sequence, the first being a process which cuts the term off from its referent, and the second being a process of de-contextualization. The element is thus raised for others to the conceptual level of a sign, and can be made to signify perhaps even the opposite of its referential meaning. It is this 'meta-capacity' which opens up language, like any other set of signs, to a paradigmatic dimension (decontextualized elements seen from the angle of their mutual differences).

This capacity sweeps across referential items of different categories, and at the semantic level (and irrespective of the particular language) permits the derivation of a verb from any noun (that is, of any item which refers to a class of stable referents). The fact that it is–or is not–attested in a given language depends on the 'ritualized ' syntactic properties of that particular language.

In a world where language exists as a system of differences, whether items are iconic or not is, in fact, immaterial. I shall illustrate this point with a few examples taken from FSL.

- [TO OPEN a door] might mean, depending on the context: *begin, to be the starting point*, but also *open* (a quality of a person's character).
- A good example of the fact that iconicity does not necessarily entail a one-to-one relationship with the referent comes from schools (e.g. Metz) which

have no finger spelling tradition (the possibility of spelling words from an oral language with a finger alphabet). The signs for the days of the week, for instance, are based on significant events of the day in question: thus, *Thursday*, *Friday*, and *Saturday* are experessed respectively by the signs [SHOWER] (the day for a compulsory shower), [FISH], [GYMNASIUM].

- Lexical creations function in a similar manner. [HEARING] signed near the forehead (a neologism) describes a deaf person who thinks and acts like a hearing one. And the same principle is used with specialized signs for games or jokes. One of my friends, a professor, specializes in electric cabling. His profession is signed [PROFESSOR + ELECTRICITY]; this latter sign is made by moving the two index fingers side by side (its origin being the representation of the two ends of an electric arc). When the professor became over-excited during a meeting, a deaf person calmed things down by signing '*It's OK, he is* (PROFESSOR + ELECTRICITY)', whilst moving his index fingers on each side of his head: ("It's not surprising; he's got electricity on the brain").

5. Sign languages as cognitive languages

The theoretical principles outlined above constitute, I believe, a starting point for an exhaustive description of French Sign Language. The verb is the distributor of actant roles; its spatial orientation manifests the semantic roles of the actants, depending on the specific position assigned to them in space. In short, I have disregarded syntactic notions and definitions such as the verb as a class of commutable units specialized in the predicate function, the syntactic subject and object, etc.

Might not syntax be due to that very slow diachronic ritualization, phylogenesis, of which R. Thom speaks? In other words, it represents the economic resolution, at a formal level, of earlier problems connected with the construction of meaning. The fact that this ritualization has been pushed to extremes in oral languages would be a consequence of the medium itself, whose constraints allow few iconic resolutions (or none at all, i.e., imagistic iconicity). Similarly, these constraints render impossible the use of space in a pertinent manner, and strongly limit the possibilities of reshaping ('anamorphizing') practical and perceptual experience. Syntax could be considered as having the same function among semantic units as phonology has among phonological units. A level of organization within individual units does indeed exist in sign languages; however, this cannot be assimilated to phonology, because the diverse parameters which enter into the formation of signs are themselves frequently meaningful. To account for this 'organizational' level, Stokoe has recently proposed the notion of 'semantic phonology' (Stokoe, 1991).

The title of this final section should be understood thus: the fact that sign languages are cognitive languages is banal in the sense that all languages are cognitive objects and all uses of a language have to do with cognitive processes. This statement is less banal, however, if it refers to the linguistic traces of cognitive operations in languages where the synthetic levels of syntax and phonology are absent and where formal, less constrained resolutions might constitute examples of a more direct contact with cognition (according to Langacker's conception of this term, 1987).

Thus, if one accepts as legitimate the linguist's choice of certain syntactic problems as points of departure for analyzing the language he works with, sign languages lead us to question the validity of models which postulate, as much from phylogenetic as ontogenetic points of view, the autonomy of a syntactic level vis-a-vis the more all-inclusive problem of the construction of meaning.

Acknowledgment

I would like to thank Jody Dochney-Lépine, Rhian Jones and Steven Schaeffer for help in translating this paper.

References

Cuxac, C. 1996. *Fonctions et structures de l'iconicité dans les langues des signes; analyse descriptive d'un idiolecte parisien de la Langue des Signes Française.* Thèse de Doctorat d'Etat, Paris: Université René Descartes, Paris V.

Cuxac, C. 1997. "Iconicité et mouvement des signes en langue des signes française", in *Actes de la 6ème Ecole d'Eté de l'Association pour la Recherche Cognitive*, Bonas, juillet 1997, 205-218.

Cuxac, C. (in press). *La Langue des Signes Française*. Bibliothèque de Faits de Langues, Ophrys.

Desclés, J.P. 1991. "La prédication opérée par les langues (ou à propos de l'interaction entre langage et perception)". *Langages*, 103: 83-96.

Frei, H. 1982. *La grammaire des fautes*. Slatkine Reprints, Genève-Paris.

Langacker, R. 1987. *Foundations of cognitive grammar*. vol. 1, Stanford University Press.

Langacker, R. 1991. *Foundations of cognitive grammar*. vol. 2, Stanford University Press.

Martinet, A. 1955. *Economie des changements phonétiques*. Francke S.A., Berne.

Petitot, J. 1991. "Syntaxe topologique et grammaire cognitive". *Langages* 103, 97-128.
Stokoe, W.C. 1991. *Semantic phonology*. Sign Language Studies, Silver Springs, Maryland: Linstock Press, 107-114.
Thom, R. 1972. *Stabilité structurelle et morphogenèse*, Paris: Ediscience.
Thom, R. 1980. *Modèles mathématiques de la morphogenèse*, Paris: Christian Bourgois.
Yau, S.-C. 1988. *Création de langues gestuelles chez des sourds Isolés*. Thèse de Doctorat d'Etat, Université de Paris VII.

Part III

Language activity: From linguistic to cognitive processes

From Natural Language to Drum Language
An Economical Encoding Procedure in Banda-Linda (Central African Republic)

France Cloarec-Heiss
CNRS-LLACAN, Paris

Introduction

As a means of communication, drum language is a unique system, as it *diverts* sound from a normal musical function into use for the transmission of information. This medium for sound transmission is in fact neither speech, nor an audible transposition of script (as in Morse code). What then is the nature of these signals, which the Banda produce by beating two wooden drums? This question cannot be answered without an understanding of one of the most widespread features of African languages, that is, *tone systems*. Indeed, Banda-Linda[1] is a tone language, in which every vowel must be spoken on a specific pitch: any change in pitch brings about a corresponding change in meaning. Since tone systems are not found in the languages which are more familiar to us, we may tend to underestimate how much information they can convey. These tones contribute to the 'mysteriousness' of drum language for those who are unacquainted with it; moreover, the role of tones in African languages has undoubtedly helped to give them an important place in colonial folklore and to make them the subject of an extensive bibliography[2].

The signal in a drum message is all that remains of speech after elimination of every audible feature provided by consonants and vowels, i.e., *the pitches assigned to each of the vowels*. It is surprising to find that communication is still possible after such a major amputation. This has nevertheless been proven to be the case by research[3] involving the recording of a set of fifteen different messages, each in two forms: one, the ordinary continuous transmission, and the other, in alternation with speech.[4] In the latter case, the drummer stopped to allow another informant who had no prior knowledge of the content of the message to decode it, step by step, into ordinary speech. The speed and accuracy of the decoding observed in the course of this study provided spectacular proof of the effectiveness of this form of communication, which does not have an audience of specialists: any Banda-Linda speaker can understand drum messages and immediately transpose each statement into spoken Banda-Linda before the start of the next.

It will naturally be asked how communication can still be possible after such compression, and how all the problems arising from tonal homophony can be solved. We shall see that loss of information is compensated for by the sociolinguistic circumstances under which the system is used and by the structure of the message itself.

1. The principles of encoding

Encoding involves the reproduction of two parameters of ordinary speech: pitch and rhythm.

1.1 Pitch

In Banda-Linda, the tone of any vowel corresponds to one of three possible pitch levels. Tones have the same distinctive capacity as consonants and vowels. They suffice of themselves to produce both lexical and morphological contrasts. For example, in Banda-Linda as in many other languages in this part of Africa, most of the verb conjugation relies on differences in tone.

In all the messages we recorded, we found a one-to-one correspondence between the pitch of the drum beats and the pitch of the vowels in the matching spoken utterances.

1.2 Rhythm

Comparison of each drum message with the matching decoded statement in Banda-Linda shows the rhythmic curve of the message in perfect superposition to the spoken utterance.
- There are shorter intervals between the tones within a given lexical item than between two successive tones in different words, allowing the listener to distinguish the repetition of a disyllabic word from a single quadrisyllabic one with identical tones.
- The final tone of a noun or a phrase is struck more heavily and held slightly longer.

- Some tone sequences provide information on medial consonants: e.g., in a $C_1V_1C_2V_2$ structure, if V_1 and V_2 are separated by a liquid consonant in C_2 [l, r, ʋ][5], the drum beats on the vowels will be closer together than if the consonant were of another kind. This is how the drum expresses the loss of the first vowel often observed in spoken language.
- The tones of two immediately following vowels with the same tone are represented by a single lengthened beat of the drum.

Here we find, in a different form, the characteristic demarcative procedures of spoken language, whereby accentual and intonational features allow segmentation into units of meaning. This close relationship between spoken language and drum language proves that the drummer formulates his message in natural language as he transmits it. Drum language is thus derivative from speech, which it encodes by copying speech intonation and rhythm.

Our work also shows that the messages sent are not part of some preconcerted set, enabling the drummer to play a sort of 'score'. A comparison of the continuous and alternate forms of each message reveals important variations in both the form and the order of its melodic and rhythmic components.

The underlying linguistic content is, with the exception of very few features (see below), exactly what the general syntax of the language demands. The messages are composed of complete utterances which are grammatical in the spoken language. There are thus no abridgements such as the elimination of articles or grammatical markers characteristic of telegraphic language.

Such a system should potentially be capable of transmitting any utterance whatsoever. It nevertheless remains to be seen how the loss of information resulting from the elimination of all segmental phonemes can be made up for. An analysis of the content of the messages and the decoding process shows that, in practice, the theoretical capability of transposing any utterance whatsoever into drum language is unrealizable. This capability is severely limited by the social requirement of comprehensibility. While *anything can be said, not everything can be understood.* Drum language thus faces, on an even larger scale, the difficulty inherent in every communicative situation, whether relying on spoken language or not: the *dysymmetry* between source and receiver, i.e., things which are not ambiguous for the speaker may often be so for the hearer.

2. How decoding takes place

The decoding strategy, based on the *availability of clues*, i.e., the possibility of figuring out a full meaning when only part of its components is known, makes use of two given elements: 1) the extralinguistic situation and 2) the structure of the message.

2.1 The extralinguistic circumstances

The listener recovers the meaning of what he hears from information external to the message as much as from internal elements, i.e., the contents of the message itself.

2.1.1 Physical circumstances

The listeners (whether or not the message is intended for them) are able to situate its geographical origin. They can tell where the message is coming from and thereby eliminate a large number of possible addressees.

2.1.2 Sociolinguistic circumstances

Under ordinary conditions, drum language is used locally and involves a fairly limited number of participants. This is because the Banda live mostly in villages of no more than a few hundred inhabitants, and the actual social function of drum language restricts its use to a few emergency situations requiring one or more people to go to the place from which the message originates. These situations include traditional social events (such as birth, death, inauguration of a chief, inaugural ceremonies for new drums), accidents (e.g., on hunting expeditions or when someone gets lost in the bush), or any of a series of events having their origin in colonial times (such as the arrival of an administrative official, an egg collection for a subprefect, a cotton market, the arrival of a team of health visitors, or tax collection). The range of messages collected is proof in itself of the fact that there is no fixed set and that the system can *generate new information*.

2.2 The structure of the messages

Analysis of our set of fifteen messages shows them to be composed of *two types* of utterance whose order of occurrence is not codified, but left to the drummer's discretion.
- **Cue formulae** (CF), i.e., utterances or parts of utterances found in every message, around which the message is organized;

- **Informative units (IU),** which are peculiar to a given message.

The CF are the vectors for transmission of the IU, in that they make up most of the body of the message and are familiar, well-known melodies which have an immediate meaning for the listener. These formulae are *semantically*, though not formally, invariant: some of them can be realized in many different ways.

There are several features which are common to any utterance in the system, whether a CF or an IU:

- constant repetition: the time allotted to sending a message is fairly long (usually around five minutes), although the number of different utterances is small (around ten CFs and one or two IUs);
- further reinforcement of negative structures, which already have a reduplicated form in spoken language: in drum messages, the first syllable of the second occurrence of the verb is repeated;
- the informative nouns peculiar to the message are systematically reduplicated;
- the addressee(s) is/are particularized in the address formulae.

2.2.1 Cue formulae

There are some ten semantic types of CF, there may be more than one formula of each kind, and each formula has variants. The semantic types are as follows:

- The *opening* is always the same: a High [H] tone representing a spoken wá. Then comes the name of the addressee, e.g.,

    wá à-màkònjì!   "Oh village chiefs!"
    wá à-yī-kɨ̄ndɨ̄ kɨ̄ndɨ̄!   "Oh farmers!"

- There are two formulae which are used *to set off the IUs*, the first to mark the beginning:

    ɔ́ pà dɔ̀ yē   "and I say that..."

    and the second to mark the end:

    ...dɔ́ mɔ̄ nɔ́ pà ndɔ́ nɔ̀ kɔ̄ ʔē kó   "...is the one I am telling you about"

- There are formulae which *confirm the message:*

    mɔ̄ fɔ́rɔ̀ tɔ́mɔ̄ fófɔ́rɔ̀ nē   "I am not 'fooling myself', not wrong (about this)"

    ávɔ́rɔ́ pɨ̄pɨ̄ dɔ́ mɔ̄ sɔ́ pà kē   "it's the truth I'm telling you"

- There are formulae which *solicit the listener's attention* (by questioning, threatening, or insulting him):

yē ngbə́rə̀ ə̀ndɨ̀ ngbə́ngbə́rə̀ nē	"don't 'play the fools'" (pretend you all don't understand)"
yē jí nɔ̂?	"have you understood all that?"
yē jí gbə̀lá gbə̀lá nɔ̂?	"have you really understood every bit of it?"
ə̀njē sə́ zà bə̀ gálə́ kâkángà nə́ kɔ̄māndá!	"they're going to throw you in jail"

- There are calls to assemble:

yē ngbùrù gù gá mə̄!	"all of you get together right away"

- There are calls to come:

yē gù gá mə̄ kèrə̀ kèrə̀ kèrə̀!	"come to me as fast as you can!"
ə̀rə̀ yēkɔ̀ də́ bə̀ sə́ kə́ngbə́rə̀ nə̀?	"what are you all up to (that's delaying you)?"

- There is a notice of the approaching end:

pà bàlē cémà mə̄ də́ mə̄ nə́ pà kē	"this is the last time I'll tell you"

- There is a *closing formula*, a [LL MM] tone sequence which can be repeated any number of times. This formula can correspond in spoken language to onomatopoeic expressions (*gbə̀là gūlū gbə̀là gūlū*) or evocative descriptions (*gə̀vɔ̀ gūlū gə̀vɔ̀ gūlū*).[6]

- The drummer has his *signature*:

wàkángà kə̀ ʔé ʔē kó	"this is Wakanga speaking to you"

It is striking from the cognitive standpoint to see that these formulae can be identified and understood despite all the variations in their acoustic form. Identification of the paradigm to which a formula belongs is made possible by the existence of a *typical minimal sequence* (a "signature") for each variant, which constitutes a *prototype* whose presence suffices to ensure a correct interpretation. Thus, the "come to me" formula may have any of the following forms, among others:

yē gûgū	gǎ mɔ̄
ɔ́ gûgū	gǎ mɔ̄
yē gûgū	gǎ mɔ̄ kèrə̀ kèrə̀ kèrə̀ gǎ mɔ̄
yē gûgū	gǎ mɔ̄ málɔ́ gōgō nɔ́ ʔē
	gǎ mɔ̄

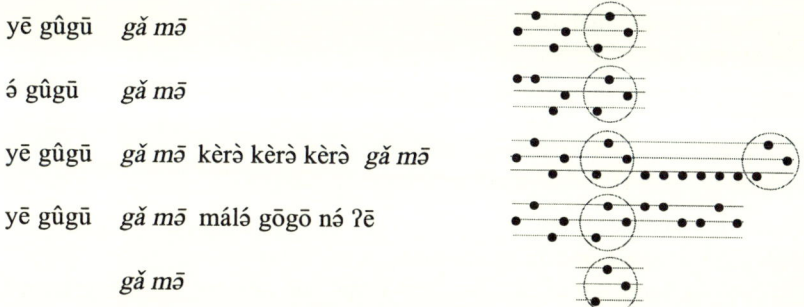

The prototype of the call to come is realized in the last example, the minimal form, by a [LHM] tone sequence, which can be played on the drum as part of any of a wide variety of sequences.

We shall see below that decoding into spoken language is carried out by one of *two different cognitive procedures,* according to whether the utterance involved is a CF or an IU. In the case of the CFs, which make up the greater part of the message, the listener, knowing the melody, thereby has immediate access to the meaning and can skip the transposition into spoken language.

2.2.2 *Informative units*

The indication of the addressee comes immediately after the opening formula. The message may be addressed to a group:

wá à-màkònjì!   "oh village chiefs!"

The plural marker à-, represented by the first [L] tone after the opening, indicates that the message comes from a higher authority than the village chief and is addressed to the entire population administered through the system of village chiefs set up in colonial times. The hearer may therefore conclude that the message is coming from the seat of local government (subprefecture).

Wá à-yī-kīndī kīndī "oh farmers!" and *wá à-kōʃē kōʃē! wá à-yāʃē yāʃē!* "oh men! oh women!" indicate messages sent by the village chief to all people who are somewhere outside the village (working their farms, hunting, or gathering). The message emanates from the village.

The message may be addressed to an individual. The addressee's name will be followed by that of his father and, if necessary, that of his lineage.

1. yālénɔ́mɔ̄ māndá rə̀málè
   "Yaleneme, *son of* Remale"

2. kòngbɔ̀ kòngbɔ̀ māndá léwā léwā
"Kongbo, *son of* Lewa"
3. yímàngā māndá kpádàkà málɔ́ gōgō làmbɔ̀là
"Yimanga, *son of* Kpadaka *of the lineage of* Lambela"
4. kíndìngō nɔ́ cà?òà málɔ́ gōgō nɔ́ ānéʃē gbàgɔ́rá
"Kindigo, *son of* Tshawa *of the lineage of* Gbagera"

When the name of the addressee has less than three syllables (as in example 2), it is systematically repeated.

The *paradigmatic set* of all IUs shows that the amount of new information transmitted in any message is very small. There are hardly more than *two or three semantically distinct units* in a given message, although each of these may have more than one form.

...sándákà sándákà màdāyè màdāyè nɔ́ wàyéwò wàyéwò...
ceremony x 2/installment/of/Wayewo x 2
[This is about] a ceremony to install Wayewo

ɨ̄pɨ̄ kùzū kùzū gōngérɔ̄ gōngérɔ̄
subject/death x 2/Gongere x 2
[This is] about the death of Gongere...

ɔ̀njē zú āméyā āméyā málɔ́ gōgō nɔ́ ʔē
they/*real*-give birth/*pl.*-twins x 2/ in/village/of/you
Twins have been born in your village

These units are usually bracketed by the CFs *and I say that* preceding and *that is what I am telling you* following.

Using these cues, the hearer can *break the message down* and identify the part whose meaning he has to recover, within the boundaries provided by recognizable preconcerted signals. Thus, in the address formulae, the name of an individual addressee is preceded by an invariant opening formula and followed by the name of his father and, if necessary, that of his lineage. These names are introduced in a codified way:

yímàngā **māndá** kpádàkà **málɔ́ gōgō** làmbɔ̀là
kíndìgō **nɔ́** cà?òà **málɔ́ gōgō nɔ́ ānéʃē** gbàgɔ́rá

The words *māndá* "behind, after, heir" and *nɔ́* "connective element" introduce the father's name, while *málɔ́ gōgō* and *málɔ́ gōgō nɔ́ ānéʃē* (literally, "in/village" and "in/village/of/children") introduce the name of the lineage. These cues are used to delimit the beginning and end of the tone sequences corresponding to an "unlisted" unit and therefore requiring interpretation.

Unlike the CFs, the IUs cannot be decoded without being transposed into natural language; the melody does not give direct access to the meaning. With the help of the opening and closing formulae and all the other cues provided by the message, the new information can be restored to spoken form. Understanding is facilitated by reference to all the contributing extralinguistic factors and by insistent repetition. The difficulties arising from the linear nature of language, aggravated here by the strictly acoustic nature of the transmission, can thus be obviated by "rerunning" the message often enough.

3. Recovery of the message as a cognitive process

Three operations are involved in the cognitive process of recovering the linguistic message: segmentation, selection, and reconstitution.

3.1 Segmentation

Rhythm, with its demarcative properties, plays a major role in allowing accurate decoding within this system. If the beats were produced at identical intervals and at a constant rate, they could only be perceived as a succession of individual entities, and it would be impossible to identify the segments containing elements requiring reconstitution. This would prevent the meaning from being recovered. Rhythm allows segmentation through its use of pauses, stresses, and holds, so that the segments requiring interpretation (words, phrases, or clauses) can be identified. The shape of the melody of each one of these segments, though the object of linear perception, is then decoded as a whole by means of processes of selection and reconstitution.

3.2 Paradigmatic selection

Having identified the relevant segments, the hearer can now decode different sets of tone sequences as wholes. Information theory, as developed by Shannon and Weaver (1975), accounts for all the observed features of this system by defining information as a measure of freedom of choice in selecting a message. Polysemy varies inversely with the number of theoretically possible tone combinations for a given sequence.

This number depends on two factors: one, the number of distinctive tone levels (which varies from language to language), is paradigmatic; the other, the number of syllables in the message, is syntagmatic, or sequential. Thus, the number of possible tone sequences in a given rhythmic unit is equal to the nth power of the number of distinctive tone levels in the language, where n is the number of syllabic tones in the unit. When the number of syllables on the syntagmatic axis is increased, the number of possible combinations increases exponentially and thereby reduces the number of interpretations for any sequence.

Thus, in a two-tone language, a disyllabic CVCV item can have four different tone patterns, LL, HH, LH, or HL, for the drum to reproduce. Whichever one is produced eliminates the other three possibilities, i.e., three-quarters of all the possible sequences.

In a three-tone language like Banda, any disyllabic CVCV sequence may have one of nine possible tone patterns (LL, LM, LH, ML, MM, MH, HL, HM, HH). Any sequence of two tones in this language will thus eliminate, not just three-quarters, but eight-ninths of the possibilities. The same acoustic material will thus transmit nearly 14% more information (8/9 – 3/4) in this language than in a two-tone language. Adding a single tone at a given point in a rhythmic unit eliminates two-thirds of the remaining possible interpretations in a three-tone language, but only half in a two-tone language.

According to the number of distinctive pitch levels, tone languages thus have a given paradigmatic "depth", i.e., a relative extent of choice and level of polysemy. This may be why some drum languages deriving from spoken languages with two tones compensate for their paradigmatic shallowness by making use of *periphrasis* on the syntagmatic axis. Only by lengthening the sequences can the sender reduce the level of indeterminacy. As Arom and Cloarec-Heiss (1976) have already shown, this disambiguating procedure, which was formerly thought to be universal in African drum languages,[7] is entirely absent from the Banda system.

3.3 Reconstitution

As the message proceeds, the listener narrows his choice from the paradigm of possible alternatives by seeking the semantic compatibility of each new tone with the preceding ones.

Reconstitution is the process by which the linguistic message is ultimately recovered. The mental process which accompanies the perception of a tone sequence is not an additive one; rather, it works retroactively, with each new tone reorganizing the message as a whole, cf. the following two nearly homophonous tone formulae:

mā fórɔ́ tá-mā fófórɔ́ nē

I/*real*+fool/myself/*neg.*+fool/not
I am not fooling myself

yē ngbə́rə̀ ə̀ndɨ ngbə́ngbə́rə̀ nē

you all/*real*+seem/fool/*neg.*+seem/not
don't play the fools

These examples show how perception of the formulae is nonlinear with reconstitution taking place by "retroidentification". Indeed, they differ only in their fourth and fifth tones. The HM pattern in one and the LL in the other allow the listener not only to interpret the two tones as either the term for "myself" or the one for "fool", but at the same time to identify *retroactively* the words corresponding to the second and third tones, which are the same in both formulae, as "to fool" in one case and "to seem" in the other, according to considerations of semantic incompatibility.

Since the name of an addressee can, as we have seen, be particularized by adding the name of his father and, when necessary, that of his lineage, there will be a sequence of not just two to four tones, but six (at the very least) to nine, when the three names are given as described above. A sequence of six tones (the smallest possible number of information-bearing tones, interspersed with cue sequences) will then be one of 729 (3^6) possibilities, and nine, one of 19,683 (3^9). The message thereby contains ample information to identify any individual in a small community.

We thus find, not sequential perception of pitch, but retroactive identification of segments by reconstitution of the whole through a process of elimination. This process assumes storage of data in memory until a threshold is reached where understanding occurs through reconstitution. This proves that the melodic pattern, though linear for perception, is decoded *holistically*.

The process of decoding of IUs, unlike CFs, is thus symmetrical to encoding: the hearer simply reverses the sender's procedure. He seeks the natural language equivalent of the tones he hears, i.e., he recovers the words underlying the audible message.

Conclusion

While drum communication uses a peculiar form of audible material, it nevertheless has features which can be found in any kind of linguistic output. One is the central role of segmentation, where the rhythm of drum language replaces prosodic phenomena such as stress and intonation in spoken language. Others are the importance of extralinguistic factors in the process of disambiguation and an organizational structure paralleling the topic/comment structure of speech. The listener operates with three pairs of *poles of reference*:

- the linguistic information contained in the message *vs.* the extralinguistic information provided by the circumstances of reception;
- new information to be recovered (from the IUs) *vs.* preconcerted material (from the CFs);
- within the IUs, new material to be recovered (the information-bearing parts) *vs.* the accompanying predefined cues.

Recovery of the linguistic message by retroidentification and reconstitution are sufficient proof of the holistic nature of perception.

The path *from perception to meaning* is thus more or less complex accordingly as the material played by the drums is familiar (the CFs) or new (the IUs). In the former case, meaning is *directly* accessible from a predefined output; in the latter, a *recovery procedure* is required. Even when the audible material is the same, the *two cognitive processes* involved are different in kind. Indeed, the frequency of the CFs has given rise to a sort of 'drum vocabulary'. When a given tone sequence is sent out at a specific rhythm, the meaning is immediately apparent. This means that an inventory of signs has been constituted. In the case of the IUs on the other hand, the hearer is obliged to recover the meaning part by part as the message is sent. To do this, he must compensate for the informational shallowness of the message by making adequate use of strategies relying on whatever linguistic and extralinguistic cues are available.

This system of communication thus retains close ties to the spoken language, even after loosening them by eliminating the greater part of the audible components of speech. A study of the strategies for compensating for this loss of information reveals a clear-cut view of the cognitive processes at work in any communicative situation, which can be taken as characteristic of human perception and understanding in general.

Notes

1. According to Greenberg's classification, Banda-Linda is a Niger-Congo language (Adamawa-Eastern branch, now called ubangian: IA6b2. It has been described in Cloarec-Heiss (1986)
2. Sebeok and Umiker-Sebeok's 1976 synthetic study lists all the essential works up to that time.
3. This research was conducted in 1973 by Simha Arom (LACITO-CNRS) and the author in Ippy, Central African Republic.
4. Recordings of each version can be heard on the cassette accompanying Arom and Cloarec-Heiss (1976).
5. ʋ represents a sound called a "labial flap" which is unknown outside Central Africa.

6. gɔ̀ʋɔ́ denotes a wreath placed on the roof of a traditional house when it is completed; gūlū is onomatopoeic.
7. See Alexandre (1969), Betz (1898), Carrington (1949), Heepe (1920), Nekes (1912), Rialland (1974), Thilenius et al. (1916), Verbeken (1920).

References

Alexandre, Pierre. 1969. "Langages tambourinés, une écriture sonore?". *Semiotica*, I: 3, 272-281.
Arom, Simha and Cloarec-Heiss, France. 1976. "Le langage tambouriné des Banda-Linda (RCA)". In L. Bouquiaux (ed.), *Théories et méthodes en linguistique africaine*. Paris, SELAF 54-55, pp 113-169, 1 cassette.
Betz, R. 1898. "Die Trommelsprache der Duala". *Mitteilungen von Forschungsreisenden und Gelehrten aus den Deutschen Schutzgebieten*. XI, 1-86.
Carrington, John F. 1949. *The Talking Drums of Africa*. London: The Carey Kingstate Press.
Cloarec-Heiss, France. 1986. *Dynamique et équilibre d'une syntaxe: le banda-linda de Centrafrique*. Paris / Cambridge: Peeters-SELAF and C.U.P.
Heepe, Marius. 1920. "Die Trommelsprache der Jaunde in Kamerun". *Zeitschrift für Kolonial Sprachen*, X, 43-60.
Nekes, Hermann. 1912. "Trommelsprache und Fernruf bei den Jaunde und Duala in SüdKamerun". *Mitteilungen des Seminar für orientalische Sprachen*, XV: 3, 69-83.
Rialland, Annie. 1974. "Les langages instrumentaux sifflés ou criés en Afrique". *La Linguistique*, X: 2, 105-121.
Sebeok, Thomas A. and Umiker-Sebeok, Donna J. (eds). 1976. *Speech Surrogates: Drum and Whistle Systems* (2 volumes). The Hague / Paris: Mouton.
Shannon, Claude. and Weaver, Warren. 1975, *Théorie mathématique de la communication*. Paris: Retz - CEPL, Les Classiques des Sciences Humaines. Traduction de *The Mathematical Theory of communication*. 1949, The Board of Trustees of the University of Illinois.
Thilenius, G. et al. 1916. "Die Trommelsprache in Afrika und in der Südsee". *Vox*, 26, 179-208.
Verbeken, A. 1920. "Le tambour téléphoné des indigènes de l'Afrique centrale". In T. A. Sebeok and D. J. Umiker-Sebeok (eds), *Speech Surrogates: Drum and Whistle Systems* 1, La Haye / Paris: Mouton, 336-365.

Electrical Signs of Language in the Brain

Marta Kutas
*Departments of Cognitive Science and Neurosciences
University of California, San Diego*

Mireille Besson
*Laboratoire des Neurosciences Cognitives
C.N.R.S., Marseille*

Introduction

How is knowledge represented in the brain? Does our knowledge of language differ in any substantive way from our knowledge of other domains such as music, for example? Are musical and linguistic chunks different? Do they interact according to a different set of principles or rules? What constitutes evidence of structural or functional identity in the case of music and language where complete identity is out of the question? Music and language are clearly different in many ways; nevertheless, they enjoy enough similarity to sustain research on the closeness of their representations and the computations in which they partake. We can ask similar questions within the domain of language for semantic versus syntactic representations, for example – for which the differences may be less obvious or less numerous than between language and music. We believe that adequate answers to such questions call for cross-disciplinary collaboration between anthropologists, cognitive scientists, cognitive neuroscientists, linguists, and psychologists. Morever, it requires the investigation not only of the structures and functions of many different languages, but those of the brain as well.

Our brains are on the one hand highly structured and on the other hand remarkably plastic. Their basic structure is imposed by the sensory input receptors (e.g., eyes, ears, nose, skin) and the motor effectors (e.g. hands, feet, tongue), but the fine structure arises out of a lifetime of experiences – spatial and temporal co-occurrences of neural activity of various orders and on multiple time scales. Which experiences are relevant to language comprehension? As we use language to convey meaning, which is admittedly an elaborate construction in our minds from the cues in the linguistic stream, much of what we experience (conscious or unconscious) *must* be relevant to how we understand and use language. It is also probable that learning one language rather than another has consequences on processing. Languages vary in what information is readily available in the linguistic input (e.g. English has almost no morphological markers for case), in the locus and nature of their linguistic ambiguities, and consequently in the demands that various of their linguistic analyses make upon working memory processes. Insofar as this is the case, the specifics of any given language must have an impact on how quickly comprehension unfolds, the types of information that are actually used in on-line processing and their relative contribution to the various and sundry linguistic operations as well as the types of misunderstandings that a reader or listener is likely to experience.

Language processing is constrained in certain ways in part because meaning is constructed via analyses in a relatively short-lived, capacity-limited working memory system; this system uses associatively- and categorically-based, hierarchically-organized sensory, conceptual, and motor memory systems, and is implemented in a brain with many hundreds of areas that perform different functions and are subject to the organizational principles of the neocortex (if we can use the 30 or so areas used by the visual system as an estimate). Thus the structure of the input and that of the processing medium mutually constrain each other in order to determine what information is processed and what information is lost. This interaction also determines which signals follow which paths from the sensory receptors to higher brain areas, whether or not signals are fed back from higher to lower areas to sustain or highlight the initial activation, or to inhibit local neighbor cells with different response properties, etc., and thereby determine what we perceive, think, and ultimately remember.

1. The brain's electrical activity

One way to look at the relations among the input, the physiology of the brain, and what we understand is to record the patterns of electrical activity at the human scalp. As long as the brain is functioning, there is some ongoing electrical activity, for the brain's currency is electrochemical. Unlike positron emission tomography (PET) and functional magnetic resonance imaging (fMRI), both the electroencephalogram (EEG) and its magnetic counterpart, the magnetoencephalogram (MEG) are *direct* measures of the electrochemical activity by which brain cells (neurons and glia) communicate. The neuroimaging measures mentioned previously as well as others based on metabolism or hemodynamic changes are at best of secondary importance for neuronal activity.

An event in the world – be it a light, a sound, a touch, a smell, or a cognitive event such as a decision or an intention to move – is reflected in the concerted activity of neurons in various parts of the brain. While the brain's response to any one specific input may be difficult to discern among all else that is going on, repeating the event (or categories of like events) and averaging across these repetitions allows the signal to emerge from the noise. The signal is a waveform of the voltage across time from the moment the stimulus is presented, although a few hundred milliseconds of prestimulus activity is recorded to serve as a baseline for analytic purposes. The waveform consists of peaks and troughs, negativities and positivities relative to the baseline (see Figure 1), although polarities are not absolute, but rather relative to the location of the two electrodes that serve as inputs to the differential amplifier that allows us to see these 1-60 uV fluctuations in the EEG.

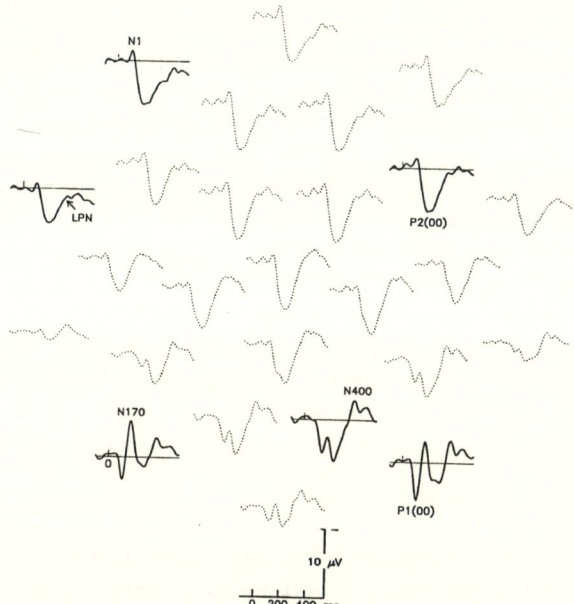

Figure 1. Grand average (across stimuli and subjects) ERPs elicited by the first noun in a set of sentences at 26 different recording locations across the scalp. Top

represents the front of the head, bottom the back of the head. Some of the typical components (peaks or troughs) elicited by various visual stimuli (e.g. N1, P1(00), N170, P2(00), lexical processing negativity or LPN, and N400) are labelled at characteristic sites. Zero represents stimulus onset. All waveforms on this and all subsequent figures are plotted with negative upwards.

Not all brain activity is volume-conducted to the surface in order to be detectable by an electrode at the scalp. For example, the activity of closed-field configurations of neurons are not; only open-field configurations of activity are volume-conducted to the surface. The neocortex, however, is essentially an open field in its functioning and meets all the necessary criteria for producing an externally observable electric potential: (1) the average distribution of sources and sinks in a patch of cortex is distributed in a non-radially symmetrical fashion, (2) the neurons are aligned in some systematic fashion, and (3) the neurons are activated in a synchronized fashion. About 70% of the cells in the neocortex are pyramidal cells; these have apical dendrites that extend from the soma towards the surface and give the cortex a columnar appearance. When these apical dendrites or the cell body are activated, the current flow in and out of the cell creates an approximately dipolar source/sink configuration, oriented perpendicularly to the cortical sheet, with its orientation determined by the actual site of the stimulation. The potential field produced by any single cortical pyramidal neuron is quite weak; however, those produced by a patch of cortex containing hundreds of thousands of such pyramidal cells can sum and produce a strong field that can be detected at the scalp. This is, in fact, primarily what we see reflected in the scalp-recorded ERPs. In short, most of the observed electric recordings at the scalp are generated by post-synaptic currents in the apical dendrites of cortical pyramidal cells in the neocortex. Being limited to seeing the activity in the neocortex is not really so limiting after all: the neocortex is the principal neural substrate of perceptual processing, is involved crucially in motor execution and planning, and underlies much of what we mean by 'higher cognition' including language.

2. What can we learn from ERPs?

Let us first examine how one reads ERPs and makes inferences from one or more. Generally, one starts with a waveform of voltage in time where zero represents stimulus onset. It is now commonplace to look at multiple (e.g. 12-128) waveforms of this kind recorded concurrently from different scalp locations to get an idea of how the waveform changes not only in time but in space (see Figure 1). Insofar as the distribution of an ERP waveform reliably changes across time, one must infer that more than one generator was active. Knowing exactly how many generators were active at any given moment would require special spatial-filtering algorithms, but the fact that there was more than one appears in changes in distribution. Classically, peaks are labelled and identified as components, which can be shown to be reliably correlated with particular experimental manipulations; although, in fact, there is nothing special about peaks as opposed to other parts of the waveform. The word component is variably used by different researchers to refer to (1) a peak, (2) a waveform feature whose polarity, latency, and scalp distribution are predictable from experimental manipulations, or (3) the reflection of the activity of a particular generator or set of generators in the brain. Since a peak is often correlated with a particular cognitive process, it has been assumed that it can be used as a physiological index of that process with its timing inferred from the latency of the peak (propagation of the potential field is essentially instantaneous), and with its degree of activation or 'strength' (somewhat mistakenly) inferred from the amplitude or area under the peak.

If two ERP waveforms differ significantly, then it is generally safe to assume that the brain activity and associated mental activities are different in the two conditions. The exact nature of the difference at the scalp is very much a function of where the recording electrodes are situated relative to the underlying generators. Also, it is important to note that one cannot assume that the electrode site where a potential is the greatest necessarily provides unequivocal information about the location of the underlying generator. One can also make reasonable inferences from the time course of the differences between the ERPs from two conditions, using the point at which two waveforms first differ as an upper limit on the time by which the brain has detected the difference between the eliciting stimuli.

2.1 Is language special?

Now that we know how to look for changes in the ERP, let us see what effects have been observed and what they might tell us about how special language really is: that is, what they have to say about the general question of whether language is separate from knowledge about other domains such as music (which we will discuss later) and the more limited question of whether different sorts of linguistic knowledge are represented differently and independently in the mind/brain.

The most relevant transient potentials are the N400, the N280 (more generally known as the lexical processing negativity - LPN) and the left anterior negativity (LAN), and the P600 or syntactic positive shift (SPS). The N400 is a negative potential between 100 and 600 ms with a peak around 400 ms after the onset of a word or pseudo-word, which provides a measure of how and when semantic constraints are imposed by context on the processing of an item. The LPN is a negativity whose latency varies between 250 and 350 ms as a function of the frequency of occurrence of the eliciting word in the language. The LAN is a negativity between 200 and 700 ms after a word onset which has been hypothesized to reflect working memory load. The P600 is a positivity between 200 and 800 ms which varies with manipulations of various syntactic constraints and their violations, and is correlated with processing difficulty due to structural factors. These are considered to be different components or effects, because they differ in their scalp distributions and because they differ in their sensitivities to experimental manipulations. The N400 shows the largest amplitude over posterior sites of the right hemisphere. The LPN has a maximal amplitude over left-anterior sites. The LAN is maximal over the frontal-central regions of the left hemisphere, and especially large over prefrontal areas. The P600 is very broadly distributed, often but not always maximal over bilateral posterior areas.

2.2 Different representational levels in language

So how can these potentials or effects be used to distinguish between representational levels in language? There have been three primary approaches. One is to violate various representational levels and see if the brain's response, in this case the ERPs, is similar or different; differences implicate the involvement of different brain areas and the existence of different levels. Here the search has been for representation-specific ERP components. In the same way, researchers have sought language-specific ERP components to support hypotheses about the modular nature of the language processor. Later we will examine this in a direct comparison of ERPs to structural violations in music versus those in language. A second approach has been to contrast the brain's responses to different categories of words such as open- and closed-class words and to compare their relative distribution, as distinct scalp topographies are usually taken to strongly suggest different neural generators. A third main approach has been to look for interactions between levels of representation; that is, to look for evidence of context effects in purportedly modular processes. This has often involved determining whether and under which circumstances higher level contextual information influences processing at lower levels.

2.3 Semantics and syntax

2.3.1 The N400 component

Much effort has gone into identifying the distinct components in the ERP which index syntactic versus semantic processing. Lexical semantic violations as in *I take coffee with cream and dog* as opposed to *sugar* elicit an N400 (Kutas and Hillyard 1980). N400s are largest for outright violations whether in written or spoken English, Spanish, French, German, Dutch, or Japanese and even American Sign Language (for review see Kutas and Van Petten 1994). Its amplitude is inversely related to the cloze probability of a word in a sentence context (Kutas and Hillyard 1984; Kutas, Lindamood and Hillyard 1984).

In fact, the response to each word has an N400 whose amplitude is determined by its semantic expectancy, which is set up by the sentence context. This was shown by Van Petten and Kutas (1990, 1991) who compared the effect of context buildup on the N400 for words in normal congruent sentences, those with only syntactic structure but no meaning, and completely scrambled sentences without meaning or structure. Only the congruent sentences showed a modulation of the amplitude of the N400, becoming progressively smaller over the sentence as the semantic context built up. They also showed a similar interaction between word frequency and semantic context on N400 amplitude, but again only for meaningful sentences; the effect of frequency is greater at the beginning of a sentence, but diminishes as semantic constraints build up toward the end of the sentence (Van Petten and Kutas 1990, 1991).

2.3.2 The P600 Component

Let us examine the types of ERP responses that have been reported for other types of violations (other than semantic) within sentences. The first direct comparison of lexico-semantic and morphosyntactic violations indicated that various morphosyntactic violations in English elicited a late positivity (a result subsequently replicated in Spanish), which has since been called a P600 or SPS, as well as some anterior negativities – but not any substantive N400 activity (Kutas and Hillyard, 1983). In subsequent reports, this positivity has been interpreted as indexing (directly or indirectly) the operation of a modular syntactic parser. Various other types of syntactic violations have since been used in English, Dutch, Finnish and German. For example, in addition to violations in subject/verb agreement, researchers have investigated violations of subcategorization constraints, violations of phrase structure, and violations of case markings. For example, Münte and Heinze (1994) found a P600 to the inappropriate genitive case marking on the word *Besens* in *Die Hexe benutzte ihren Besens, um zum Wald zu fliegen* ("The witch used her broom's to fly to the forest") relative to the correct word *Besen* (see Figure 2).

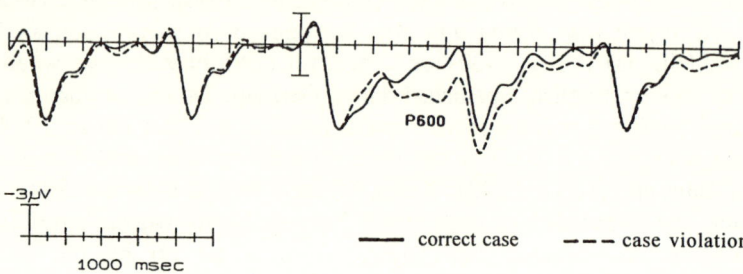

Figure 2. Comparison of the grand average ERPs to a five-word segment of German sentences containing syntactic violations (dashed line) with those containing the syntactically correct forms (solid line); these sentences were read one word at a time. The recording was taken from an electrode at the top of the head (vertex). Figure adapted from Münte and Heinze (1994).

The presence of N400s in response to lexical semantic violations and P600s in response to many (although not all) types of syntactic violations has been offered as evidence for a corresponding division between semantic and syntactic processors (e.g. Osterhout and Holcomb 1992). But subcategorization violations in Dutch do not elicit a P600. Should this result be considered an indicator of a linguistic difference? Moreover, the various positivities (so-called P600s) in the different experiments varied in their scalp distributions and their relative latencies. These differences in scalp distribution imply different configurations of neural generators. Thus, the P600 does not appear to be a unique index of syntactic processing. Moreover, Coulson, King and Kutas (1998) showed that the amplitude of the P600 (like that of the P300, elicited by task-relevant, unexpected *non-language* events) is sensitive to the probability of violations. That is, if syntactic violations are frequent and the syntactically correct form is infrequent, then the difference in the P600s between the two conditions is much less than if the syntactic violation also occurred infrequently. The non-additivity of the effects of syntactic violations and frequency of occurrence of the violation argues against the independence of their generators.

2.3.3 The Left Anterior Negativity and N280

In fact, the left-anterior negativity (LAN) as in WH-movement seems to be a more consistent response to syntactic violations. At present however, it is unclear how it differs from a similar negativity seen in a number of situations where there are no syntactic violations, but merely loads on short-term memory such as in WH-questions in English. Kluender and Kutas (1993a) hypothesized that the LAN reflected cognitive operations involved in entering a filter into working memory, storing it, and subsequently retrieving it to assign fillers to gaps (also see King and Kutas 1995a).

In a second approach, cognitive electrophysiologists have also contrasted scalp distributions of various lexical classes such as open-class versus closed-class words. The idea is based on the loose association of open-class words with semantics and closed-class words with syntax. This division has been supported electrophysiologically by the argument that the response to open-class words has a large N400 component over right-posterior sites and that the response to closed-class words has a large negativity (N280) over left-frontal sites (near Broca's area). However, even this division is questionable. First, N400s are not restricted to open-class words. For instance, Kluender and Kutas (1993b) observed N400s in response to the closed-class words *that*, *if*, and *who* in questions like *Can't you remember that/if/who*, with the largest N400 to *who*.

Moreover, there are data indicating that not all open-class words show a large N400 component. For example, a semantic violation repeated for the second time does not elicit an N400 response (Besson et al. 1992), nor does a content word at the end of a sentence (Van Petten, 1993; Van Petten and Kutas 1990; 1991). Closed-class words are more predictable from context than open-class words, and we believe this difference in contextual predictability explains why open-class words generally have larger N400 components.

It is also possible to show that N280 responses are not specific to closed-class words. In fact, the ERPs to all words over left-frontal regions contain a negativity; however, its latency varies with the eliciting word's frequency. Figure 3 illustrates the lexical processing negativity (LPN) to definite articles, adverbial prepositions, adjectives, verbs and nouns.

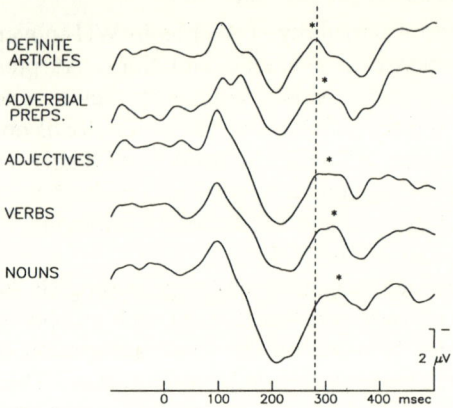

Figure 3. Grand average ERPs (across 24 subjects) recorded over a frontal site in the left hemisphere (F7) for representative word types that are subclasses of the broad Open Class (adjectives, verbs, nouns) versus Closed Class (definite articles, adverbial prepositions). The dashed line is at 280 ms post-word onset; asterisks mark peak latencies for the word types.

A linear regression of the peak latency of the LPN and word scarcity (a transformation of frequency) accounts for, on average, 90% of the variation. Thus, the LPN is definitely not a marker for closed-class words; it is present with the same distribution across the scalp for both word classes, but at a shorter latency for the higher frequency closed class words than for the lower frequency open-class words. And, a 50 ms processing difference of this sort may well lead to real functional differences in the processing of open- versus closed-class words, which obviates the need for the proposed special closed-class processor (located in Broca's area) to account for the observed differences (King and Kutas 1995b, 1998).

While neither the N400 nor the LPN are specific to any lexical class, they can, nevertheless, be used to investigate linguistic representations. We have already mentioned that semantic context modulates N400 amplitude in sentences. N400s are also sensitive to category membership (e.g. Fischler et al. 1983; Boddy and Weinberg 1981; Heinze et al. 1998). Following the presentation of a word belonging to a semantic category, responses to members of the category have much smaller N400s than do non-members. Moreover, the ERPs of more typical members have smaller N400s than those to less typical members. Kara Federmeier took advantage of the fact that both sentential context and category membership influence N400 amplitude, to investigate how constraints arising from the organization of categories in long term memory interact with constraints arising from sentence fragments during on-line reading. She asked people to read sentences that ended either with the name of an object predicted by the context, the name of an object from the same category but not predicted by the context, or an unexpected name of an object from a different category. For example, *Checkmate! Rosaline announced with glee. She was getting to be really good at* CHESS (expected), MONOPOLY (same category), *and* FOOTBALL (different category). The preliminary results showed that the ERP corresponding to the expected ending included a large positivity between 300 and 600 ms, whereas both unexpected endings were characterized by N400 responses – the ERP to the item from the different category being larger. It seems that expectations as people read are not only for specific words but also for more general categories. These results suggest that items from the expected taxonomic category are more easily integrated even if they are not more plausible, which is consistent with the hypothesis that context operates through the use of category structure for objects in long-term memory. We are now looking for similar effects using pictures of objects and categories of actions.

2.3.4 The Slow Potentials

By focusing on the response to various types of violations, the emphasis in ERP studies of language has remained at the level of single words, even if these words occur within a sentential context. This is like the majority of neuroimaging investigations of language, which have been based mostly on isolated words taken from word lists. But language is more than this, involving not only the registration of single words but also the computation of the syntactic, semantic, and thematic relationships among words. Moreover, at least some of these processes must extend temporally over a series of processing events such as for anaphoric reference and the comprehension of WH-questions in English. ERPs are well-suited to track these extended brain processes.

Such slow processes are reflected in slow potentials and revealed by applying a low-pass digital filter to the cross-sentence ERPs, so that only the slow activity remains. Even after filtering, there remains a temporally and spatially rich and complex pattern of electrical activity over the head; these are potentials that fluctuate with the structure of the clause and the functional structure of the brain. As simple as these sentences are, they still require analysis at multiple linguistic levels and must utilize working and long-term memory to be understood.

There are many features to these slow potentials that allow one to track the course of the processing of a clause. In brief, we have identified four laterally asymmetric slow potential effects (see Figure 4):

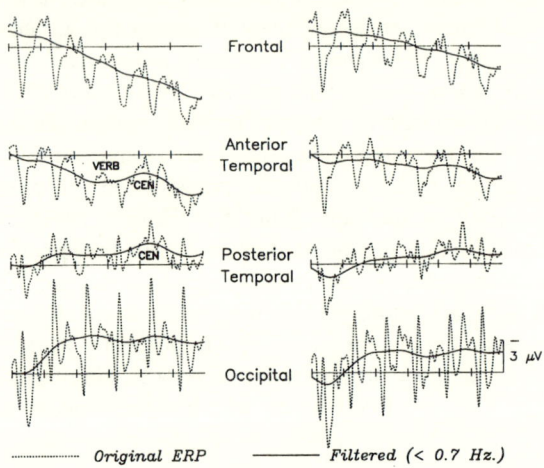

Figure 4. Original ERPs (dotted line) recorded from 18 subjects, and slow potential activity (solid line), low pass-filtered at 0.7 Hz for 4 pairs of sites going from front to back of the head over left and right hemispheres, shown in the left and right columns, respectively. The ERP reflects the response to the first six words of a transitive clause (e.g., The secretary answered the phone because...). The region of the verb and the clause ending negativity or CEN are labelled. Reprinted by permission of MIT Press, Kutas and King (1996).

(1) A sustained negative shift over occipital sites associated with early visual processing,
(2) a temporal positivity reflecting verb processing (perhaps thematic role assignment),
(3) a negativity over temporal sites indexing clause ending (clause ending negativity or CEN), and
(4) a very slow-going frontal positivity that might reflect the building of a mental model or schema of the sentence from an integration of items in working memory with representations in long-term memory.

Moreover, all of these are taking place simultaneously but over different brain regions with different time courses.

We have recorded similar slow potential effects for a variety of sentence structures such as subject- and object-relative constructions (e.g. subject relatives: *The reporter who harshly attacked the senator admitted the error.* versus object relatives: *The reporter who the senator harshly attacked admitted the error.*). Without going into great details, King and Kutas (1995a) found that the processing of these two differ and these differences can be linked to differences in their demands on working memory. Moreover, we have found that the effects were very similar, whether the sentences were written or spoken (Müller, King and Kutas, 1997). Perhaps most important for present purposes is the fact that these can be used to examine potential interactions between supposedly different linguistic levels of analysis. For example, Jill Weckerly (1995) used these to examine whether noun animacy (a semantic factor in English, although not in all languages) is used on-line during reading of sentences with object-relative constructions which varied only in the order of the animacy of the nouns in the main and relative clauses.

In brief, we observed many of the same cross-sentence patterns as in previous studies: namely, the ultra-slow frontal positivity, the verb positivity, the CEN, and LAN effects on the verbs. Moreover, the brain was shown to be sensitive to noun animacy as soon as the noun was read, which had consequences on the upcoming ERPs including the complementizer, the relative clause subject, and the relative and main clause verbs (see Weckerly and Kutas, in press). We have argued elsewhere that these data support our hypothesis that the animacy information is combined (1) with word order to make tentative grammatical role assignments and (2) with the complementizer (*that*) to set up expectations for the object relative construction. We thus have evidence that semantic and pragmatic knowledge are brought into the initial parsing analysis. More generally, our results show cross-talk between supposedly separate, independent levels of linguistic analysis.

To sum up, we have shown how it is possible to examine the brain's activity during language processing via ERP recordings from the human scalp. Both word- and sentence-level responses reflect the brain's sensitivities to linguistic analyses of various types. To date, none of our data support any unequivocal presence of encapsulated linguistic representations that do not interact prior to their full processing. We have found no unique markers of any language-specific processes. Next, we will examine how the modularity hypothesis fares when we compare language versus music representations and processes.

2.4 ERPs and music

The first experiment that we conducted in music perception research (Besson and Macar 1987) was aimed at testing the functional significance of the N400 component. We wanted to determine whether or not the presentation of an incongruous note (out of key) at the end of a musical phrase would elicit an N400, as does the presentation of an incongruous word at the end of a sentence. Our results show that only incongruous words are associated with N400s. Incongruous notes, in contrast, elicit late positive components (LPCs), peaking around 500 ms after terminal note onset over parietal sites. Should we then have concluded that N400 is language-specific? Several reasons led us to reserve judgment. First, musical phrases were highly familiar and incongruous notes were so obvious that they did not require any specific musical knowledge to be noticed. Furthermore, since participants were not musicians, they could not access musical knowledge. It is still an open question whether the N400 reflects the access to and the computations performed on knowledge, regardless of its content.

2.4.1 Harmonic violations

We conducted a second series of experiments (Besson, Faita and Requin, 1994; Besson and Faita, 1995) in which we manipulated:
- musical expertise: musicians with a classical background, professionals or with at least 7 years of training at the regional musical school and non-musicians participated in the experiments;
- the familiarity of the materials: we used well-known musical phrases, from the classical repertoire (Vivaldi *Four Seasons*, Mozart *Turkisch March*, etc...), and new, unknown musical phrases, composed for the experiment following compositional rules of classical music;
- the type of incongruity: musical phrases, known or new, ended with a congruous note, an incongruous note out of key (nondiatonic) or in key but not as expected – as a function of the melodic contour (diatonic incongruity), or with a congruous note delayed by 600 ms (rhythmic incongruity). Note that each type of terminal note had the same probability of occurrence.

As illustrated in Figure 5, compared with congruous notes, nondiatonic incongruities elicited large LPCs, as was shown by Besson and Macar (1987). Diatonic incongruities also elicited LPCs, but of smaller amplitude than the nondiatonic incongruities. These effects were larger in size for known than for unknown melodies, and larger for musicians than for non-musicians.

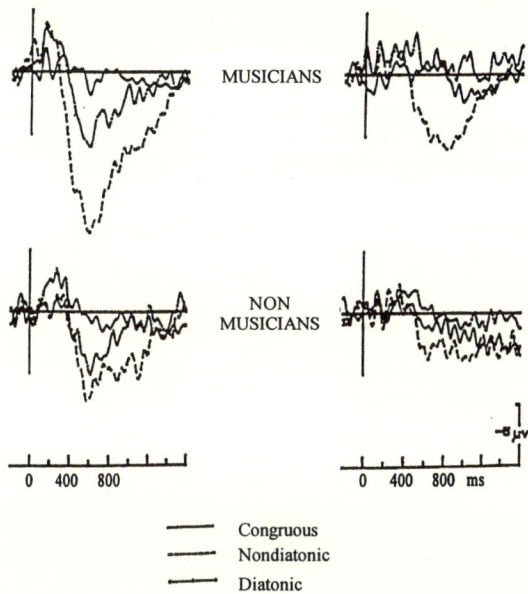

Figure 5: ERPs recorded from musicians (15 participants) and non-musicians (15 participants) in response to congruous note (solid line), nondiatonic incongruity (dashed line) and diatonic incongruity (dashed-dot line) ending known (left column) and unknown (right column) melodies. Recordings are from parietal site (Pz). Adapted from Besson and Faita (1995).

Therefore, nondiatonic and diatonic incongruous notes are associated with LPCs but not with the N400 component. As mentioned above, late positivities, such as P600, have also been elicited in response to syntactic incongruities. Thus, it may be that the similarities between language and music emerge at the level of harmonic and syntactic structures rather than at the level of semantic representations. Recently, this hypothesis was directly tested by Patel et al. (1998). Musicians were presented with linguistic and musical phrases, in which syntactic violations and harmonic violations were introduced, respectively. The results showed that the LPCs elicited in the two linguistic and musical conditions were not significantly different.

2.4.2 Rhythmic violations

Results for rhythmic incongruity are presented in Figure 6. A large positive component is associated with the absence of the note; that is, this component appears when the terminal note should have been presented, but was not. The amplitude of this positive component does not differ for musicians and non-musicians, but is larger for known than for unknown melodies.

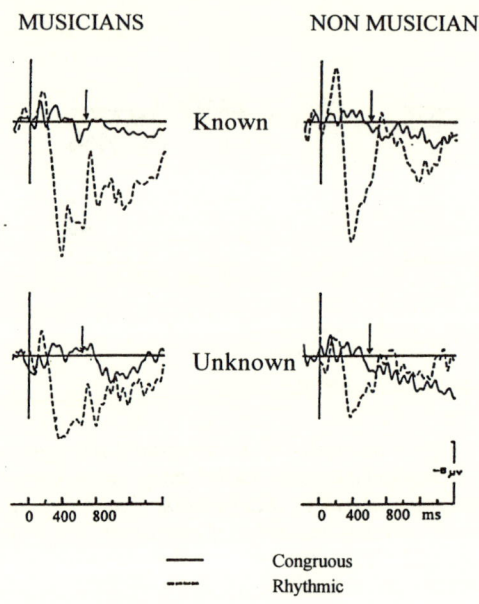

Figure 6: ERPs recorded from musicians (15 participants) and non-musicians (15 participants) in response to congruous note (solid line), and rhythmic incongruities (dashed line) ending known and unknown melodies. The vertical bar shows when the terminal note should have been presented, and the arrow when it was actually presented. Recordings are from parietal site (Pz). Adapted from Besson and Faita (1995).

These results demonstrate that ERPs are sensitive to rhythm and consequently, to the temporal structure of musical phrases. We recently conducted a series of experiments in which we added some unexpected pauses in written or spoken sentences, such that the sentence terminal word was either presented when it should have been, or with a 600 ms delay (Besson et al, 1997). The effect of temporal structure violation in spoken sentences was found to be very similar to that observed in previous music experiments.

Therefore, it seems that temporal information is processed similarly in linguistic and musical phrases. Experiments are now in progress, using different brain imaging techniques, such as fMRI and MEG, to determine whether or not the same brain areas are activated by the processing of temporal information in both language and music.

2.4.3 Lyrics

In another series of experiments, we directly compared the effects of semantic and musical incongruities. To this end, we selected excerpts from French opera, which were then sung a capella by a professional singer. These excerpts lasted for 15-20 seconds, and ended either with a congruent word sung in or out of key, or with an incongruous word sung in or out of key (Bizet, *Carmen*: "The fabric floated in the breeze / blood"). They were presented to professional musicians from the Opera in Marseille who were asked to detect the linguistic and musical incongruities. Results showed that N400s were elicited by incongruous words, and that LPCs were elicited by words sung out of key. Most importantly, both components, the N400 and the LPC, were elicited by the double incongruity (incongruous words sung out of key). Thus, these results demonstrate the strong additivity of the ERP components associated with semantic and musical incongruities. As such they point to the independence of semantic and musical processing.

Conclusion

In conclusion, comparing language and music processing reveals both similarities and differences. Differences are mainly demonstrated when studying semantic representations and the computations that allow access to a word's meaning. On the other hand, similarities arise when the focus is on syntactic, harmonic, and temporal information processing. Overall, these results favor the idea according to which the cognitive operations that subserve language and music processing obey similar, if not common, functional principles. Our data are, therefore, inconsistent with a strong modular view of linguistic and musical processing.

Acknowledgments

Some of the work reported herein was supported from grants NIMH (MH52893), NIA (AG08313), and NICHD (HD22614) to M. Kutas, and from grants MRT (92.C.0420) and G.I.S., "Science de la Cognition" (1995-1997) to M. Besson.

References

Besson, Mireille and Macar, Françoise. 1987. "An event-related potentials analysis of incongruity in music and other non-linguistic contexts". *Psychophysiology*, 24: 14-25.

Besson, Mireille, Kutas, Marta and Van Petten, Cyma. 1992. "An Event-Related Potential (ERP) analysis of semantic congruity and repetition effects in sentences". *Journal of Cognitive Neurosciences*, 4: 132-149.

Besson, Mireille, Faïta, Frédérique and Requin, Jean. 1994. "Brain waves associated with musical incongruity differ for musicians and non-musicians". *Neuroscience Letters*, 168: 101-105.

Besson, Mireille and Faïta, Frédérique. 1995. "An Event-Related Potential (ERP) study of musical expectancy: Comparison of musicians with non-musicians". *Journal of Experimental Psychology: Human Perception and Performance*, 21 (6): 1278-1296.

Besson, Mireille; Faïta, Frédérique; Czternasty, Claire and Kutas, Marta. 1997. "What's in a pause: Event-Related Potential analysis of temporal disruptions in written and spoken sentences". *Biological Psychology*, 46, 3-23.

Boddy, John and Weinberg, Hal. 1981. "Brain potentials, perceptual mechanisms and semantic categorization". *Biological Psychology*, 12: 43-61.

Coulson, Seana; King, Jonathan W. and Kutas, Marta. 1998. "Expect the unexpected: Event-related brain responses to morphosyntactic violations". *Language and Cognitive Processes*, 13: 21-58.

Fischler, Ira; Bloom, Paul A.; Childers, Doug G.; Roucos, S.E., and Perry, Nathan W. 1983. "Brain potentials related to stages of sentence verification". *Psychophysiology*, 20: 400-409.

Heinze, Hans; Münte, Thomas and Kutas, Marta. 1998. "Context effects in a category verification task as accessed by Event-Related brain Potentials measures". *Biological Psychology*, 47: 121-137.

King, Jonathan and Kutas, Marta. 1995a. "Who did what and when? Using word- and clausal-level ERPs to monitor working memory usage in reading", *Journal of Cognitive Neuroscience*, 7(3): 376-395.

King, Jonathan and Kutas, Marta. 1995b. "A Brain Potential whose latency indexes the length and frequency of words", *CRL Newsletter* October, 10(1).

King, Jonathan and Kutas, Marta. 1998. "Neural plasticity in the dynamics of visual word recognition". *Neuroscience Letters*, 244: 61-64.

Kluender, Robert E. 1991. *Cognitive Constraints on Variables in Syntax*. Dissertation. University of California, San Diego.

Kluender, Robert and Kutas, Marta. 1993a. "Bridging the Gap: Evidence from ERPs on the processing of unbounded dependencies". *Journal of Cognitive Neuroscience*, 5(2): 196-214.
Kluender, Robert and Kutas, Marta. 1993b. "Subjacency as a processing phenomenon". *Language and Cognitive Processes*, 8(4): 573-633.
Kutas, Marta. and Hillyard, Steven A. 1980. "Reading senseless sentences: Brain potentials reflect semantic incongruity". *Science*, 207: 203-205.
Kutas, Marta. and Hillyard, Steven A. 1983. "Event-Related brain potentials to grammatical errors and semantic anomalies". *Memory and Cognition*, 11: 539-550.
Kutas, Marta and Hillyard, Steven A. 1984. "Brain potentials during reading reflect word expectancy and semantic association". *Nature*, 307: 161-163.
Kutas, Marta; Lindamood, Timothy and Hillyard, Steven. 1984. "Word expectancy and event-related brain potentials during sentence processing". In S. Kornblum and J. Requin (eds), *Preparatory states and processes* (217 - 237). Hillsdale: Lawrence Erlbaum.
Kutas, Marta and Van Petten, Cyma. 1994. "Psycholinguistics Electrified: Event-related potential investigations". In M.A. Gernsbacher (ed.), *Handbook of Psycholinguistics*, Academic Press, 83-143.
Kutas, Marta and King, Jonathan W. 1996. "The potentials for basic sentence processing: differentiating integrative processes", In T. Inui and J.L. McClelland (eds.), *Attention and Performance* XVI. MIT Press.
Müller, Horst M., King, Jonathan W. and Kutas, Marta. 1997. "Event related potentials elicited by spoken relative clauses". *Cognitive Brain Research*, 5: 193-203.
Münte, Thomas and Heinze, Hans. 1994. "Event-Related negativities during syntactic processing of writtent words". In H. Heinze, T.F. Münte and G.R. Mangun (eds), *Cognitive electrophysiology*. Boston, MA: Birkhauser.
Patel, Ani; Gibson, Edward; Ratner, J.; Besson, Marta and Holcomb, Phillip. 1998. "Processing syntactic relations in language and music: An Event-Related Potential study". *Journal of Cognitive Neurosciences*, 10: 717-733.
Osterhout, Lee and Holcomb, Phillip. 1992. "Event-Related brain potentials elicited by syntactic anomaly". *Journal of Memory and Language*, 31: 785-806.
Van Petten, Cyma and Kutas, Marta. 1990. "Interactions between sentence context and word frequency in event-related potentials". *Memory and Cognition*, 18: 380-393.
Van Petten, Cyma and Kutas, Marta. 1991. "Influences of semantic and syntactic context on open- and closed-class words". *Memory and Cognition*, 19: 95-112.
Van Petten, Cyma. 1993. "A comparison of lexical and sentence-level context effects in event-related potentials". *Language and Cognitive Processes*, 8: 485-531.

Weckerly, Jill. 1995. *Object Relatives Viewed Through Behavioral, Electrophysiological, and Modeling Techniques*. Dissertation. University of California, San Diego.

Weckerly, Jill and Kutas, Marta. "Electrophysiological analysis of animacy effects in the processing of object relative sentences". *Psychophysiology*, in press.

Linguistic Variations and Cognitive Constraints in the Processing and the Acquisition of Language

Michèle Kail
Laboratoire Cognition et Développement
CNRS - Université Paris V

Introduction

For some years, on-line research has been the dominant methodology in psycholinguistic research. More recently, developmental studies of on-line sentence processing have begun to provide some general principles on temporal resolution, taking into account both cognitive capacities and linguistic variations. In this article, we present data on this topic, focusing mainly on morphosyntactic variations. A thorough evaluation of the method used in these experiments calls for a short summary of the previous off-line sentence processing principles. We examine these principles in the context of a functional and probabilistic model of language acquisition and language processing, the Competition Model.

Real-time language comprehension requires that the listener or reader integrate linguistic cues into the ongoing sentence representation. The main controversy in the field revolves around the following question: is structural information processed autonomously during an initial phase, while lexical-semantic information is processed later, when the parser's first analysis has failed? Or, on the contrary, is the parser immediately able to integrate all the available linguistic information, so that the distinction between phrase structure representation and interpretation gets no longer very useful?

The hypothesis of autonomous processing has been mainly put forward by Frazier and tested in a series of experiments using the 'garden-path' paradigm, where sentences with syntactic ambiguities force the parser to choose that syntactic analysis which minimizes memory load and optimizes processing (Frazier 1990).

This conception has been called into question by various models, mainly interactive ones (Altmann and Steedman 1988; Perfetti 1990), that are based on the assumption that the computation of syntax is obligatory even though non structural information (lexical, semantic and contextual) can be processed in parallel. These models vary according to the degree of autonomy they grant the syntactic parser (Schelstraete 1993).

Integrative models, unlike autonomous and interactive models, propose that syntactic and conceptual information are 'inextricably intertwined'. According to this integrative view, there is a single system in which all the linguistic cues guide the construction of a unique representation as a function of their relative weights.

Among other integrative models such as "the Multiple Constraint Satisfaction Model" developed by MClelland et al. (McClelland, St John and Taraban 1989), the Competition Model (MacWhinney 1987 a, b, c; MacWhinney and Bates 1989) provides a framework for the cross-linguistic study of language use looking at both the ways languages differ and the ways in which they are alike. This comparative approach draws on the pioneering work of Slobin (Slobin 1980; 1985). Since the emergence of this model, we have emphasized its heuristic value for language acquisition (Kail 1983 a and b) and we have, along with other colleagues, contributed to an enriched version of the model and its application to various psycholinguistic fields: language acquisition, processing in normal and aphasic adults, second language acquisition and bilingual processing.

1. Off-line principles of sentence processing

Following earlier traditions within functional linguistics (Lakoff and Thomson 1975; Li and Thomson 1976; Givón 1979), the Competition Model does not characterize linguistic knowledge in terms of rules but in terms of a complex set of weighted form-function mappings. Each language provides linguistic cues (lexical, syntactic, morphological or prosodic) which indicate semantic functions, for example the role of agent. Nevertheless, the strength of the connection between forms and functions vary not only from one language to another but also within one language.

The assignment of functions is derived from the mapping of the formal level where all the surface forms are available, and the functional level where all the meanings and intentions to be expressed in a sentence are represented. The mapping of the relationship of form to function is stated as directly as possible but is not assumed to be a one-to-one mapping: one form may be plurifunctional, while one function may be expressed through various forms. The direct mapping of form to function means that it is possible for the parser to integrate all the linguistic cues on a single level for sentence processing. The parser exploits various configurations of these cues: lexico-semantic cues (animacy contrast) morphological cues (nominal and verbal agreement) word order cues (preverbal position, for example) and prosodic cues (contrastive stress).

Form-function mappings involve vertical correlations, whereas form-form mappings or function-function mappings involve horizontal correlations. For example, in English, the preverbal position is highly correlated with the syntactic subject (form-function correlation). On the other hand, the syntactic subject is composed of a set of formal devices linked together, such as preverbal position and initial position in the sentence, nominal case marking, definite determiner, default stress and so forth (form-form correlations). Finally, at the functional level, the syntactic subject is very often correlated with the semantic agent. Both functions are usually assigned to a specific referent sharing a set of recurrent properties such as being human, animate and capable of intentionality. These properties distinguish this referent as fullfilling these functions in the sentence (function-function correlation).

According to the Competition Model, these three types of mappings do not work independently in the language system. Instead, they tend to act together in the form of coalitions. These coalitions seem to be a necessary characteristic of all languages, due to resource limitations in the channel of communication and the temporal constraints of the processing system. In the Competition Model, grammatical categories are stuctured in a manner similar to the category stuctures proposed in Rosch's theory of prototypes (Rosch 1977). An instance of the prototypical category of subject is that found in English, where coalitions at the formal level (preverbal position, verbal agreement) and coalitions at the functional level (agent of a transitive action, discourse topic) coincide. In English, when an element different from the agent is topicalized, the coalition between agency and topicality breaks down: this is an instance of passive construction.

In some cases, the parallel activation of the formal and functional levels leads to competition between the different sources of information for role assignment. In these instances, a co-evaluation of sources becomes necessary and is directly determined by the relative validity of these cues in a given language.

The notion of cue validity is the central predictive construct of the Competition Model. It represents the informative value of a given source of information (for example, preverbal position) for the assignment of a particular communicative function or meaning (for example, the role of agent). Cue validity is defined by two properties, availability and reliability. If a cue is there whenever needed, it is maximally high in availability. If a cue is never ambiguous and always leads to the correct interpretation, it is maximally high in reliability. An example of a very valid cue in English is preverbal position, which is both available and reliable. This is contrary to what happens in Italian and Spanish.

Another fundamental notion is cue strength. Whereas cue validity is an objective property of the stimulus measured directly in samples of inputs given to the language learner, precisely quantified (McDonald and MacWhinney 1989) cue strength is a subjective property of the language user: it is a psychological construct inferred from data obtained in precise experimental conditions.. Cue strength is the probability assigned by the subject to a specific piece of linguistic information in order to assign a specific function.

According to the processing hypotheses proposed by this probabilistic and integrative model, cue strength depends on cue validity in a given language. In adults, cue strength and cue validity are isomorphic when form-function mappings are optimally 'adjusted'. In children, the central hypothesis is that the order in which cues for sentence comprehension emerge in a language is largely a function of the relative validity of cues in that language.

The heuristic value of cue validity is supported by a substantial body of experimental data on comprehension obtained in contrasted languages: English and Italian (Bates, McNew, MacWhinney, Devescovi and Smith 1982, Bates, MacWhinney, Caselli, Devescovi, Natale and Venza 1984), German (MacWhinney, Bates and Kliegl 1984), Hebrew (Sokolov 1988), Hungarian (MacWhinney, Pléh and Bates 1985), French (Kail 1987, 1995; Kail and Charvillat 1986, Amy and Vion 1986), French and Spanish (Charvillat 1988; Kail and Charvillat 1988, Kail 1989; Charvillat and Kail 1991), Dutch (Kilborn and Cooreman 1987; McDonald 1986), Japanese (Sasaki 1991), Chinese (Liu, Bates and Li 1992; Li, Bates and MacWhinney 1993), Serbo-Croatian (Smith and Mimica 1984) Warlpiri (Bavin and Shopen, 1989), Arabic (Taman 1993; Bamhamed 1996; Bamhamed and Kail, 1996), Modern Greek (Kail and Diakogiorgi 1994; Diakogiorgi 1996; Diakogiorgi and Kail 1996). In these studies, subjects (children and adults) are asked to identify the agent or the patient in simple transitive sentences. Classical off-line procedures are used to decide which of the two nouns is the agent: acting out for children, and reaction times for adults.

A very robust conclusion that emerges from all of these crosslinguistic studies is that there is a strong correlation between cue validity and cue strength in sentence processing. These results also support the assumption that children acquire sentence comprehension strategies in a sequence that is predictable from the cue validity of the grammatical devices in the adult language.

However, a number of exceptions to predictions based on cue validity, especially in French (Kail 1987; Kail and Charvillat 1986), have been found. Young French children initially base their sentence interpretation on word order (like English children). Later, from six years upwards, they rely on the animacy contrast of the nouns (like Italian children). In order to explain the incompatibility of such results with the model's developmental predictions, we proposed to implement the Competition Model with the notion of cue cost. Cue cost must be distinguished from cue validity in terms of the differential processing demands imposed by different types of cues. The relationship between cue validity and cue cost has been explored in a series of experiments on sentence processing conducted with French and Spanish children and adults (Charvillat 1988; Kail and Charvillat 1988; Kail 1989). These studies found first that for French and Spanish adults, the more local a linguistic cue is, the stronger it is; and second, for French children, a linguistic cue is all the stronger the more topological it is (verbal agreement < clitic pronoun < word order), whereas for Spanish children, a cue is all the stronger the more local it is (word order < clitic pronoun < verbal agreement < accusative preposition *a*). With development, children tend to rely more on local cues (those that are costless) than on topological ones. The fact that Spanish children's latencies are always shorter than those of French children must be related to the effect of the preposition *a*, which permits efficient role assignment at minimal cost. These results stress the importance of locality in sentence processing and indicate that in the course of their development, children keep adjusting their strategies, taking both cue validity and processing cost into account.

Cross-linguistic cue hierarchies seem to follow a general principle that is captured by the locality processing principle: the use of local processing strategies increases to the greatest extent allowed by the language to be acquired (See table below).

Table 1: Hierarchical ordering of cues for agent assignment by language (adapted from MacWhinney and Bates 1989)

English
Adults: SVO > VOS, OSV > Animacy, Agreement > Stress, Topic
5-7 years: SVO > Animacy > Agreement > NNV, VNN, Stress
under 5:   SVO > Animacy > Stress, SOV,VSO > Agreement

Italian
- Adults: SV Agreement > Clitic Agreement > Animacy > SVO > Stress, Topic
(NNV,VNN interpretable only in combination with stress, clitics)
- under 7: Animacy > SVO > SV Agreement > Clitic Agreement > SOV, VSO
(no interactions of NNV, VNN with stress, clitics)

French
- Adults: SV Agreement > Clitic Agreement > Animacy > SVO > Stress
- under 6: SVO > Animacy > VSO, SOV (agreement not tested)

Spanish
- Adults: Accusative preposition > SV Agreement > Clitic Agreement > Word order (animacy not tested)
- under 10: Accusative preposition > SV Agreement > Clitic Agreement > Word order

German
- Adults: Case > Agreement > Animacy > SOV, VSO, SVO

Dutch
- Adults: Case > SVO > Animacy
- under 10: SVO > Case > Animacy

Serbo-Croatian
- Adults: Case > Agreement > Animacy > SVO, VSO, SOV
- under 5: Animacy > Case > SVO, VSO, SOV > Agreement

Hungarian
- Adults: Case > Agreement > Order
- under 3: Animacy > Case > SVO > Stress (agreement not tested)

Turkish
- Adults: Case > Animacy > Word Order
- under 2: Case > Word Order (animacy not tested)

Hebrew
- Adults: Case > Agreement > Order
- under 10: Case > Order > Agreement

Warlpiri
- Adults: Case > Animacy > Order
- under 5: Animacy > Case > Order

Chinese
- Adults: Animacy > SVO

Japanese
- Adults: Case > Animacy > SOV

Greek
- Adults: Case > Animacy > SVO
- under 3: Animacy > Case > SVO

Arabic
- Adults: Case > VSO

Each language is characterized by a specific cue configuration which is optimal for sentence processing. As has been shown in Spanish and French (Kail and Charvillat 1988), Serbo-Croatian (Mimica et al. 1984) and Hungarian (MacWhinney and Osman-Sagi 1991), an increasing number of convergent cues does not necessarily result in shorter processing times.

2. On-line principles of sentence processing

On-line sentence processing is governed by temporal constraints that involve different cognitive resources than those required in off-line interpretations.

To study the microstructure of on-line sentence processing, three main experimental methods have been used successfully in adults and children from five years of age upwards. These techniques have provided reliable new data on cue integration: a) on-line sentence interpretation gives a direct measure of processing time by placing inaudible clics on the signal, thus providing information about anticipatory strategies; b) on-line error detection is used to assess the extent to which children and adults can make on-line judgments about grammaticality. This technique is particularly relevant for highly inflected languages (case violations, violations of verbal agreement), even though it can also be extended to word order violations. According to a general assumption of the Competition Model, the more valid a cue in a language, the quicker subjects will detect its violation; c) on-line interpretation with noise superimposed has been extensively used by Kilborn (1991) with bilingual and aphasic subjects to study the relative vulnerability of morphological cues.The noise can prevent cue integration by reducing the availability and accessing of cues for timely processing.

According to Bates and MacWhinney (1987), it is assumed that the parsing system allows for an ongoing updating of the assignment of nouns to case roles. For example, when processing a sentence such as "the cats are looking at the bird", the assignment of "cats " as the agent is first suggested by its appearance as the initial noun in a preverbal position.The fact that "are looking" agrees with "cats" in number further supports this assignment. Finally, "bird" as a singular postverbal noun does not agree with the verb and is thus disqualified as a good candidate for the agent role. In this way, the mapping from the lexical item "cats" to the agent role is updated at each point in sentence processing. In this particular case, updating increases the strength of this assignment.

Whereas form-function mappings are at the core of off-line sentence processing, form-form mappings are the central determinants in this on-line processing view. Highly inflected languages such as those we have selected – Modern Greek and Moroccan Arabic – are good candidates for revealing constraints of the system on processing ability. In other languages such as French, morphological variations between oral and written language are evident and consequently one finds limitations in the perception of morphology (auditory vs. visual input).

2.1 Cue Assignability

The general principle of the ongoing updating outlined above is based on the assumption that the processing system tries to assign cues to meanings as soon as possible, integrating each piece of linguistic information into larger structures compatible with the information obtained up to that point. In this processing model, attachments between units that can be made locally place less load on the processor.

The assignability of a linguistic cue lies in its capacity for integration. In a language such as Turkish, case suffixes are maximally high in assignability: the semantic role of a noun is assigned as soon as the suffix for that noun can be classified. This is what Ammon and Slobin (1979) refer to as a 'local cue'. In contrast, a cue can involve discontinuous fragments. This discontinuity can be an inherent property of the morphological system of a particular language (Moroccan Arabic for example) or can be the result of experimental conditions (variations of the distance between the subject and the verb in experiments on verbal agreement).

2.1.1 Cue assignability and morphological marking
A series of experiments have been conducted to examine what factors constrain the assignability of morphological cues during on-line interpretation of sentences (cleft sentences). The main value of Moroccan Arabic lies in the fact that it is a highly inflected language that allows for the control of the continuity vs. discontinuity of case marking, the position of the affixes (pre- vs. postverbal morphology) and the length of morphological marking (phonemes vs. syllables). In Moroccan Arabic, the basic word order is VSO and the verb is pivotal for the assignment of various functions (agency, temporality).

For example, in agentive cleft sentences, preverbal marking is obligatory: it is continuous for singular NPs (/j/ masculine, /t/ feminine) and discontinuous for plural NPs (/j...u /). When the first noun of the sentence is not the agent, postverbal marking is obligatory and expressed in continuous suffixes (/u/

masculine, /ha/ feminine, /hum/ plural). The main results of these experiments showed that, in Moroccan Arabic, the preverbal personal prefix is the decisive cue used to assign the agent function to one of the two nouns. The experiments confirmed that the position of affixes is a crucial determinant of assignability. Sentences with continuous preverbal marking (singular nouns) are more rapidly processed than sentences with discontinuous marking (plural nouns).

In Moroccan Arabic, the assignment of the agent and the patient in cleft sentences is very difficult when the two nouns share the same gender and number. In the case of identical morphological marking, subjects tend to rely on word order and their processing times increase. In addition, when word order and morphology are in competition (ungrammatical sentences), subjects are more efficient if they rely on a local strategy based on morphology rather than using a word-order configuration strategy (Bamhamed 1996; Bamhamed and Kail 1996).

These on-line results are consistent with previous results obtained in off-line comprehension studies emphasizing the prevalence of morphology in Arabic (Taman 1993). They provide new data on the way some decisive dimensions of morphological marking are integrated into ongoing sentence processing.

2.1.2 Cue assignability and distance

Recent studies conducted in various languages, such as English and Italian (Wulfeck, Bates and Capasso 1991), French (Kail and Bassano 1997) and Modern Greek (Kail and Diakogiorgi 1994; Diakogiorgi 1996), have examined how some fundamental grammatical constraints such as word order configurations and morphological devices (verbal and case agreements) are integrated as cues during on-line sentence processing.

Experiments with adults have shown a close relationship in these languages between cue validity and error detection times in sentences where grammatical violations affect the selected cues. Thus, English adults are more sensitive to word order violations while Italian subjects are more sensitive to agreement violations. Greek subjects detect morphological violations more rapidly, but they are also quite sensitive to word order violations. This is an unexpected result in a highly inflected language where – as shown in off-line sentence processing – morphology is a very dominant cue. In addition, Greek on-line data indicate that error detection times for word-order violations depend on the hierarchical relations between the elements affected by sequential transposition: violations of elements belonging to different main constituents (for example, transposition of the noun and the verb) are more quickly detected than violations of elements belonging to the same constituent (for example, transposition of the article and the noun).

In French, the results indicate that there are complex interactions governing on-line processing. First, the ability to detect a grammatical violation depends on the input modality; word-order violations are more rapidly detected in the auditory modality, while agreement violations are more quickly detected in the visual modality. This difference in the apprehension of agreement violations is explained by the greater perceptibility of agreement cues in written French, in contrast to their opacity in oral French. Second, when a linguistic sequence is interposed between the subject and the verb, the error detection times for verbal agreement are generally delayed, and the delay seems to be influenced not only by the structural, but also the semantic properties of the interposed sequence (Kail and Bassano 1997). Such results have to be confirmed by other cross-linguistic investigations in order to substantiate the idea that the parser can immediately integrate both structural and lexico-semantic information.

2.1.3 Cue assignability and word order

The importance of word order to the on-line processing of morphology was underscored in research done with Greek adults and children over six years of age. In a task which required the interpretation of sentences with varied word order and case morphology, we showed (Kail and Diakogiorgi 1994) that the decision time for agent attribution is contingent on the sequential organization of the nouns. For example, the juxtaposition of nouns case-marked in a NNV order permit a much faster assignment of semantic roles than those possible if the marking is distributed (NVN), or placed at the end of the sentence (VNN).

Analogous results have been found in Italian (Bates, personal communication). In general, Italian subjects (normal and aphasic) process VNN sequences faster than NVN or NNV sequences. Given that the agreement of the verb is the most valid interpretive cue in this language, the assignment of the semantic function of agent in VNN is a quicker and more accessible way to access this cue. It is interesting to remark that in Italian, VNN is not the dominant word-order (S(VO) is dominant), just as NNV is not the dominant word order in Greek. In fact, it seems that the constraints of on-line processing places word order and its functional aspects at the service of morphology.

2.2 Cue perceptibility, cue detectability and context

If the role of the perceptibility of cues – that is, their capacity to initiate processing – has been proven for off-line sentence interpretation (Pléh 1990), this role becomes absolutely essential in the processing and integration of on-line cues. Applying the paradigm for detecting violations in case agreement in Greek (agreement of the marked article and the marked noun), Diakogiorgi (1996) showed that after 6.6 years of age, the perceptibility of violations–given the acoustic/phonetic gap between the target stimulus and the correct response– is a measure of sensitivity to case agreement violations. The target stimuli consist of case substitutions (article in nominative case and noun in accusative case) using morphemes that are not identically frequent in Greek. The nominative morpheme (a fundamental case in the Greek nominal system), and the accusative morpheme (the case of the majority of verbs), are far more common than genitive morphemes (a case reserved for very specific functions in Greek). The results indicate a strong correlation between the perceptibility of violations and their detectability, thus underlining the interdependence of the cues' objective and subjective properties (such as detectability). As is true of the development of phonological consciousness, itself linked to learning to read and write, one becomes progressively more able to perceive these violations with age.

Perceptibility can also compete with another parameter of the detection of case violation – frequency. For example, genitive substitutions are very perceptible but not frequent, and thus more time is required for identifying violations. There thus exists a minimum frequency threshold, short of which the activation of case morphemes is not sufficient to detect violations.

One very strong finding has emerged from cross-linguistic research on on-line processing which uses this paradigm of error detection: violations which occur late in the sentence are more rapidly detected than those that occur earlier. This difference has been shown for children aged six and older, normal adults, and aphasics. This phenomenon provides information regarding the temporal components underlying detection processes. It has been understood to reveal the subjects' capacity to rapidly integrate linguistic properties of the context in order to formulate hypotheses about what is to follow.

It is in this perspective that research was undertaken looking at the detection of case agreement violations between articles and nouns in preverbal and postverbal NPs, using Greek-speaking 6- and 10-year-olds and adults as subjects (Kail and Diakogiorgi 1994, 1998; Diakogiorgi 1996). Aside from the fact that postverbal violations are more quickly detected than preverbal violations at all ages – thereby emphasizing the global effect of context – other interesting phenomena emerged. First, if the detection of agreement violations rests on the local mapping of the case markings of the article and noun, no differences should be observed between the article and the noun. This is the case for preverbal violations. Second, for all age groups, errors which are localized in the postverbal article are more rapidly detected than those that are localized in the postverbal noun. These findings indicate that both children and adults are capable of processing the morpho-syntactic information made available by context, and can rapidly integrate this information in the course of sentence processing, thereby formulating precise expectations with respect to subsequent information in the sentence. It is in this way that they are able to detect the violation when it occurs. Additionally, the results imply that contextual information of a morphological and nonsemantic nature facilitates processing (Tyler and Marslen-Wilson 1981). They suggest the existence of activation resources, highly developed even in young children, that allow for both the rapid activation of representational elements of the sentence and the maintenance of this activation for subsequent use in the course of sentence processing.

However, in spite of the uniformity of these processing strategies, some differences do exist. Adults integrate contextual morpho-syntactic information far more rapidly than do children. In addition, the effect of context is not always the same: in the absence of particular problems of perceptibility, context facilitates the detection of case violations–violations that occur after the verb are more quickly detected than those occurring before. However, when the violation is only slightly perceptible, the strong anticipation of the correct form inhibits the rapid activation of the perceived form, and this considerably slows its detection. The effect of context thus depends both on the perceptibility of the violation and the frequency of case substitute suffixes.

One sees the facilitating effects of context as early as ages six and seven. The inhibiting effects do not appear until a child is eight years old, when detection time diminishes considerably. The differential effects of context as a function of development are compatible with the idea that there exist two types of on-line linguistic processing. First, there is a conscious processing, controlled and relatively slow, which is most likely the source of the slow facilitating effects observed at six and seven years of age. In contrast is the more rapid automatic processing – initially non-attentional but followed, in certain cases, by slower controlled processing – which could account for the inhibiting effects found 8- and 10-year-old children and adults. This progressive automation is optimal in adults, where violations of the postverbal article are detected before the noun is presented, in other words, in the strictest sense of real time.

3. Final remarks

The cross-linguistic work done by various teams in the past twenty years utilizing the Competition Model has examined both the general principles governing off-line interpretation of sentences and the development of interpretive capacities in the child. Studies of on-line sentence processing, on the other hand, are so recent and conducted with such a restricted number of language samples, that a comparative evaluation can not be undertaken.

Nevertheless, the Competition Model must integrate new constraints linked to the microstructure of on-line processing. We have attempted to show how the assignability of cues, their perceptibility and detectability, must be articulated, as must the sequential and hierarchic constraints of context. The facilitating and inhibiting effects of context in the course of sentence processing must be pursued, especially in a developmental perspective. The phenomena reported here, derived mostly from languages that are morphologically rich, leave questions as to their generalization. This must be resolved with the help of further cross-linguistic research, the heuristic value of which has been amply demonstrated.

References

Altmann G. T. and Steedman M.J. 1988. "Interaction with context during human sentence processing". *Cognition*, 30: 191-238.

Ammon M.S. and Slobin D.I. 1979. "A cross-linguistic study of the processing of causative sentences". *Cognition*, 7: 3-17.

Amy G. and Vion M. 1986. "Les indices de traitement des phrases clivées chez l'enfant". *Bulletin de Psychologie*, Numéro spécial "Jugement et Langage", 39: 377-386.

Bamhamed M. 1996. *Traitement en temps réel des énoncés complexes: études comparatives interlangues arabe / français*. Thèse de Doctorat de Paris V.

Bamhamed M. and Kail M. 1996. "Mode d'appropriation des langues et traitement psycholinguistique: cas de l'arabe marocain et du français". *Dialogos Hispanicos*, 17: 45-66.

Bates E. and Mac Whinney B. 1987. "Competition, variation and language learning". In B. MacWhinney (ed.), *Mechanisms of Language Acquisition*, Hillsdale N.J., Lawrence Erlbaum.

Bates E., MacWhinney B., Caselli C., Devescovi A., Natale F., and Venza V. 1984. "A cross-linguistic study of the development of sentence interpretation strategies". *Child Development*, 55: 341-354.

Bates E., McNew S., MacWhinney B., Devescovi A. and Smith S. 1982. "Functional constraints on sentence processing: a cross-linguistic study". *Cognition*, 11: 245-299.

Bavin E.L. and Shopen T. 1989. "Cues to sentence interpretation in Walpiri". In B. MacWhinney and E. Bates (eds), *The crosslinguistic study of sentence processing*. Cambridge, New York: Cambrige University Press, 185-205.

Charvillat A. 1988. *Etude développementale de la compréhension et du traitement en temps réel des phrases pronominales en français et en espagnol*. Thèse de Doctorat, Université de Paris V.

Charvillat A. and Kail M. 1991. "The status of 'canonical SVO sentences' in French: a developmental study of the on-line processing of dislocated sentences". *Journal of Child Language*, 18: 591-608.

Diakogiorgi K. 1996. *Contraintes morphologiques et séquentielles dans le traitement de phrases en grec / étude développementale*. Thèse de Doctorat, Université de Paris V.

Diakogiorgi K. and Kail M. 1996. "De l'intérêt psycholinguistique d'une langue minoritaire: cas du grec". *Dialogos Hispanicos*, 17: 111-135

Frazier L. 1990. "Exploring the architecture of the language system". In G.T. Altmann (ed.), *Cognitive models of speech processing: Psycholinguistics and computational perspectives*. Cambridge, Mass: MIT Press, 409-433.

Givón T. 1979. *On understanding grammar*. New York: Academic Press.

Kail M. 1983 a. "L'acquisition du langage repensée: les recherches interlangues. Partie I. Principales propositions théoriques". *L'Année Psychologique*, 83: 225-258.

Kail M. 1983 b. "L'acquisition du langage repensée: les recherches interlangues. Partie II. Spécificités méthodologiques et recherches empiriques". *L'Année Psychologique*, 83: 561-596.

Kail M. 1987. "The development of sentence interpretation strategies from a cross-linguistic perspective". In C. Pfaff (ed.), *First and Second Language Acquisition Processes*. Cambridge, MA: Newbury House, 28-55.

Kail M. 1989. "Cue validity, cue cost, and processing types in sentence comprehension in French and Spanish". In B. MacWhinney and E. Bates (eds), *The Cross-Linguistic Study of Sentence Processing*. Cambridge, New-York, Cambridge University Press, 77-117.

Kail M. 1995. "Variations interlinguistiques et développement du langage". *Revue de Phonétique Appliquée*, N° Spécial, 112-113: 239-261.

Kail M. and Charvillat A. 1986. "Linguistic cues and processing types in French sentence comprehension". In I. Kurcz, G. W. Shugar and J. H. Danks (eds), *Knowledge and Language*. Amsterdam: North Holland, 349-357.

Kail M. and Charvillat A. 1988. "Local and topological processing in sentence comprehension by French and Spanish children", *Journal of Child Language*, 15: 637-662.

Kail M. and Bassano D. 1997. "Verb agreement processing in French: A study of on-line grammaticality judgments", *Language and Speech*, 40: 1, 25-47.

Kail M. and Diakogiorgi K. 1994. "Morphology and word order in the processing of Greek sentences". In I. Philippaki-Warburton, K. Nicolaidis and M. Sifianou (eds), *Themes in Greek linguistics.* (Current issues in linguistic theory 117). Amsterdam: John Benjamins, 325-332.

Kail M. and Diakogiorgi K. 1998. "On-line integration of morphosyntactic cues by Greek children and adults: A crosslinguistic perspective". In N. Dittmar and Z. Penner (eds), *Issues in the theory of language acquisition.* Bern: Peter lang, 177-201.

Kilborn K. 1991. "Selective impairement of grammatical morphology due to induced stress in normal German listeners: Implications for aphasia". *Brain and Language*, 41: 275-288.

Kilborn K. and Cooreman A. 1987. "Sentence interpretation strategies in adult Dutch-English bilinguals". *Applied Psycholinguistics*, 8, 415-431.

Lakoff G. and Thomson H. 1975. "Introducing cognitive grammar", Proceedings of the Berkeley Linguistic Society.

Li C. N. and Thomson H. 1976. "Subject and topic: a new typology for language". In C.N. Li (ed.) *Subject and topic.* New york: Academic Press.

Liu H., Bates E. and Li P. 1992. "Sentence interpretation in bilingual speakers of English and Chinese". *Applied Psycholinguistics*, 13: 451-484.

Li P., Bates E. and MacWhinney B. 1993. "Processing a language without inflections: A reaction time study of sentence interpretation in Chinese". *Journal of Memory and Language*, 32: 169-192.

MacWhinney B. 1987a. "The Competition Model". In B. MacWhinney (ed.) *Mechanisms of language acquisition.* Hillsdale, NJ: Erlbaum, 73-136

MacWhinney B. 1987b. "Applying the competition model to bilingualism". *Applied Psycholinguistics*, 8: 315-325.

MacWhinney B. 1987c. "Competition and transfer in second language learning". In R.J. Harris (ed.), *Cognitive processing in bilinguals.* Amsterdam: North-Holland, 371-390

MacWhinney B. and Bates E. (eds) 1989. *The crosslinguistic study of sentence processing.* Cambridge: CUP.

MacWhinney B., Bates E. and Kliegl R. 1984. "Cue validity and sentence interpretation in English, German and Italian". *Journal of Verbal Learning and Verbal Behavior*, 23: 127-150.

MacWhinney B., Pléh C. and Bates E. 1985. "The development of sentence comprehension in Hungarian". *Cognitive Psychology*, 17, 178-209.

MacWhinney B. and Osman-Sagi J. 1991. "Inflectional marking in Hungarian aphasics". *Brain and Language*, 41: 161-183.

McClelland J.L., St John M.J. and Taraban R. 1989. "Sentence comprehension: A parallel distributed processing approach". *Language and Cognitive Processes*, 4: 287-335.

McDonald J. L. 1986. "The development of sentence comprehension strategies in English and Dutch". *Journal of Experimental Child Psychology*, 41: 317-335.

McDonald J. L. and MacWhinney B. 1989. "Maximum Likelihood models for sentence processing". In B. MacWhinney and E. Bates (eds), *The crosslinguistic study of sentence processing.* Cambridge, CUP, 397-421.
Mimica I., Sullivan M. and Smith S. 1994. "An on-line study of sentence interpretation in native croatian speakers". *Applied Psycholinguitics*, 15: 237-261.
Perfetti C.A. 1990. "The cooperative language processors: Semantic influences in an autonomous syntax". In D.A. Balota, G.B. Florès d'Arcais, K. Rayner (eds), *Comprehension processes in reading.* Hillsdale: Erlbaum, 205-230.
Pléh C. 1990. "Word order and morphophonological factors in the development of sentence understanding in Hungarian". *Linguistics*, 28: 1449-1469
Rosch E. 1977. "Principles of categorization". In E. Rosch and B. Lloyd (eds). *Cognition and categorization.* Hillsdale, NJ: Erlbaum, 18-49.
Sasaki Y. 1991. "English and Japanese interlanguage comprehension strategies: An analysis based on the Competition Model". *Applied Psycholinguistics*, 12: 47-73.
Schelstraete M.A. 1993. "La conception du traitement syntaxique en compréhension de phrases". *L'Année Psychologique*, 93: 543-583
Slobin D.I. 1980. "Universal and particular in the acquisition of language". In L.R. Gleitman and E. Wanner (eds). *Language Acquisition, State of the art.* New York: Academic Press, 128-170.
Slobin D.I. (ed) 1985. *The crosslinguistic study of language acquisition.* Hillsdale, NJ: Erlbaum.
Smith S. and Bates E. 1987. "Accessibility of case and gender contrasts for agent-object assignments in Broca's aphasics and fluent anomics". *Brain and Language*, 30: 49-60.
Sokolov J. 1988. "Cue validity in Hebrew sentence comprehension". *Journal of Child Language*, 15: 129-155.
Taman H.A.1993. "The utilization of syntactic, semantic and pragmatic cues in the assigment of subject role in Arabic". *Applied Psycholinguistics*, 14: 299-317.
Tyler L.K. and Marslen-Wilson W.D. 1981. "Children's processing of spoken language". *Journal of Verbal Learning and Verbal Behavior*, 20: 400-416
Wulfeck B., Bates E. and Capasso R. 1991. "A cross-linguistic study of grammaticality judgments in Broca's aphasia". *Brain and Language*, 41: 311-336.

Universal *vs* Language-Specific Constraints in Agrammatic Aphasia
Is comparatism back?

Jean-Luc Nespoulous
Laboratoire de Neuropsycholinguistique Jacques-Lordat
Université de Toulouse-Le Mirail

Introduction

From the pioneering work of Roman Jakobson onwards, a few linguists – not that many to be sure (!) – do not hesitate to examine the different symptoms that can be observed in the verbal behavior of aphasic patients due to focal brain damage which is localized most of the time in the left hemisphere. Their main goal within the context of such an enterprise is to gather "external evidence" capable of validating, whenever possible, the structural architecture and the theoretical constructs put forward by such and such a linguistic theory to account for the intrinsic structure of natural languages.

From a psycholinguistic and neuropsychological point of view, the analysis of the same pathological phenomena attempts to specify the *functional architecture* of language within the human brain/mind. Indeed, on the basis of the observation of 'double dissociations' within aphasic patients' verbal performances, neuropsycholinguists try not only to better characterize the underlying determinism of pathological surface manifestations produced by such and such a patient but also – at a more general level – to identify the representations and the processes which are thought to be involved in language production and comprehension in normal individuals. Even if such an extrapolation – from pathology to normality – may amaze non-specialists, it is made possible (and legitimate) by the well-established fact that the linguistic symptoms generated by aphasics are by no means random: on the contrary, they have an underlying logic which, moreover, happens to be qualitatively similar to that which governs performance errors observed in normal-speaking subjects (Fromkin, 1973; Garrett, 1980).

In their attempt to identify structures and processes underlying language behavior in general, both of the above-mentioned (and complementary) approaches suffer however from an important shortcoming: until very recently, the vast majority of aphasiological studies have only dealt with a small number of languages: English, French, German, Dutch and Italian. These are, moreover, languages which are fairly similar from a structural and genetic point of view. When confronted with the structural diversity of languages, on the one hand, and with the (postulated) unity of the human brain and of its language faculty, on the other, a two-fold question emerges, quite obviously, from the observation of symptoms generated by aphasic patients belonging to quite different linguistic communities:

- which phenomena are *brain-dependent*, i.e., common to aphasic patients speaking structurally highly-contrasted languages?- which phenomena are *language-dependent*, i.e., variable from one language to another, on the basis of the structural properties of each one of them?

Among several research programs (formulated at Dan Slobin's instigation) which have been launched in the cognitive sciences in an attempt to answer both of these questions on the respective roles of 'cerebral hardware' and 'linguistic software' in the underlying determinism of aphasic symptoms, I will (briefly and partially) outline one of them, the "Cross-Linguistic Aphasia Study" (C.L.A.S), which was initiated by Lise Menn and Lorraine Obler in 1982, and which is currently supervised by Gonia Jarema and myself. Its goal is to analyze intra-linguistically and to compare cross-linguistically the disturbances observed, within 14 different languages,[1] in the processing of grammatical morphemes (both bound and free) as observed in what is classically labelled '*agrammatism*' in neurological wards (Menn and Obler, 1990).

1. Agrammatism: From the description of symptoms to their interpretation

Coined by Küssmaul (1887), and defined more accurately by Pick (1913), the word 'agrammatism' refers to the verbal behavior, either oral or written, that can be observed in some Broca's aphasics, most of the time after a left hemisphere lesion. Its main symptomatological features are, in Alajouanine's terms (1968): "reduction of sentences to their skeleton, relative preservation of nouns, constant use of verbs in the infinitive with omission of little words and absence of tense, gender and number markings" (our translation):

> *Ah, aujourd'hui, bonne soirée, parler littérature*
>
> *Salle à manger avec papa manquant; maman apporter bouillon avec fille; fils mettre table; la table, chat; enfin sept heures, travail fini.*
> (Alajouanine, 1968)[2]

Of paramount interest for clinicians is the distinction between agrammatism and *paragrammatism*. The latter type of symptoms appears within the context of Wernicke's aphasia – following a retro-rolandic lesion – and is classically characterized by *substitutions* of grammatical morphemes (instead of omissions, as in agrammatism):

> *Elle portait une galette **sur** sa grand-mère.*
>
> *J'étais **dans** la couturière*
> (Lecours and Lhermitte, 1979)[3]

In relation to the omission vs. substitution dichotomy – crucial for Alajouanine because it allows him to buttress a differential diagnosis between two clinical types of patients whose symptoms and lesions are different – one should nevertheless note the qualifications introduced by Lecours and Lhermitte (1979) when they define agrammatism by the following features:

> A slowing down of the speech rate, a general reduction in lexical availability, a reduction in the number and simplification of syntactic structures, reduced phrase length, a tendency to juxtaposition, deletions and substitutions specifically affecting grammatical morphemes (our translation).

From a psycholinguistic point of view, agrammatism is most often interpreted as the manifestation of an underlying *syntactic deficit*[4] – a deficit which, moreover, may also be observed, in some cases, in comprehension (Zurif, Caramazza and Myerson, 1972). As for paragrammatism, it could be the outcome of multiple lexical substitutions (=paraphasias), sometimes affecting more specifically grammatical morphemes (Pillon and Nespoulous, 1994).

2. The case for a cross-linguistic description and interpretation of agrammatic symptoms

As we have already mentioned, only a few languages have so far been examined in 'classical' aphasiological studies, and clinicians do not seem to worry much about this situation. In other words, the symptomatological convergence of data gathered from English, French and German aphasic patients does seem sufficient to them to posit, explicitly or implicitly, a 'universalist', and thus 'brain-dependent', interpretation of agrammatism. Only with considerable difficulty does one find the following comment in Alajouanine (1968), just after the above quotation: "the richer a language in such markings, the more massive the agrammatism" (our translation) but he does not go any further along these lines – as he could well have done, obviously, on the basis of a comparison between, for instance, agrammatism in English and in German. After all, following Alajouanine's logic, it is perhaps not a matter of chance if agrammatism was first identified in the German language!

Not until the eighties, however, did one begin to see the launching of cross-linguistic studies (Cf. supra. C.L.A.S). In what follows, we will only provide the reader with a limited overview of cross-linguistic agrammatic symptomatology, going from French and English to Hebrew, before observing Italian and coming back to French. We will only concentrate, all the way through, on manifestations of *omissions vs. substitutions* of grammatical morphemes.

2.1 French

In French, as is clearly stated by Alajouanine (cf. supra), the deletion of grammatical morphemes constitutes a defining feature of agrammatism. Such a symptom is usually considered as the surface manifestation of an underlying syntactic deficit: patients are thus no longer able adequately to compute syntactic matrices, and particularly complex ones. Patients tend to simplify language processing a) by abruptly juxtaposing a few lexical items, such as nouns or nominalized verbs (e.g. the infinitive in French, the gerund in English) and b) by deleting the grammatical morphemes. In French (and in English), these morphemes determine the major lexical constituents (articles, possessives, demonstratives) or indicate their syntactic function (prepositions, relative pronouns, subordinating conjunctions). Hence the frequent use of such an expression as "telegraphic style"[5] to grossly characterize the nature of verbal strings whose only residual syntactic marker relies on word order. It remains for the receiver to compensate for the missing elements on the basis of contextual and pragmatic inferences and, interestingly enough, such a 'guessing' process is fairly often successful with agrammatic patients, with whom communication thus remains possible; this is certainly not the case with other clinical types of aphasics.

2.2 Hebrew

Now, what happens when the patient, instead of speaking French or English, expresses himself in a language such as Hebrew? From the outset, one must recognize that Broca's aphasia – with its predominantly expressive symptomatology, usually following a pre-rolandic lesion (cf. supra) – does exist in each and every one of the 14 languages studied within the context of the C.L.A.S project: this no doubt gives some credit to the opinion of neurologists who are particularly interested in the functional specificity of some areas, or modules, in the cerebral cortex. Now the question arises which form the problem will take – what we will call, for the sake of brevity, a 'problem in the processing of grammatical morphemes' – in Hebrew (or Arabic), a language that inserts vocalic infixes within triconsonantal lexical matrices.

Ex: *k.t.b*   (= general concept of writing)
     katab   = he wrote, a reporter
     hiktib   = he dictated
     miktab   = letter
     ktobet   = addresses
     miktaba   = desk
(Baharav, 1990)

For an agrammatic patient speaking Hebrew, to resort to the deletion of the grammatical markers of his language is clearly impossible. It would condemn the patient to absolute mutism, since he could not, from a strictly phonological point of view, produce consonantal strings without any vowels! As a matter of fact, and as Grodzinsky (1982) hypothesized, Hebrew-speaking Broca's aphasics do indeed generate *substitutions* of grammatical morphemes and not deletions, thus demonstrating that *the structural properties of a language constrain*, up to a point, *the symptomatology to be observed*. Whatever neurologists may think, such a symptomatology is thus not only generated by the functional specificity of some cerebral areas; it is also (and perhaps above all) governed by the intrinsic characteristics of the language spoken by the patient.

Such an observation is of course not without consequences on the dogma of classical aphasiologists in relation to the differential diagnosis between patients with agrammatism and patients with paragrammatism (cf. supra). Indeed, when one considers that some patients, in some languages, substitute grammatical morphemes whereas other patients, in other languages, tend to omit them, the distinction between agrammatism and paragrammatism loses part of its 'historical' interest. Moreover, the fact that such substitutions are intra-category and not cross-category paraphasias tends to indicate clearly that those patients do not suffer from a deficit affecting the underlying planning of the category to which such morphemes belong. Their only difficulty lies in the selection of appropriate morphemes within an adequately activated category. Aside from a contiguity (or syntagmatic) disorder, in Jakobson's terms, agrammatism, in languages such as Hebrew, thus becomes a similarity (or paradigmatic) disorder. Far from being syntactic, the underlying deficit of agrammatic patients – at least in Hebrew – might very well turn out to be morphological!

2.3 Italian

Let us now move on to Italian, keeping in mind however the type of phenomena we have just observed in Hebrew. In Italian, as in many other Romance languages (excluding French), nominal and verbal roots can only exist with bound morphemic markers. Given its structural property, it follows that if agrammatism manifested itself – as it does in French and in English – by the deletion of grammatical morphemes (even when they are bound), one would be left with the production of a great number of non-words: e.g.: *pens-*, instead of *penso, pensi* or "*-pensa* (Miceli et al., 1989). In contrast with Hebrew though, such errors would not lead to the production of unpronounceable phonological strings.

Work by Miceli and his collaborators (1983, 1990) clearly shows that such deletions do not occur in the agrammatic corpora they studied. As in Hebrew, Italian agrammatics indeed generate intra-category substitutions of bound morphemes, which does not prevent them, at the same time, from omitting the free-standing grammatical morphemes that their language also contains – as in English and French.

It follows from these observations that the processing problem that agrammatic patients do have with the grammatical morphemes of their language cannot violate its canonical structural properties. Such a difficulty would manifest itself, within different languages (Hebrew vs. English) as well as within a single language (Italian, in our example), either by the deletion of free-standing grammatical morphemes (easily omitted, after all), or by the substitution of bound grammatical morphemes, when the deletion of the latter would lead to the production of bare stem forms that do not exist in some languages. Moreover, the coexistence, within the same patient, of both omissions and substitutions of grammatical morphemes would seem to invalidate again – as in Hebrew, although for different reasons – the classical clinical distinction between agrammatism and paragrammatism.

2.4 Back to French

Let us now come back to French, bearing the fruits of this brief cross-linguistic journey. Indeed, as indicated by Alajouanine and all French-speaking aphasiologists, the omission of grammatical morphemes is very frequent among French agrammatic patients. But is it not possible also, in these patients, to come across substitutions of grammatical morphemes, such as the ones that are produced, in this same language, by Wernicke's aphasics with paragrammatism?

The study of Mr. Clermont,[6] a French-speaking agrammatic patient with whom I have been working for over ten years (Nespoulous et al., 1990), seems to me particularly relevant in relation with the issues being discussed in the present paper.

Briefly stated, Mr. Clermont, six months post onset (of his illness), showed evidence of a prototypical clinical picture of agrammatism for any French-speaking neurologist: his oral performances systematically revealed most of the symptoms that were grouped together by Alajouanine in the above-mentioned definition, including the omission of grammatical morphemes.

However, on a closer examination of his verbal behavior – carried out, though, four years post onset – several phenomena emerged which deserve to be mentioned:

- If Mr. Clermont indeed resorts quasi-systematically to the omission of free-standing grammatical morphemes when he is producing spontaneous speech or narrative discourse, it is clear that his inflectional morphology remains adequately formed. Not a single error can be noted in his handling of verbal paradigms in particular. From such an intra-language observation, it can be postulated that the processing of free-standing grammatical morphemes, on the one hand, and that of bound morphemes, on the other, may depend upon distinct psycholinguistic (and possibly neural) systems. This is a result that many hard core linguists might appreciate, if only they were eager to look into aphasic data for 'external evidence' likely to substantiate their theoretical frameworks (Cf. supra)!

- In relation to free-standing grammatical morphemes (articles, prepositions, pronouns, in particular), a comparative analysis of Mr. Clermont's performances in different types of tasks (spontaneous speech, written production, repetition and oral reading, for instance) shows very clearly that error types vary a great deal from one task to another. Indeed, the frequent omission of grammatical morphemes only occurs in spontaneous speech and in oral narrative discourse (= "Little Red Riding Hood"). In contrast, when asked to narrate the same story in written form, the number of omissions

decreases and the number of substitutions increases – *on the same types of grammatical morphemes.* In oral reading, similarly, the number of substitutions is definitely greater than the number of omissions.
- Finally, if we compare Mr. Clermont's performances in spontaneous speech (a) when agrammatism appeared in his oral production (i.e. six months post onset) and (b) when the Cross-Linguistic Aphasia Study began (four years later), one notes that the quasi-systematic omissions of free-standing grammatical morphemes – a characteristic of the initial phase – have been replaced by more and more substitutions affecting the same grammatical constituents. Undoubtedly, there are very few clinicians and investigators who will dare interpret such a symptomatological change as a change in the underlying deficit!

In summary, on the common basis of (a) the data gathered in different languages within the C.L.A.S Project and of (b) the data coming from the in-depth analysis of Mr. Clermont's performances, it clearly appears:
1) that there indeed exist problems in aphasic pathology which disrupt the processing of grammatical morphemes, regardless of the language spoken by the patient before his cerebral lesion;
2) however, that such problems manifest themselves differently – omissions vs. substitutions – in relation to the intrinsic structural properties of the different languages under analysis;
3) that within languages admitting of such phenomena, the simultaneous appearance of both manifestations – omissions and substitutions – can be observed;
4) that consequently, in languages that admit the omission of free-standing grammatical morphemes (e.g. French), the latter phenomena may legitimately be re-interpreted as substitutions by a "null morphematic element" – such an interpretation being further strengthened by the fact that omissions and substitutions come to bear on the same grammatical constituents;
5) that considering the fact that the substitutions of free-standing grammatical morphemes – when observed (as in Mr. Clermont's case) – are intra-categorical, the hypothesis of the existence of an underlying syntactic deficit which would prevent the patient from constructing syntactic matrices seems to be invalidated. In contrast to this, the alternative hypothesis according to which agrammatic patients have problems in selecting the adequate grammatical morpheme within its correct paradigm seems to deserve attention. Such an interpretation finds further support from the agrammatic data gathered (by other teams within the C.L.A.S Project) in highly inflected

languages such as Finnish and Polish, in which substitutions are indeed prevalent;
6) that the distinction between agrammatism and paragrammatism – although traditional in French, English and German neurological wards – ought to be given up, as Heeschen proposes (1985).

3. What kind of deficit?

The observation in different languages of processing problems (subsequent to brain damage) in relation to grammatical morphemes raises, of course, another crucial question: are such problems – appearing at the surface level as omissions and/or substitutions – the consequence of a disruption in the access to closed-class lexical items from correctly computed semantic representations, or are they the result of a cognitive, and representational deficit at a deeper, semantic level of processing?

It is still not easy to give a definite answer to such a question. Nevertheless, in most cases, the general behavior of the patients makes it possible to answer the former question positively and the latter negatively. To back up such an interpretation, three phenomena, frequently observed in agrammatic patients, can be mentioned:

- First, *performance variability*, according to which, for instance, a preposition may be omitted here and adequately produced there. Such a variability clearly indicates that agrammatism is not the outcome of a competence deficit, or of a "loss", in Jakobson's terms.[7] It suggests that the omission and/or substitution of grammatical morphemes finds its source in the limitation of certain processing capacities, rather than in a representational deficit;
- Second, the presence of *self-correction*, particularly when the patient produces substitutions. Whether such attempts be successful or whether they fail – which is very often the case – they indeed seem to show that the patient is utterly conscious of the inadequacy of his production in relation to the underlying representation which had been activated in his mind;
- Third, the use of *adaptive, "palliative", strategies*. Agrammatic patients often resort to alternative lexical resources available in their language to make up for their inability to produce grammatical morphemes adequately. We have demonstrated elsewhere (Nespoulous, 1973), for instance, that such patients, often unable to produce verbal *tense markers* (with the exception of Mr. Clermont!), tended to use temporal adverbs (such as "yesterday",

"tomorrow") as well as the names of days or months in order to provide their message with temporal information (e.g.: *demain, partir, campagne; dimanche, montagne*)[8]. Similarly, whenever they are unable to indicate *number* via articles or verbal inflections, we have noted the tendency for some patients to resort to quantifiers and numerals. As far as spatial prepositions are concerned, some patients tend to replace them by the adequate gestures. All such strategies tend to indicate that it is lexical access only which is disturbed in those patients, an observation that is corroborated – as mentioned above – by the fact that substitutions, when present, are "intra-category": preposition/preposition, article/article, and so on.

4. By way of a conclusion...

The existence subsequent to brain damage, of a selective impairment in the processing of grammatical morphemes – whatever the language, including Sign Language (Poizner et al., 1987) – clearly indicates that such constituents indeed have a specific status both in the *structural architecture* of the languages of the world and in *the functional architecture* of language in the human brain/mind.

The fact that the surface manifestations of the deficits to be found in agrammatic patients may vary, due to the canonical structural properties of each and every language, reveals the prominent role that such properties exert upon cognitive and cerebral processing.

It follows from this double observation that, if neuropsycholinguistics indeed is widening its scope to include the analysis of pathological phenomena generated by patients speaking highly contrasted languages, it is equally able to provide relevant data for whomever is interested in *universals*, be they cognitive or cerebral. Properly conceived, such an approach requires the inclusion of at least three cognitive sciences: linguistics, psycholinguistics and neuropsychology. All three disciplines, whose terminological fusion yields the word "neuropsycholinguistics", are clearly *complementary*:

- *linguistics* specifies the structural properties a particular language;
- *psycholinguistics* characterizes the underlying mental processes which manipulate such structures (or representations) in language production and comprehension. By doing so, it sometimes forgets that the human mind is located in the brain;
- and it is *neuropsychology* which – mainly on the basis of in-depth studies of brain-damaged subjects – correlates the psycholinguistic processes of the human mind with the neurophysiological mechanisms of the human brain, in an attempt to reduce the classical Cartesian brain/mind dualism.

Complementary though they may be, all three above-mentioned disciplines are nonetheless *hierarchically related*. In fact, if it is indeed possible to be a linguist without being a psycholinguist, it seems utterly impossible to be a psycholinguist without a strong background in linguistics. Similarly, if it is conceivable to be a psycholinguist without dabbling in neuropsycholinguistics, it seems utterly impossible to have an interest in language pathology without a strong background in psycholinguistics and in linguistics.

The fact that linguistics, within the context of such a hierarchical approach to interdisciplinary relationships, gains the status of *central discipline* – the "inner circle" around which both psycholinguistics and neuropsychology revolve – should put the hard-core linguists' minds at ease. Indeed, why would language pathology be considered any longer as a marginal discipline within the context of 'language sciences' when such a core status is offered to general linguistics? The current development of the cognitive sciences, and the important and frequent participation of linguistics in such a development, should more than ever substantiate the fruitfulness of observations which, even if (or when) they are not *stricto sensu* linguistic, are nonetheless crucial if one's intention is finally to better understand, through language, the functioning of human cognition.

Notes

1. English, Dutch, German, Icelandic, Swedish, French, Italian, Polish, Serbo-Croatian, Hindi, Finnish, Hebrew, Chinese and Japanese (in the chronological order of their presentation in Menn and Obler's volume, 1990).
2. "Well, to-day, nice evening, speaking literature", "dining-room with father absent; mother bringing soup with daughter; son setting table; the table, cat; at last seven o'clock, work over" (our translation).
3. "She was bringing a cake on her grandmother", "I was in the dressmaker" (our translation).
4. Other interpretations, which we cannot present at length here, exist however in the aphasiological literature: a deficit in accessing grammatical morphemes (Bradley, Garrett and Zurif (1980); a phonological deficit (Kean, 1977, 1979, 1980); a morphological deficit (Lapointe, 1987); agrammatism = the manifestation of adaptive strategies and not a deficit (Kolk *et al.*, 1985).
5. On the inadequacy of such an expression, see Nespoulous (1973).
6. A pseudonym given to the patient on account of the fact that he was taken care of in the hospital at Clermont-Ferrand.
7. The stability of errors, and omissions in particular, can only be observed in agrammatic patients in the acute stage at the beginning of their illness, when their clinical picture is very severe (cf. the clinical evolution of Mr. Clermont, Nespoulous et al., 1988).
8. "tomorrow, going countryside"; "Sunday, mountain" (my translation).

References

Alajouanine, T. 1968. *L'aphasie et le langage pathologique*, Paris: Baillière.
Baharav, E. 1990. "Agrammatism in Hebrew: two case studies". In L. Menn and L. Obler (Eds.) *Agrammatic aphasia*, Amsterdam: John Benjamins, Vol.2., 1087-1190.
Bradley, D., Garrett, M. and Zurif, E. 1980. "Syntactic deficits in Broca's aphasia. In D. Caplan (Ed.) *Biological studies of mental processes*, Cambridge (Mass.): The M.I.T Press, 269-286.
Fromkin, V. 1973. *Speech errors as linguistic evidence*, The Hague; Mouton.
Garrett, M. 1980. "Levels of processing in sentence production". In B. Butterworth (Ed.) *Language Production*, Vol. 1. New-York: Academic Press, 177-220.
Grodzinsky, J. 1982. *Syntactic representation in agrammatism: evidence from hebrew*, Paper presented at the Academy of Aphasia, New York.
Heeschen, K. 1985. "Agrammatism vs. paragrammatism: a fictitious opposition". In M-L Kean (Eds.) *Agrammatism*, London: Academic Press, 207-248.
Kean, M-L. 1977. "The linguistic interpretation of aphasic syndromes: agrammatism in Broca's aphasia, an example", *Cognition*, 5: 9-46.
Kean, M-L. 1979. "Agrammatism: a phonological deficit?", *Cognition*, 7: 69-83.
Kean, M-L. 1980. "Grammatical representations and the description of language processes". In D. Caplan (Ed.) *Biological studies of mental processes*, Cambridge (Mass.): The M.I.T Press.
Kolk, H., Van Grunsven, M. and Keyser, A. 1985. "On parallelism between production and comprehension in agrammatism", In M-L Kean (Eds.) *Agrammatism*, London: Academic Press, 165-206.
Kussmaul, A. 1887. *Die Störungen der Sprache*. Leipzig: Vogel.
Lapointe, S. 1983. "Some issues in the linguistic description of agrammatism", *Cognition*, 14: 1-39.
Lecours, A.R. and Lhermitte, F. 1979. *L'aphasie*, Paris: Flammarion.
Menn, L. and Obler, L. (Eds.) 1990. *Agrammatic aphasia*, Amsterdam: Benjamins.
Miceli, G., Mazzuchi, A., Menn, L. and Goodglass, H. 1983. "Contrasting cases of Italian agrammatism without comprehension deficits", *Brain and Language*, 19: 65-97.
Miceli, G. and Mazzuchi, A. 1990. "Agrammatism in Italian: two case studies". In L. Menn and L. Obler (Eds.) *Agrammatic aphasia*, Amsterdam: John Benjamins, Vol.1., 717-816.
Poizner, H., Klima, E. and Bellugi, U. 1987. *What the hands reveal about the brain*, Cambridge (Mass.), The M.I.T Press.
Nespoulous, J-L. 1973. *Approche linguistique de divers phénomènes d'agrammatisme*, Thèse pour le Doctorat de 3ème cycle, Université de Toulouse-Le Mirail.

Nespoulous, J-L., Dordain, M., Perron, C., Ska, B., Bub, D., Caplan, D., Mehler, J. and Lecours, A.R. 1988. "Agrammatism in sentence production without comprehension deficits: reduced availability of syntactic structures and/or of grammatical morphemes? A case study", *Brain and Language*, 33: 273-295.

Nespoulous, J-L., Dordain, M., Perron, C., Jarema, G. and Chazal, M. 1990. "Agrammatism in French: two case studies". In L. Menn and L. Obler (Eds.) *Agrammatic aphasia*, Amsterdam: Benjamins, Vol.1., 623-716.

Pick, A. 1913. *Die agrammatische sprachstörungen*, Berlin: Springer.

Pillon, A. and Nespoulous, J-L. 1994. "Perturbations syntaxiques dans le langage aphasique". In X. Séron and M. Jeannerod (Eds.) *Neuropsychologie Humaine*, Bruxelles: Mardaga, 390-407.

Zurif, E., Caramazza, A. and Myerson, R. 1972. "Grammatical judgments of agrammatic aphasics", *Neuropsychologia*, 10: 405-417.

Schizophasia and Cognitive Dysfunction

Bernard Pachoud
Université de Picardie

Introduction

Psychopathology should attempt to account for disorders observed in patients by making hypotheses concerning the underlying mechanisms in cases where the dysfunction of these mechanisms may help explain the disorders, and where the same mechanisms are responsible for behavior in normal individuals. According to the logic of psychopathology, it can be assumed that schizophrenic language disturbances are caused by an impairment of the cognitive processes involved in speech production, which illustrates the importance of their role. In order to test this hypothesis, we will begin by reviewing the basic characteristics of schizophasia, before attempting to study both the disorders and cognitive dysfunctions which are currently cited as offering explanations for the principal symptoms displayed by schizophrenics.

1. Indeterminacy of meaning in schizophrenic speech

There is general agreement in recent psycholinguistic research which recognizes the fact that schizophrenic alterations to speech cannot be reduced to a simple language skill disorder: it is commonly held that these alterations are not merely equivalent to an impaired command of the rules governing the syntax and semantics of language, but that they basically depend on a pragmatic dimension (Schwartz, 1982). While there are exceptions to this observation, i.e. the schizophrenic practice of producing neologisms (creating portmanteau words or 'blends') and semantic paraphasia (using words with the wrong meaning), which are semantic disturbances, these anomalies alone cannot adequately account for the disorganization of the schizophrenic discourse which is often observed in the absence of any such semantic disorders. This schizophasic disorganization actually depends on the pragmatic dimension, if pragmatics can be extended to cover the principles of coherent discourse and therefore of the interpretability of the discourse (Trognon, 1987, 1988; Frith, 1992). What often makes schizophrenic speech discontinuous and 'difficult to follow', even incoherent or hermetic, is basically the fact that the listener is unable to make the inferences required to determine the meaning of the utterances or to grasp their coherence. Since Rochester and Martin (1979), the focus has been on this inferential aspect of the disorder: the inferences required to understand frequently cannot be made by the listener, as the information needed (extra-linguistic or contextual) is not available. Typical characteristics of schizophrenic speech are:

(a) Indeterminability of the referents of 'deictic' terms: it is not unusual for patients to use pronouns referring to persons not introduced in previous statements and who do not belong to the context shared with the interlocutor, thus making it impossible to understand who is being referred to.

(b) The use of polysemic terms making disambiguation impossible gives rise to the same type of indeterminacy of meaning in schizophrenic utterances. As in the previous case, the disorder is usually related to the schizophrenic's inability to take the context into account, and specifically the context shared with his (or her) interlocutors.

(c) Coherence and discourse continuity disorders are clearly the most prevalent and most typical (Rieberо, 1994). Again, when no interpretation making it possible to restore coherence at an implicit level is readily accessible, judgement is made by inference. Indeed, the most typical feature of schizophrenic discourse is its discontinuity, with sudden changes of topic (what current psychiatric semiology refers to as 'derailment'), utterances abruptly cut off in mid-sentence (i.e. 'blocking') and all sorts of breaks in discourse such as, according to the psychiatric semiology, elusive answers (or 'tangentiality') and digressions, related to a thought disorder referred to as 'dissociative process' ever since Bleuler (1911).

To present a more accurate description of such cases of discontinuity, a distinction can first be made between those that appear in the patient's utterances, referred to as *'intra-discursive or monologue breaks'* and those affecting the course of sequencing between the interlocutors, i.e. *'inter-discursive or dialogue breaks'*.

In the case of *monologue discontinuity*, breaks in coherence can be considered as a result of violating the constraints of textual coherence. Research has mostly studied the lack of cohesion between adjacent utterances in schizophrenic discourse, with fewer and fewer conjunctions being used and, most importantly, misuse of pragmatic anaphora, as patients use 'deictic' terms with ambiguous referents (Blanchet, 1994). The analysis of the textual coherence of narrative speech by schizophrenics (speaking English) also clearly showed that the hierarchical organization of utterances had been lost, reflecting a disturbance in the planning of the discourse. Consequently there were difficulties of interpretation due to the difficulty of identifying the central statements (which determine the overall meaning) and the subordinate statements (intended as a complement to the central meaning) (Hoffman, 1986).

In the case of *dialogue discontinuity*, when two interlocutors are involved, such disturbances to coherence are apparent in the unexpected, inadequate or apparently incongruous comments made by the patient in the exchange, violating the linking constraints which guarantee the cohesion and coherence of turn-taking. These constraints, as described by Moeschler (1985), require the second utterance to be on the same topic as the first, to take into account the content of the utterance and to respond to the illocutionary force of the previous utterance. In addition to these different dialogue breaks, there are also the breaks described by Trognon (1987) as "conversational declutching": while they may respect linking constraints, there is a change of referential context without any explicit warning sign being given.

The detailed analysis of discourse breaks has not yet been completed and an objection could be raised, as schizophrenics are not the only people to answer elusively, to lose track of what they are saying or to suddenly change topic. What makes such infringements of conversational coordination pathological is firstly their high frequency in schizophrenic discourse and secondly the fact that patients virtually never "repair" the statement, nor produce any linguistic or vocal markers of these shifts; it seems that they are not even aware of them. It may be that, under normal circumstances, the choice of topic for the conversation results from some sort of agreement (albeit tacit) between the parties, and therefore from some kind of negotiation, similar to those described by Goffman (1967, 1981) for the opening and closing of conversational exchanges. A sudden change of focus, under normal circumstances and in the absence of any negotiation, would therefore lead into a repair sequence designed to maintain the cooperative framework for the exchange. It is these requirements, necessary for cooperation or coordination, which schizophrenics turn out to be unable to meet.

(d) This inability to carry out 'self-repair' extends to self-correction of all speech errors; compared to control subjects, schizophrenic patients make fewer attempts to correct such errors, and when they do so, it is often in an inappropriate manner (Leudar, 1992).

2. Examples of schizophrenic discourse breaks

A small number of examples of discourse breaks have been selected from transcripts of clinical interviews with a 29-year-old French schizophrenic. The patient is hospitalized, his medical condition has been developing over the past eleven years and he shows signs of severe dissociation; in the excerpts quoted, he expresses delusions concerning his parentage, speculating as to whether his mother might actually be one of the nurses.

> Excerpt No. 1 (D = Doctor, A = Patient) (Translated from French)
> D 44: Yes (4 sec.) *You were talking about your mother and Mrs. Frame [a nurse]*.
> A 44: Yes (3.) *I - I* (4.8) *I don't recognize my mother... I was too-raumatized*.
> D 45: *You were..?*
> A 45: *Too-raumatized. I was too-raumatized,* (11.) *You could have a look at my appendicitis... it hurts*.
> D 46: *What hurts?*

A first discourse break is seen in A 44 between *I don't recognise my mother...* and *I was too-raumatized*. When asked about his doubts on his parentage, the patient tries to find a justification, begins articulating one and then follows up with what can be seen as a change of focus that is neither marked nor repaired: *I was too-raumatized*. What produces a break here is the fact that the connection between the two assertions is not immediately accessible, even if possible links can be inferred *post hoc*. The difficulty in interpretation, as shown by the interrogative reaction of the doctor, can therefore be explained by the neologism *too-raumatized* ("traumaté" in French), the agent deletion after the passive and the transitional coherence which cannot be immediately inferred. In answer to the doctor's question, the patient merely repeats his own statement and then continues, after 11 seconds silence, by changing focus; again the change is not negotiated, 'repaired' or even marked. While *post hoc* conjectures can provide semantic links between the different verbal speech acts (between *I don't recognise my mother, I was too-raumatized* and *have a look at my appendicitis... it hurts*), it is still quite clear that the patient's intention as a speaker is discontinuous. And it is this discontinuity in his overall discourse purpose which makes any interpretation indeterminate and gives the impression of a break.

> Excerpt No. 2
> A 47: *When you hear a mother... the very first second... you're the... happiest person on earth.*

D 48:   *Is that what you feel when your mother comes to see you?*
A 48:   *Yeah, I am delighted... delighted.*
D 49:   *You're delighted*
A 49:   *Yeah*
D 50:   *But you said it was the first second? As if afterwards... it didn't last... why do you say the first second?*
A 50:   *... Eh... because it's: she's my mother to me* ((*very softly*))
D 51:   *Because?*
A 51:   *She's my mother to me* (4.) *there's a wall between us I think.* (8.) *Is my problem serious?* (5.) *Isn't it serious?* ((*laugh*))
D 52:   *What do you think your problem is actually?...*
A 52:   *Eh* (12.5) *actually I used to have money in:: in the bank* (7.5)
(...)

The break between the last two utterances consists of an 'inter-discursive or dialogue break'. It follows a request for information related to the patient's concern about his own state of health as expressed in the previous utterance (A 51: *Is my problem serious?*). When asked to explain what he means, he is unable to do so (*eh::* 12 seconds silence) and then he goes on (*actually I used to have money in:: in the bank*). Thus the illocutionary constraint is met (having the question answered), but the coordination constraint on the content of the utterance is not; *what do you think your problem is actually?* refers to the patient's own question, *Is my problem serious?*, while the patient's answer in A 52 is: *actually I used to have money in:: in the bank*. It is noteworthy that this utterance complies nevertheless with a form of (strictly local) coordination which is based on the last word of the question asked, so in answer to *what do you think your problem is actually?*, the patient answers *actually I used to have money in:: in the bank*. The patient here presents a number of examples of this adjacency-based type of coordination, 'bouncing off' the last word of the previous utterance, at the expense of more general or context-based constraints governing coordination and therefore the overall coherence of the exchange.

What therefore makes schizophrenic discourse pathological, regardless of the content, is first the difficulty in ascertaining the actual significance, working out what the patient 'means'. The recent contribution of pragmatics has been to analyse the indeterminability of the meaning in terms of a misuse of pragmatic functions (mainly referential), breaks in coherence that can be described in terms of violations of linking constraints.

The perspective as observed to date remains descriptive; in particular what we refer to as 'breaks' can be observed as such by the hearers who are in fact interrupted in the flow of their interpretative activity in such a way that the continuity of meaning is lost. However, if we wish to go beyond these formalized descriptions and attempt to explain the disorders of schizophrenia, then the study should focus on the point of view of the patient as speaker rather than the point of view of the hearer, and consequently emphasize the viewpoint of speech production. Attention will then be focused on the schizophrenic's inability to make his speech coherent and to coordinate turn-taking, i.e. on the impairments in planning, adjusting and controlling speech production.

At this stage, the study of schizophasia can be associated with recent research into cognitive disorders that may explain schizophrenic behavior patterns, particularly as this research tends to concentrate on the processes involved in action management and control.

3. A cognitive hypothesis for a motor control disorder in schizophrenia

My intention is not to present the different directions investigated by cognitive research into schizophrenia. The current trend is towards hypotheses focusing on motor skills due to the wealth of explanations they offer for the main symptoms of the condition. Influences are observed on motor skills, either as a deficit (apragmatism) or as a disorganization of action and an abnormal experience of action. These disorders also prove to be eminently observable in speech produced by patients.

The present study will refer only to the cognitive model of schizophrenia developed by Frith (1992), which focus on the mechanisms involved in action and can be summed up in three hypotheses:

1) an inability to carry out intentional actions, i.e. turning intentions into acts; this may be a cause of impoverished action and speech observed in the negative forms of schizophrenia.
2) a planning disorder may account for the disorganization of action and of speech in schizophrenic patients, this being exacerbated by the increase in automatic behavior patterns, with certain environmental stimuli triggering motor routines. This could explain, among others, the 'distractible speech' of schizophrenics, with sudden changes in discourse topic in response to irrelevant stimuli in the environment.
3) the third, more specific hypothesis aims at explaining 'agency disorders' as expressed by the patient feeling that he is not the initiator or the subject of his own acts. This gives rise to pathological phenomena such as the

experience of alien control where the patient has the impression of acting under the influence of outside forces, and the phenomenon of thought insertion, involving a feeling of being dispossessed of one's own thoughts or a feeling of a loss of control over one's own thoughts.

Such 'agency disorders' may be caused by an impairment of the process known as monitoring of action, through which individuals become aware both of their current action and their initiative to act, and by which they can exercise control over the action and change its course. This mechanism is now explained by a neurophysiological theory of movement control whereby any motor command transmitted to the effector system is simultaneously sent as a 'corollary discharge' to the central integrative structures. Here the effects of the movement are anticipated and are continuously compared to the effects observed, thus providing continual adjustment of the movement in progress. This theory could not only account for the ability to make early corrections to motor errors (in less than 50 milliseconds, and therefore before any perceptive feedback of motor effects), but could also explain our feeling of agency. The hypothesis that this mechanism may be impaired in cases of schizophrenia has been confirmed by experiments involving an error correction task in which schizophrenics record low scores (Frith, 1992).

These hypotheses can be synthesized by stating that they all focus on the processing of intentions. This involves both a deficit in the initiation of action (hence the negative signs of schizophrenia such as poverty of action and of speech), and a deficit in the awareness of intention and the subsequent control of action (hence the disorganization of the discourse and pathological phenomena such as thought insertion or delusions of control by alien forces).

One problem with this type of model, however, is that it is founded on the key presupposition of 'prior intentions', whose subsequent processing is the only aspect taken into account – one which is moreover assumed to put these intentions into effect, or to ensure one's awareness of them. Thus the problem of the origin of intentions or their production is not addressed. The philosopher Dennett (1991) was the first to criticize this reasoning when referring to the speech production model proposed by Levelt (1989), which similarly presupposes initial intentions (described as the speaker's intentions) and for which the language system would only serve as a means of providing a verbal format. In intuitive terms, however, it seems quite unlikely that any utterance could be the result of processing prior thought into words, where this is taken as a thought which the subject may access non-linguistically. In verbal exchanges in particular, a number of utterances seem to be 'reactions' to the previous utterance, with the connotation of automatism inherent in the notion of reaction. Can such 'reactive' utterances be considered intentional? Surely it is ultimately the very idea of intentionality of speech that needs to be re-assessed.

Recent contributions in the philosophy of action have helped give a clearer idea of the concept of intention. On the basis of the main conclusions of conceptual analyses by Livet (1995), it can be shown that action, even intentional action, is only very partially specified by the initial intention, which simply sets the expected or target effects. It is invariably in the course of performing the action that the action become specified, and this performance is basically controlled by motor automatisms. Yet various processes are involved in the course of action: processes of adjusting, fine-tuning the automatisms used by the agent to fully specify the action and to appropriate it in intentional terms. Intentionality of action is not therefore distinct at the point of initiation, but is rather acquired over the automatism of the action by means of control, error correction and adjustment processes, which combine to make up the *monitoring* process. The monitoring process is therefore less important as a means of access to a prior intention and more important as a means of enabling the subject to specify what was initially an inadequately determined intention (being nothing more than the identification of a target); the process then influences the intentional appropriation of the action through the control exercized over the actual process of its unfolding in time.

Such a view can naturally be extended to speech production and would seem well suited to this domain. It is clear that when we speak, we do not usually conceive of what we are going to say before we articulate the utterance; our intention to convey meaning being, as it were, immediately an act in itself. Moreover, there are quite clearly times when there is a discrepancy between intention and the verbal realization of the intention, as indicated by expressions of hesitation – particularly when efforts are being made to produce certain effects, in other words when the speaker wants to increase his control over his speech. Such control nonetheless presupposes that the effects of the spoken word are anticipated and are the result of a choice, the choice of 'editing' or 'censoring' certain turns of phrase, a selective exercise that then occurs at a relatively late stage in speech production. The intentionality of speech may then be seen as operating more as a control exercized over expression, i.e. 'monitoring' the speech act, rather than the point at which the intentions are generated and which basically is beyond our conscious control.

Such a view, while somewhat speculative, finds an approximate illustration in schizophrenic language disorders and the relevant cognitive models proposed. If it is clear that the monitoring process is impaired in schizophrenics who no longer have the capacity to anticipate the effects of their speech early enough to be able to modulate the course of their utterances, all that is then left for patients to do is to observe the effects of their utterances. This is also the reason why they cannot realize what their intentions are until after they have completed the articulation of their utterances. Being unable to make adjustments in the course of action, they are also unable to appropriate the action as an intention. The difference in time between the subject who is aware of his intention in the course of action and the schizophrenic who can only understand after the action is completed is a mere fraction of a second, but this could well be crucial in relation to the intentionality of action, as a tiny but decisive time lapse required for an awareness of the effects of the action.

This hypothesis tallies with the schizophrenic's failure to correct errors in utterances. A timed study of verbal production by schizophrenics showed that when they did make corrections, they did so later than normal subjects (Leudar, 1992).

The difficulties faced by schizophrenics in planning their discourse and coordinating it with utterances made by others (all of which underlie schizophasia), are equally related to the role played by intentions in verbal exchanges. They are involved in understanding, if understanding is considered to be the grasping of meaning, and therefore of the speaker's intention as claimed by Grice (1957). They are also involved in conversational coordination, for which the intentions of one's interlocutor need to be grasped. The coordination of discourse with another party in the context of conversation is quite a complex task requiring not only the planning of discourse (in compliance with the linear structure of language), but also the situation imposed by dialogue, with turn-taking, adjustments with reference to what has just been said and therefore the need to improvise an utterance appropriate to the situation, which will have to be re-appraised at each new turn. In a situation of interaction and from the viewpoint of speech production, there is therefore a neat blend of improvization and planning, which means that the speaker's plan has to be reframed each time he speaks. It is particularly important to be able to delay certain speech acts because of the linearity of language – the ultimate purpose being not to lose the thread of what one intends to say, of the general subject of conversation and even of certain illocutionary obligations which the speaker may choose to delay. The ability not to lose the thread (i.e. not to lose track of one's goals), and the ability to delay certain acts depend basically on the ability to conceive of the action as an intention. And in the end, what is involved in the coordination of individual discourse with another party, if not the ability to rearrange intentions and therefore one's overall framework at every turn in the interaction? Verbal interactions thus appear as an excellent situation for the study of the management of intentions, which has a bearing on the pragmatic skill of the individual to coordinate his own discourse and also to coordinate himself with reference to the other party in verbal interactions.

Conclusion

In conclusion, it would seem that schizophasic coherence disorders are basically the result of a deficit in discursive and interlocutory coordination; the deficit itself appears as secondary to a disorder in the monitoring and processing of intentions, in accordance with one of the key cognitive models for schizophrenia. If the hypothesis is accepted, it means that schizophrenic language disorders, being of a pragmatic nature and therefore considered to involve 'high level' cognitive processes (involving inferences), may actually depend on an elementary (i.e. 'low level') cognitive process which is not specifically linguistic and which, for the case in question, is a process involved in motor control and for which a neurophysiological model is available. This would explain why observations to date have not, as far as we can ascertain, shown any language-specific variability in schizophrenic disorders.

References

Andreasen, N. C. 1979. "Thought, language and communication disorders: 2; diagnostic significance". *Archives of General Psychiatry*, 36: 1325-1330.
Bange, P. 1992. *Analyse conversationnelle et théorie de l'action*. Paris: Didier.
Blanchet, A. 1994. "Pragmatique et psychopathologie". In D. Widlöcher (ed.), *Précis de Psychopathologie*. Paris: P.U.F.
Bleuler, E. 1911. *Dementia praecox, oder Gruppe der Schizophrenien*. Leipzig / Wien: Deuticke. Trad. fr. 1993: *Dementia praecox ou groupe des schizophrénies*. E.P.E.L.
Dennett, D. 1991. *Consciousness explained*. Boston: Little, Brown and Company.
Frith, C. D. 1992. *The cognitive Neuropsychology of Schizophrenia*. Hove: LEA.
Goffman, E. 1967. *Interaction Ritual: Essays on Face to Face Behavior*. New York: Doubleday Anchor.
Goffman, E. 1981. *Forms of talk*. Oxford: Basil Blackwell.
Grice, P. 1957. "Meaning". Reprinted in P. Grice, 1989. *Studies in The Way of Words*, Cambridge Mass.: Harvard University Press.
Hoffman, R.E. 1986. "Verbal hallucinations and language production processes in schizophrenia". *The Behavioral and Brain Sciences*, 9: 503-548.
Leudar, I. *al.* 1992. "Self-repair in dialogues of schizophrenics: effects of hallucinations and negative symptoms", *Brain and Language*.
Levelt, W. J. 1989. *Speaking; from Intention to Articulation*, Cambridge Mass.: M.I.T. Press.

Livet, P. 1994. *La communauté virtuelle; action et communication*. Combas: L'éclat.
Moeschler, J. 1985. *Argumentation et conversation*. Paris: Hatier.
Rochester, S. and J. R. Martin. 1979. *Crazy Talk. A Study of the Discourse of Schizophrenic Speakers*. Plenum Press.
Ribeiro, B. T. 1994. *Coherence in Psychotic Discourse*. Oxford: Oxford University Press.
Schwartz, S. 1982. "Is there a schizophrenic language?". *The Behavioral and Brain Sciences*, 5: 579-626.
Trognon, A. 1987. "Débrayages conversationnels". *DRLAV*, 36-37.
Trognon, A. 1988. "L'utopie du schizophrène". In *Autrement dire*, Nancy: Presses Universitaires de Nancy.
Trognon, A. 1992. "L'approche pragmatique en psychopathologie cognitive". *Psychologie française*, 37 (3-4): 191-202.
Widlöcher, D. and M. C. Hardy-Baylé. 1989. "Cognition and control of action in psychopathology". *Cahiers de Psychologie Cognitive*, 9 (6): 583-616.

Index

Subject index

A

abstraction 37; 38; 40; 49
accessibility 44; 48
accidental relation 110; 111; 112
 See also : permanent relation
agency disorders 214; 215
agent
 agent assignment 180–91
 agentivity 40; 41; 42; 44
agrammatism 204–5
agreement
 case – 187; 189
 verbal – 181–88
algebra, algebraic 5; 12; 15; 16
analogy 59; 67
animacy contrast 181; 183
antonymy 24; 33
aphasia 197; 199
arbitrariness 23; 139
as, aus (Old French) 58
assertion 39; 48; 49
attractor 46; 49

B

biology, biological 7; 10
body 22; 38; 39
bondedness 115; 116
branching path, branching point 40; 41; 42; 46; 47; 49; 50

C

categorization 5; 6; 7; 14; 15
 linguistic categories 22; 32; 33
ce (Old French) 57–62
cels (Old French) 57; 58; 60; 66
celui, cestui, icelui, icestui (Old French) 55–62
celui-ci, celui-là (Modern French) 55; 56; 59; 60; 62; 65
CEN (Clause Ending Negativity) 170; 171
centralization, centralized 115 See also : decentralized
ces (Old French) 57–62
cestes, celes (Old French) 57; 58; 60; 65
cette, cet (Old French) 56; 61; 62
change (linguistic) 37; 53; 54; 55; 61; 62; 63; 66; 67
chemistry, chemical 9
children's processing 182–90
cil (Old French) 55; 57–62
cis (Old French) 59
cist (Old French) 57–62
cognitive agent 51
cognitive grammar 9
cognitive operations 7
cognitivism, cognitivist 12
coherence 209–14; 218
communication 145; 146; 155; 156
comparative 45; 46
competition 181; 187
 Competition Model 179–91
complexity 37
comprehension 179; 182; 183; 187
computation, computational 5; 10; 11; 12; 51
concatenation 22; 28
connectionism, connectionist 9
connotation 33

construction of meaning 22; 26; 27; 32
constructivism, constructivist 12; 15
context 21; 24; 25; 27; 28
contextual constraints 180; 190
continuity, continuous 15
continuum 108–14
coordination
 conversational –, interlocutory – 211; 213; 217; 218
cross-cultural cognition
 experiments in – 93
 gender and – 98; 100
cross-linguistic studies 5; 10; 12; 85; 91; 100; 114; 180; 182; 183; 189; 3–202
cues
 Cue Assignability 186; 187; 188; 191
 Cue Cost 183
 Cue Detectability 188; 189; 191
 Cue Perceptibility 188; 190; 191
 Cue Strength 180; 182; 185
 Cue Validity 181; 182; 183; 187
cultural experience 21; 24
 gender and – 98

D

data bases (Medieval French) 55
decentralized 115; 116 *See also*: centralization
decoding 146; 147; 148; 151; 153; 155
deformation 40; 50
deixis, deictics 10; 55; 66; 67
demonstratives 55–62
deontic 40
depth dimension 21–33
 third dimension 24; 26; 33
des (Old French) 58; 62; 65; 67
deterministic 23
diathesis 40
diffusing 29
dimension
 dimensional conversion 22; 25; 26; 33
 dimensional reduction 26; 31
 multidimensional 22; 26
 third dimension 24; 26; 33
directional system 73–82
 anthropocentric references 73; 74; 82; 83
 cardinal system 74; 75; 76; 77
 deictic directional markers 80; 82
 fixed directional system 76
 topocentric or geocentric directional markers 79; 80
disambiguation 210
discourse 25
discourse breaks 210; 211; 212; 213
drum language 145–56
dynamic 9–16; 37; 40; 46; 50; 108; 112; 113; 115; 117

E

electrical activity 160; 169
elicitation (interactive method of) 90
enunciative, enunciator 31

É

épaisseur du langage 24

E

error detection 185; 187; 188; 189
event-related brain potential (ERP) 160–75
extension 24
Exterior 40; 46; 49

F

fictive construct 44; 47
fictive motion 9
focal zone 14; 15
focus 30
forms 38
fragmentation 27

G

generative grammar 4; 5; 6; 14
geography 87; 88; 89; 91; 92; 99; 100; 103
geometry, geometrical 8; 13
Gestalt psychology 9
gradient 49
gradualness, gradual 9; 15
grammaticalization 6; 14; 15

H

harmonic violation 173

harmonics 25
hyperlanguage 24

I

iconicity 123–41
il, lui (Medieval and Modern French) 61; 62; 63
ille, ecce ille (Latin) 55; 57
indeterminacy 25; 27
indicative, indicativity 108; 114; 116
inference 210
information 145–56
information curve 29
  informational structure 30; 33
intention 212; 214; 215; 216; 217
Interior 40
intonation 147; 155
invariance, invariant 7; 8; 10–15; 37; 38; 40; 43; 46; 50; 51
isolates of experience 7
isolates of meaning 7
isotopic (semantic -) 28; 29
iste, ecce iste (Latin) 55; 57

K

knowledge representation 159; 163; 171; 172

L

LAN (Left Anterior Negativity) 164; 167; 171
language comprehension 169
latent value 27
layering, formal layering 28; 38; 39; 50
lexical semantic violation 165; 166; 167
linear axis, linearity 22; 26; 28; 31; 32
linguistic relativism 7; 8
linkage 24; 25; 27; 29
literacy 93; 95; 97; 104
localization 107; 108; 109; 115; 116; 117
location 115
logics, logical 5; 9; 10; 12; 13

LPC (Late Positive Component) 175
LPN (Left Processing Negativity) 162; 163; 168

M

marginalizing 116
mathematics, mathematical 5; 8; 9
meaning
  meaning (construction of) 22; 26; 27; 32
  meaning deployment 37; 42; 43; 44; 47; 50
mental movement 115; 116; 117
mental space 9
metaphor 24; 25; 117
metonymy 24; 33
modal markers, modality 31; 40; 42
  See deontic
modifiers 30
modular, modularity 5; 10; 171
monitoring process 215; 216; 218
motivated, motivation 23
motor control 214; 218
multidimensional 22; 26
music 33; 171
  musicians 172; 173; 174; 175

N

N400 160–75
negation 39; 48; 51
neocortex 160; 162
neologism 212
network 21; 23; 24; 28; 29
neural networks 9; 202
neuropsychology,
  neuropsycholinguistics 204–5
notional domain 44; 45; 48

O

object relatives 171
opera 175
orientation, oriented relationship 38; 41; 45; 46

P

P600 164; 165; 166; 173

paradigms
  change of   53; 56; 57; 58; 59; 66
parameters   4; 5; 15
paraphrase   13
parsing   171
passivization   40; 41
path   38–50
permanent relation   112 *See also*: accidental relation
phenotype *vs.* genotype   10
physics, physical   8; 9
pitch   145; 146; 154; 155
planning of discourse   211; 214; 217
polysemy   15; 27; 28; 32; 37; 154
position (neutral -)   39; 40
pragmatics   209; 211; 213; 217; 218
predication, predicative   107; 108; 109; 115; 116; 117; 119
predictability   33
principles   4
projection   22; 26
pronouns
  personal -   55; 61; 62
prototype   27; 150; 151
psycholinguistics   202; 204

R

receiver   147
reconstitution   153; 155; 156
reductionism   37
reference, referential   21; 22; 23; 26; 27; 33
  referential power   23
  referential space   26; 28
regulation   43
representations, representational   9; 11; 12; 15; 21; 23; 25; 32; 38–50
  representational power of language   25
retroaction, retroidentification   28; 29; 32
retroaction, retroidentification, retroidentification   27; 155; 156
right-left   87; 88; 91; 92; 99; 100

S

salience, salient   8; 12; 15
scale of reference   22
schematic form   32; 37; 46; 47; 50
  schematic relationship, schematicity   23; 24
schizophasia   209; 214; 217
scope   30
segmentation   147; 153; 155
selection   153
semantic content   23
semantic depth   24; 29
semantic field   23; 28
semantics   57; 63
sequence   22; 25; 26; 29; 30; 31
sign languages   204
simultaneity   130; 131; 132
slow potentials   169; 170
solidarity   115; 116; 117
source   147
space   8; 10; 13; 14; 15
  conceptualization of -   73; 82; 83
  spatial cognition   82; 98
  spatial orientation   37–46
    relative orientation   75; 78
  spatialization   133
speech act, speech production   21; 25; 26; 29; 31; 32
stochastic   23
structural model   42
structuralism, structuralist   6
subject relatives   171
subjectivity   42; 44; 49; 50
suffix   59; 60
synonymy   23; 24; 32; 33; 37
syntactic violation   165; 166; 167; 173

T

teleonomy, teleonomic   40; 41; 45
thematic role assignment   169; 170
thought and language   21; 32
time   10
  time bomb   29
tone language   145; 154
topic   30
topology, topological properties   12; 37; 47
transitory   41
translation, translatability
  automatic translation   13

true 64; 65; 66
turning point, t.p. 111; 112
type 49
typical property 11; 12; 23

U

universals 12; 13; 14; 15; 204
   universal grammar 4
utterance 21–31
   situation of 62; 66
utterer 54; 63; 64; 67

V

variation 3; 5; 10; 11; 14; 15
   semantic – 51
verai, vrai, voir / reel (Old and Modern French) 64–66
vision 92; 104

W

word history 37
word order 181; 183; 185; 186; 187; 188
working memory 160; 164; 170

Author index

A

Adelaar, K. 75; 76
Alajouanine, T. 3–201
Alexandre, P. 157
Altmann, G. 180
Ammon, M. 186
Amy, G. 182
Arom, S. 154; 156
Auroux, S. 24

B

Baharav, E. 199
Bamhamed, M. 182; 187
Barden, J. 11
Bassano, D. 187; 188
Bates, E. 180–91
Bavin, E. 182
Benveniste, E. 11; 46; 109
Besson, M. 167–74
Betz, R. 157
Bleuler, E. 210
Blust, R. 75
Boas, F. 32
Boddy, J. 168
Bradley, D. 205
Brettschneider, H. 14
Broschart 117
Brown, C. 74; 82
Brown, P. & S. Levinson 82
Buck, C. 75

C

Capasso, R. 187
Caramazza, A. 197
Carrington, J. 157
Caselli, C. 182
Chafe, W. 33
Charvillat, A. 182; 183; 185
Chomsky, N. 4; 5
Churchward, C.M. 78
Cloarec-Heiss, F. 154; 156
Comrie, B. 14
Corbin, D. 23; 32; 33
Culioli, A. 10; 23; 30–32; 38; 39; 41; 48; 51; 67
Cuxac, C. 126; 127; 130

D

Dees, A. 58; 59; 67
Dennett, D. 215
Desclés, J. P. 129; 138
Devescovi, A. 182
Diakogiorgi, K. 182; 187; 188; 189
Drossard, W. 113–16

E

Edelman, G. 12

Epstein, S. 4; 5

F

Firbas, J. 33
Fischler, I. 168
Fodor, J. 5; 10
Franckel, J.J. 33
Frazier, L. 179
Frege, G. 23; 32
Frith, C. 210; 214; 215
Fromkin, V. 196
Fuchs, C. 3; 5; 13; 15

G

Garrett, M. 196; 205
Givón, T. 33; 180
Goffman, E. 211
Goldap 117
Greenberg, J. 14
Greimas, A. 33
Grice, P. 217
Grodzinsky, J. 199
Gross, M. 5
Grunig, B.N. 29
Guillaume, G. 10

H

Hébert, J.-C. 76
Heepe, M. 157
Heeschen, K. 203
Heinze, H. 165; 166; 168
Hillyard, S. 165
Hockett, C. 6
Hoffman, R. 211
Holcomb, P. 166

J

Jackendoff, R. 10; 11; 12
Jarema, G.. 196
Johnston, J. 112; 113; 114
Joseph, J. 7

K

Kail, M. 180-89
Kean, M-L. 205
King, J. 167; 168; 170; 171
Kleiber, G. 67
Klein, W. 110

Kliegl, R. 182
Kluender, R. 167
Kolk, H. 205
Kutas, M. 165-71

L

Lakoff, G. 10; 23; 33
Landaburu, J. 82
Langacker, R. 10; 23; 32; 33; 125; 137; 141
Lapointe, S. 205
Lasnik, H. 4
Laury, R. 56
Lavondès, H. 78
Lazard, G. 14; 15
Lecours, A. 197
Lee, P. 7; 9
Lentin, A. 5
Leudar, I. 211; 217
Levelt, W. 215
Levinson, S. *See* Brown, P. & –
Lhermitte, F. 197
Liddell 111
Lindamood 165
Livet, P. 216
Lucy, J. 7

M

Macar, F. 171; 172
Martin, J. 210
Martinet, A. 6
McClelland, J. 180
McDonald, J. 182
McNew, S. 182
Menn, L. 196; 205
Miceli, G. 200
Milner, G.B. 78
Mimica, I. 182; 185
Moeschler, J. 211
Mossé, F. 43
Müller, H. 171
Münte, T 165; 166
Myerson, R. 197

N

Natale, F. 182
Nekes, H. 157

Nespoulous, J-L.   197; 201; 203; 205
Nuyts, J.   9

O

Obler, L.   196; 205
Osterhout, L.   166

P

Patel, A.   173
Perfetti, C.   180
Petitot, J.   138
Pick, A.   196
Pillon, A.   197
Pinker, S.   10; 12
Pléh, C.   182; 188
Poizner, H.   204
Premper   115

R

Ramseyer, U.   77
Rastier, F.   33
Requin, J.   172
Revel, N.   77
Rialland, A.   157
Robert, S.   24; 30
Rochester, S.   210
Rosch, E.   181

S

Sapir, E.   7; 8; 13
Sasaki, Y.   182
Schelstraete, M.   180
Schultz, E.   7
Schützenberger, M.   5
Searle, J.   12
Seboek, D. & T.   156
Seiler, H.   14; 115
Shannon, C.   33; 153
Shopen, T.   182
Slobin, D.   33; 112; 113; 114; 180; 186

Smith, S.   182
Sokolov, J.   182
St John, M.   180
Steedman, M.   180
Stokoe, W. C.   141
Svorou, S.   73

T

Talmy, L.   10
Taman, H.   182; 187
Taraban, R.   180
Temple, M.   23; 32; 33
Thilenius, T.   157
Thom, R.   138; 140
Traugott, E.   53; 54
Trognon, A.   210; 211
Tyler, L.   190

V

Van Petten, C.   165; 167
Vennemann, T.   14
Venza, V.   182
Verbeken, A.   157
Victorri, B.   15
Vion, M.   182

W

Wackernagel   110
Weaver, W.   153
Weckerly, J.   171
Weinberg, H.   168
Whorf, B.   7; 8; 9; 13; 32
Wulfeck, B.   187

Y

Yau, S.   124; 138
Yvon, H.   59

Z

Zurif, E.   197; 205

Language index

A
Agul 114
Andoque 82
Arrernte 87; 90; 92
Australian Aborigine languages 74; 82; 83; 87
Austronesian languages 73–83
Avaro-Andic 114
Awar 116

B
Balinese 77
Banda 145–56
Belhare 103
Budux 114

C
Cesisch 114
Chinese 182

D
Dutch 48; 50; 86–97; 103; 182

E
English 4; 11; 22; 29; 74; 86; 88; 104; 181; 182; 183; 187
  Old English 43

F
Finnish 56; 113; 114
Finno-Ugric 113; 114 *See also*: Lappic, Finnish, Hungarian, Ugric
French 4; 10; 21–31; 43; 44; 45; 50; 182–88; 204–5
  Middle French 55; 60; 63; 64
  Old French 55; 56; 57; 61–67

G
German 22; 182
Germanic 43; 44; 47; 50
Gothic 42; 43
Greek 22; 23; 24; 42; 46; 48
  Ancient Greek 107–12; 118
  Modern Greek 108; 111; 182–90

H
Hai//om 103
Hebrew 182; 198; 199; 200; 205
Hungarian 113; 114; 182; 185

I
Icelandic 50
Italian 107; 112; 182; 183; 187; 188; 196; 198; 200; 205

J
Japanese 51; 86; 103; 182

K
Kgalagadi 103
Kilivila 103

L
Lakkisch 114
Lappic 114
Latin 44; 51; 55; 62; 64; 65; 67
Lesgisch 114

M
Malagasy 74; 76; 77; 83
Malay 76; 77
Marquesan 78; 79
Maya languages 74; 82
Mopan 89–101

N
Native American languages 7
Nemi 79–81

O
Occitan 51
Oceanic languages 77; 78

P
Palawan 77
Provençal 51

R
Romance Languages 55; 62; 74

S

Sanskrit 76
Sign Language (French) 123; 129; 130; 140
sign languages 123–41
Spanish 48; 182; 183; 185
Swahili 115

T

Tahitian 78
Tamil 103
Turkish 10; 186
Tzeltal 82; 83; 87; 93; 103

U

Ugric 114

V

Vietnamese 38; 40; 41

W

Welsh 119
Wolof 22

Y

Yucatec 103

In the series HUMAN COGNITIVE PROCESSING (HCP) the following titles have been published thus far or are scheduled for publication:

1. NING YU: *The Contemporary Theory of Metaphor. A perspective from Chinese.* 1998.
2. COOPER, David L.: *Linguistic Attractors. The cognitive dynamics of language acquisition and change.* 1999.
3. FUCHS, Catherine and Stéphane ROBERT (eds.): Language Diversity and Cognitive Representations. 1999.
4. PANTHER, Klaus-Uwe and Günter RADDEN (eds.); *Metonymy in Language and Thought.* 1999.